ROUTLEDGE LIBRARY EDITIONS: POLITICAL SCIENCE

MARX'S 'CAPITAL' AND CAPITALISM TODAY

MARX'S 'CAPITAL' AND CAPITALISM TODAY

By

ANTONY CUTLER, BARRY HINDESS,
PAUL HIRST AND ATHAR HUSSAIN

Volume 52

Routledge
Taylor & Francis Group
LONDON AND NEW YORK

First published 1977

This edition first published in 2010
by Routledge
2 Park Square, Milton Park, Abingdon, Oxon, OX14 4RN

Simultaneously published in the USA and Canada
by Routledge
711 Third Avenue, New York, NY 10017

First issued in paperback 2012
Routledge is an imprint of the Taylor & Francis Group, an informa business

British Library Cataloguing in Publication Data
A catalogue record for this book is available from the British Library

ISBN 13: 978-0-415-49111-2 (Set)

Publisher's Note
The publisher has gone to great lengths to ensure the quality of this reprint but points out that some imperfections in the original copies may be apparent.

Disclaimer
The publisher has made every effort to trace copyright holders and would welcome correspondence from those they have been unable to trace.

ISBN13: 978-0-415-64990-2 (PBK)

ISBN13: 978-0-415-55594-4 (HBK)

Marx's 'Capital' and Capitalism Today

Antony Cutler
Department of Sociology, Middlesex Polytechnic

Barry Hindess
Department of Sociology, University of Liverpool

Paul Hirst
Department of Politics and Sociology, Birkbeck College, University of London

Athar Hussain
Department of Economics, University of Keele

Routledge & Kegan Paul
London, Henley and Boston

First published in 1977
by Routledge & Kegan Paul Ltd
39 Store Street,
London WC1E 7DD,
Broadway House,
Newtown Road,
Henley-on-Thames,
Oxon RG9 1EN and
9 Park Street,
Boston, Mass. 02108, USA
Photoset in 10 on 12 Times
by Kelly and Wright, Bradford-on-Avon, Wiltshire
and printed in Great Britain by
Lowe & Brydone Ltd.

British Library Cataloguing in Publication Data

Marx's 'Capital' and capitalism today.
Vol. 1.
1. Marxian economics
I. Cutler, A J
335.4'12'0924 HB97.5 77-30216

ISBN 0-7100-8745-4

ISBN 0-7100-8746-2 Pbk

Contents

Preface

Marxist economic theory has enjoyed a renaissance in the last decade. The extent and vigour of contemporary debates and discussions has not been equalled since the turn of the century. Unfortunately it is also true that despite this investment of effort the questions elaborated at the beginning of this century and the answers then given to them continue to dominate contemporary work. For example, discussions of those transformations in capitalist social relations which are signalled by the concepts of 'monopoly' and 'finance' capital have not in substance advanced beyond the work of Hilferding, Bukharin, and Lenin. And need for advance there certainly is. This is not merely because capitalist social formations and their interrelations on a world scale have changed radically in the interval, but also because these conceptions were in many respects inadequate at the time of their formulation. The most systematic of these works, Hilferding's *Das Finanz Kapital*, published in 1910, by and large develops and synthesises the positions on money, banking capital, credit, the effects of the concentration and centralisation of capital advanced in *Capital* and presents on this basis a conception of monopolised production dominated by 'finance capital'. This conception is elaborated on the basis of, and is closely tied to, the classic forms of industrial cartelisation and the control by banking capital then prevailing in Germany. Bukharin and Lenin followed him in this and developed on the basis of this conception of the monopoly stage of capitalism a theory of the inter-imperialist struggle of the Great Powers. Imperialism is conceived as the terminal phase of capitalism and the outcome of the evolution of tendencies immanent in its basic structure. It is now widely accepted (for a variety of reasons) that this theory of imperialism is no longer tenable.

It is by no means accepted, however, that the theory of monopoly capital on which it is based or some modern revision of that theory is also untenable. It is certainly not realised that Marxism currently has no adequate theory of modern monetary forms, of financial capitalist institutions and their differing modes of articulation into the financial systems of capitalist national economies, and of the forms of organisation of large-scale industrial capitalist enterprises and the types of economic calculation they undertake. These deficiencies are real and salient ones. They cannot be gainsaid by dismissing them as quite secondary to the determination of capitalist relations in production and exploitation. That sort of response and the theoretical stance which makes it possible comprise one of the main reasons for the weakness of Marxist economic theory when confronted with new forms of contemporary capitalist relationships which do have important effects. The deficiencies we have mentioned in large measure explain the failure of Marxist theory to come to terms with the changes that have taken place in capitalist social formations since the turn of the century. This failure is revealed by the sterility and dogmatism of the responses of most Marxist economic theorists to the current depression, by a sigh of relief at what is conceived as the return of the devil we know, and by, in all too many cases, an earnest searching for signs of the re-emergence of terminal tendencies too long deferred.

It is not merely that later generations of Marxists have failed to build on the achievements of *Capital*. This is all too clearly what Hilferding did, and therein lies his main limitation. *Capital* does not provide us with the basis for the kind of work we need to undertake. In key areas of theory it is either inadequate in what it does say or it enforces silence through the intervention of the questions and concepts which it brings to the fore. The theorisation in *Capital* of, for example, money, credit, capitalist organisation, and calculation are all seriously inadequate. It is not simply that the difficulties in *Capital* are confined to what might be considered as certain relatively specialised bodies of theory. In fact the difficulties involved in these bodies of theory stem in the main from the effects of their articulation on the basis of concepts and problems which are central to the discourse of *Capital*.

Much of the sterility of modern Marxist economic theory is an effect of the point of departure to which it attempts to be all too loyal, *Capital* (that this 'loyalty' is often a travesty is another matter). Many of the central concepts and problems in *Capital*, far from constituting a point of departure, are actually *obstacles* to the new kinds of theoretical work socialists need to undertake if they are to come to terms with modern capitalism. We will outline here three areas of concepts which have had crippling effects on Marxist analysis and which are discussed in this book:

1 The category of 'value' and the forms of analysis of capitalist accumulation connected with it. This type of analysis effectively limits any conception of circulation based on credit money, limits the role of finance capital to the redistribution of the surplus value already produced and silences the discussion of the range of determinants of industrial capitalist profits.

2 The conception of the capitalist mode of production as a general entity and one involving necessary 'laws of motion' of general application. This conception has hegemonised discussion of capitalist social formations. The specific structures of capitalist national economies are suppressed as objects of theorisation, being considered as exemplars of capital*ism*-as-generality and of its 'laws'. This conception of 'laws of motion' has channelled questions about change and development in capitalist social formations into two directions, the postulation of a general 'monopoly stage' of capitalism, and the search for 'crises' and other terminal phenomena as necessary general effects of the capitalist mode of production. Both of these directions seem to us to be valueless in considering the types of questions about capitalist social formations which would be of use in formulating a socialist strategic programme.

3 The mode of discussion of economic agents. Agents are conceived as 'personifications' of economic functions to which are given definite interests and outlooks. This conception of 'personification' makes it necessary for economic agents to be confined to human individuals, it also makes possible a conception of social relations as relations *between human subjects* (even when these relations take on a fetish form). This conception makes it impossible to conceive of economic agents which are not directly represented by human subjects, and of forms of economic calculation which are not given by the structure and which differ between enterprises. This conception of agents as human subjects and social relations as relations between such subjects makes possible a sociologistic conception of classes of economic agents in which they form groups of individuals with definite interests; these

groups and interests are then represented in politics and ideology.

This book began in work which was an attempt to use Marxist theory to construct a concept of the capitalist mode of production dominated by 'monopoly' and 'finance' capital. It rapidly became clear in the course of this work that these concepts were anything but adequate and that *Capital* itself presented real problems if we were to come to terms with a range of questions about economic forms prevailing in contemporary capitalist social formations which we had formulated. This book is the product of a seminar which the authors have conducted for the past two years. This seminar has taken the form of two separate but related tasks, the criticism and modification of *Capital*, and the analysis of contemporary capitalist relations, particularly money and state monetary policy, banking and credit, and financial institutions and systems. The initial results of this seminar are collected in the two volumes of this book. We will briefly outline the content of the two volumes here.

The first volume is directly concerned with the three areas of problems in *Capital* outlined above. It is divided into three parts. The first involves a critique of the category of 'value' and the way that the category hegemonises Marxist discussions of the distribution of the product among the agents and of the nature and determinants of the profits of capitalist enterprises. The second is a critique of Marx's conception of economic 'laws of motion' and the theoretical consequences this has. The third part is a discussion of classes and economic agents which builds on the critique of the theory of surplus value in Part I and the critique of the representation of the process to the economic subject or agent in Part II. This volume is therefore confined in the main to a few key problems and concepts in the discourse of *Capital*. It is mainly concerned with the status of these concepts and the pertinence of those questions. It considers this by examining how it is that certain concepts appear in discourse and what their consequences are on that discourse. We are not concerned to review and directly to intervene in the various technical debates which have arisen on the basis of and around such concepts as 'value' or the 'law of tendency of the rate of profit to decline'. This is because we are challenging the theoretical ground of those debates. This book cannot be considered merely as a work of Marxist 'economics', that is, a definite contribution within a given field of problems. It is primarily a work on Marxist *theory*, an attempt to analyse and to redefine that field of problems itself.

The second volume continues the critique of *Capital* and also attempts to theorise certain capitalist economic forms. It is concerned with three main issues. The first is a critical discussion of the theory of money in *Capital* and also an examination of the conditions of existence and consequences of credit-money systems. The second is an analysis of the different forms of financial capitalist institutions (banks, finance companies, insurance companies, etc.), an attempt to explain why these different forms exist, and an examination of the consequences of modern interlinked financial systems, in particular the question of credit creation. The third is a critique of Marx's conception of capitalists' calculation in *Capital*, an attempt to consider modern forms of capitalist calculation employed by enterprises and their differential effects (on investment strategies, rates of profit, etc.).

These two volumes are considered by us as the start of work on these questions. We do not pretend to offer a comprehensive analysis of the discourse of *Capital* nor an overall investigation of modern capitalist economies. The implications and consequences of the criticisms we have made and the attempts at alternative theorisation are no doubt diverse, and we cannot at present hope to elaborate and come to terms with all of them. That is a task for our future work and the basis for the continuation of this discourse. Given our rejection of the rationalist conception of theoretical discourse as a logical unity (see Hindess and Hirst, 1977), the effect of its basic governing concepts, we could not pretend to be the possessors of the consequences of our work. It follows that these two volumes cannot be summed up in an authoritative introduction which sets its imprimatur on the rest of the text.

Equally, there can be no definitive conclusion. However, as this book is written by socialists concerned to produce theory relevant to the struggle for socialism in this country, some concluding remarks on this score are politically necessary whatever their limitations. At the end of the second volume we attempt to draw out some of the political implications of our work. In particular we will consider the importance of the concept of capitalist national economies as objects of analysis and the ways in which the analysis of such forms can contribute to the political strategy of socialist forces and parties in the states in question.

Finally, we should explain that while this text is the product of co-operative work its composition is the product of a division of labour. The effects of distinct portions of the text being composed by different individuals are various; the text is more repetitive than if it had been written by one hand, emphases and expositional styles differ, and minor contradictions are inevitable. We consider this to be of secondary consequence and certainly not worth emphasising by signalling who drafted what. All four authors are responsible for the basic format and agree on the basic substance of the text.

An index will be included at the end of Volume Two. References to works cited in this volume are listed at the end of this volume.

Part I

Value

The chapters in this part are devoted to a critical discussion of the concept of 'value'. In the first chapter the pertinence of labour-time as a measure of the distribution of the social product in capitalism is challenged, and in particular the pertinence of the assessment of the labour contributions of agents to the product as a means of explaining its distribution among different categories of those agents. In the second and third chapters attempts by two leading Marxist thinkers, Rudolf Hilferding and I. I. Rubin, to defend Marx's theory of value against attacks, notably that of Böhm-Bawerk, will be considered. What makes their discussions of special interest is that they both locate the concept of 'value' as a central part of the Marxist theory of history and of the social totality, rather than confining themselves merely to technical economic debates. In consequence certain of the possible implications of the category 'value' for the Marxist theory of social relations can be drawn from their work, complementing and reinforcing our analysis of Marx's *Capital*. In a short appendix the status of the notion of reproduction as posed in *Capital* is considered.

A point of caution needs to be made here. Our discussion of the concept of 'value' and the notions of a 'law of value' in *Capital* is a critical one and does not attempt to reconstruct all references to 'value' in the exposition in *Capital*. Marx's use of this concept in *Capital* is often ambiguous, his various references to a 'law of value' involve different possible formulations of this 'law' and these references are frequently marginal to the main line of the argument. There is no simple, comprehensive and unambiguous treatment of 'value' or of the 'law of value' (the form of its operation and its different modes of expression) in *Capital.* What we have done here is to criticise a definite conception of value and the law of value which is present in the discourse of *Capital* and to show how it is related to other central concepts in that discourse, notably 'surplus value' and 'exploitation'. This critique leads us to the conclusion that this concept and the concepts and problems dependent on it should be rejected. In consequence we regard a comprehensive review of Marx's references to value and the subsequent critical literature on this question redundant. The implications of abandoning the concepts 'value' and 'surplus value' for the analysis of classes are discussed at length in Part III of this volume.

One apparent notable omission needs to be explained at this point. Although the 'neo-Ricardian' critique of the Marxist theory of value and the resultant debate have occupied a prominent place in contemporary literature on this question no reference will be found to it in this part of the text. This literature is discussed in a separate chapter in Volume Two which is a critical review of theories of reproduction prices, and in particular of the work of Sraffa.

Chapter 1

Value, Exploitation, and Profit

Marx's 'theory of value' has generated a vast amount of debate amongst economists. This debate has centred on the technical possibility or the empirical validity of labour-time functioning as the measure of the proportions in which commodities exchange one with another. Thus, for example, it has been objected that this measure is in contradiction with the theory of prices of production and the formation of an average rate of profit in capitalism, and that commodities do not in fact exchange in ratios determined by their respective labour-times, that some have negative labour-times, etc. Defenders of *Capital* have replied to these critiques, in general concentrating on refuting the notion that Marx's theory of value is primarily a theory of exchange and of exchange-value, and insisting that the concept 'value' explains the way in which production-relations govern exchange-relations. Nevertheless, what is central in the theory of 'value' is the function of labour-time as a social standard of measurement.

What we will be concerned with in this chapter is not this debate but rather what it has ignored: *the theoretical pertinence and conditions of existence of the measure.* We will consider why it is that the measure takes this definite form, for what reasons this form is considered to be significant, and why the problem of measurement is considered as significant at all. Why is the labour-time used in the production of commodities (or non-commodity forms of the social product) of theoretical significance? Why should it be more important than, say, the weight of commodities? Why is the labour-time utilised in production employed not merely as the measure of the ratios in which commodities exchange but as a theoretical device to analyse the distribution of the social product between the agents? If these questions have been asked hitherto it has generally been merely to serve as the preface to the repetition of Marx's own arguments. Here, however, we will examine the discourse of *Capital* to see why these arguments Marx advances could be considered as *answers* to those questions. Central to this problem of the way the discourse defines the answers appropriate to it is *Capital*'s conception of the *nature of the operation of measurement* which is to be performed by the category of labour-time. 'Measurement' (in this case the relation of apparently distinct phenomena one to another as quantities) is not a simple non-theoretical notion or a simple non-theoretical exercise. To comprehend value as a measure in *Capital* we must understand the *conception of exchange* in which labour-time is to function as a measure and the theoretical doctrine of measurement adopted in that conception.

Value, exchange and measurement

Marx poses the problem of value-in-exchange in a specific way. Marx conceives exchange as an *equation*, as being effected through the *identity* of the objects exchanged. Posing exchange in this way leads directly to a paradox, the apparent absurdity and impossibility of the equation. What is the possibility of the form of equation 'x commodities A = y commodities B' (say, 1 cwt of iron = 1 ton of coal)? Why does *one hundredweight* of iron equal *one ton* of coal? The equation supposes a definite relation (an identity) between the things which are exchanged, yet that relation cannot be found in the distinct commodities themselves (iron = coal?), or in the ratio in which they exchange (1 cwt = 1 ton?) as such. The relative values of exchange of commodities are definite and yet are inpenetrable as such, as mere relative values:

> A given commodity, a quarter of wheat for example, is exchanged for x boot polish, y silk or z gold, etc. In short, it is exchanged for other commodities in the most diverse proportions. Therefore the wheat has many exchange values instead of one. But x boot polish, y silk or z gold, etc., each represent the exchange-value of one quarter of wheat. Therefore [they] . . . must, as exchange-values, be mutually replaceable or of identical magnitude. (*Capital*, vol. 1, Penguin edn, p. 127)

But that magnitude, the unit of measure in which these things count as the same is not given in these equivalences and Marx says:

> It follows from this that, firstly, the valid exchange-values of a particular commodity express something equal, and secondly, exchange-value cannot be anything other than the mode of expression, the 'form of appearance' (*Erscheinungsform*), of a content distinguishable from it. (*ibid*., p. 127)

The equation is, in its 'phenomenal form' as exchange-proportions, an effect.

Exchange-relations 'can always be represented by an equation':

> What does this equation signify. It signifies that *a common element of identical magnitude exists in two different things*, in 1 quarter of corn and similarly in x cwt of iron. Both are therefore equal to a third thing, which in itself is neither the one nor the other. Each of them, so far as it is exchange-value, must therefore be reducible to this third thing. (*ibid*., p. 127—our emphasis)

The equation (x commodities A = y commodities B) is possible because this phenomenal form is the effect of an identity established between the two distinct qualities (A and B, iron and coal) and their relative quantities (x and y, 1 cwt and 1 ton) in the third term. In this term xA and yB represent equal-identical quantities of the same common substance, and Marx insists that 'the exchange values of commodities must be reduced to a common element, of which they represent a greater or lesser quantity' (*ibid*., p. 127). Marx goes on to say that this common element cannot be identified in any 'natural property' of the commodities but only in the 'property . . . of being products of labour' (*ibid*., p. 128).

What is interesting here is not that 'labour' forms the basis of the 'common element' but the notion of the common element itself. Marx conceives exchange as an *equation*, exchange-values expressing an *equality of properties of the things exchanged* (identity of their labour-times). Hence the discourse of *Capital* is organised so as to pose the problem of the possibility of this equality of the things in question and to show it to be a problematical phenomenal form, inexplicable in itself and requiring the category of the third term to render it possible. The third term and the discrepancy of the physical form of the things exchanged thereby create the place for labour-time as an answer.

But it is by no means inevitable that exchange be conceived as an equation. Exchange may be conceived as being *equivalent*, in the juridical sense, that is, that both parties to it agree to the equity of the terms of the exchange and receive what they were promised, *but not as an equation* (there not being any substantive identity between the things exchanged). Likewise, in marginalist theories exchange rests neither on the identity of some property of the things exchanged nor on an identity of the estimations of utility concerning them. Exchange is possible because the utility of the things exchanged is different for the parties to the exchange—these different utilities intersect in a definite ratio, say a willingness to part with 1 cwt of iron for the utility of 1 ton of coal and *vice versa*. The relative values express or measure the utilities, but the exchanges are the product of *differing* and not equal utilities. Marx's conception of exchange is not a universal one.

Again, suppose we argue that relative exchange-values are non-pertinent. If one gives a £10 note for 1 cwt of iron, or 1 cwt of washing powder, or a gallon of wine, what does this signify? That there is some necessary relation between iron, washing powder and wine, or, the merely incidental fact that £10 of money will buy different quantities of all of them. To ask what it is that makes these quantities other than incidental (of theoretical pertinence) is to ask a question about the *necessity* of the proportions in which commodities exchange, to see exchange-values as representative of something general and which goes beyond them. To seek a general answer to the question of the necessity of these proportions, to insist that they are not incidental, is to postulate a theory of value. Marxism and marginalism, for example, share this problem and the need to answer it.

Exchange as equation and exchange proportionality as necessity are products of definite theoretical conditions, conditions which give certain questions pertinence. Marxists do not regard exchange as equation as anything other than second nature. Economists assume the need for a general theory of prices and exchange-values which assigns them a universal status, a specific function and a definite origin. That these questions are *theoretical* rather than an inevitable part of the nature of things (and for which answers must be sought) is often forgotten. It is possible to argue that prices and exchange-values have no *general* functions or general determinants, and that there is in general no necessity for the proportions in which commodities exchange. Such a change of pertinence of problems would put us not only outside of the Marxist theory of value but also conventional economic theory (we will return to these points later in this section and in Volume Two).

Marx's conception of exchange as an equation follows closely certain important elements of Hegel's theory of measurement as developed in *The Science of Logic* (Book 1, section 3). To give a short account of Hegel's position is by no means a digression. Hegel discusses measure in the context of his doctrine of *being*. Measure is not a mere formal operation but a relation of definite ontological significance. In measure the attributes of being, quantity, and quality, are reconciled. For Hegel measure is *quantified quality*. It is a quantitative expression of specificities of existence (specificity in and as quantity). Hegel develops a *realist* theory of measurement in which the object is definite relations between specific forms of quantity and forms of being. The nature of measurement varies with the different natures and divisions of being: abstract matter, the domain of mechanics (in which 'qualitative differences . . . are essentially quantitatively determined', *Science of Logic*, p. 331), organic and inorganic matter, and spirit all have different forms and capacities of measure determined by their form of being (measure is largely indeterminate in the realm of spirit). Quantified quality states the determinative effect of a quantity on specific unities of being thus measured. Unlike a formalist theory of measure (in which differences of application are determined by the purpose of the measurer) this relation does not correspond to every set of possible proportions but only to determinative proportions (that is, those in which quantity defines quality). Thus a man may lose a hair without being bald. However, at a certain point quantitative changes constitute a change of *quality*, a change in the nature of the thing and therefore of its measure. A man who loses sufficient hairs becomes bald and quantity of hair ceases to be an applicable measure. There is in Hegel's position no possibility of accepting measure as convention, as a mere standard applied to things for specific purposes. Hegel's position is quite different from positivist or formalist doctrines of measurement. So is Marx's theory of measurement in *Capital* which corresponds in certain crucial respects with the position in Hegel's greater *Logic*.

'In measure, the qualitative moment is quantitative; the determinateness or difference is indifferent and so is no difference sublated' (*Science of Logic*, p. 330). This conception of the relation of quality and quantity serves to explain Marx's conception of exchange as an *equation*. In exchange the distinct qualities of the objects exchanged are negated in their identity as quantities. Identity in the third term, as quantities of the third term, is the sublation of qualitative difference. It is this negation/sublation of quality in quantity that makes exchange possible. This measure, the third term, is not, however, merely conventional, pure quantity which in numerical identity obliterates difference. The measure between the qualitatively distinct terms is not accidental but expresses a real relation. For distinct objects to be exchangeable they must be real identities, for their difference to be negated their sameness must be expressed in (identical) quantities of a property common to them all. This property must both be *quantitative* (transcend difference) and yet not be *indifferent* (it must express real properties of the objects, properties of necessity to their nature as objects, as exchangeable products).

Marx conceives exchange as an equation, as the identity of distinct commodities in a third term which is a property common to both. Why must exchange be an equation? Why must one definite property (labour-time) be the form in which it is attained? To explain why exchange is conceived as an equation is to go beyond any question of the relative proportions in which commodities exchange. Exchange must be conceived as an equation if the discourse of *Capital* is to produce its particular concept of value and that concept is necessary to the theory of *surplus value*. Exchange must be conceived in terms of the equation of *labour-times* if Marx's concept of value is to be possible. Thus labour-time and value as categories hegemonise in the discourse the analysis of exchange-proportionality. Exchange is conceived as an equation because only in this way can it be conceived as the phenomenal form of an identity of labour-times. The notion of an equation necessitates a third term and hence opens the discursive space for labour-time as that term.

What makes the ratios in which goods exchange against one another necessary rather than incidental? What makes these necessary proportions the forms of equation of labour-times? Here we see that in *Capital* value is a concept which both explains (gives a definite form to) and goes beyond exchange-relations. The reason for this necessary proportionality in exchange and this equation of labour times which underlies it is the 'law of value' as a law of distribution of social labour. Despite the ambiguity of its various formulations in *Capital* this 'law' is a concept which provides the underpinnings in social relations for the specific conception of value-in-exchange (equation) advanced in vol. 1, pt 1. It is a 'law' necessary to all systems of social production. In the case of this 'law' taking the 'form of value' (value-in-exchange) it expresses the fact of the division and interdependence of the members of society as independent producers. Why should the members of this society be united *by the equation of their divided labours*? This division of the members of society is a division of labours which are interdependent, the products of these labours must be exchanged against one another. Why should they be equated and equated as labour-times? These questions pose the problem of the *foundation* of the *form* of the measure (labour-time). Its necessity as a measure is justified by variants of the law of distribution of social labour. We will discuss Marx's attempts to explain the pertinence of labour-time in this way later in this chapter (and Hilferding and Rubin's attempts in following chapters). The thesis of the necessity of the ratios in which commodities exchange and that there are general determinants of these ratios takes us beyond exchange in seeking the foundation of this thesis.

Marx's concept of exchange as equation makes possible a definite range of questions concerning profits. If profit is defined as the difference between the receipts from the sale of a product and the cost of its production it may be asked what determines this difference. Various economic theories attempt to give a single general explanation of this difference and to connect it with the 'revenues' of the different classes or 'factors' entering into production. Thus profit may be conceived as the return on the factor of production 'capital', as the reward for entrepreneurial skill and as compensation for risk-taking. All these explanations are dominated by a conception of bourgeois right in that they suppose 'profit' is the 'reward' for effort spent, opportunities forgone or risks taken: such actions by the possessors of capital or skill require in equity returns of a roughly commensurate or equivalent nature. As we have seen part 1 of *Capital* conceives exchange as the *equation* of the labour-times necessary to produce the commodities entering into exchange. There is no scope here for any conception of returns for 'risk' or 'entrepreneurship' being added to the cost of production. If the possessor of the commodity is a non-labourer (as the capitalist is, *qua* possessor of capital) then his activities do not enter into the determination of the ratios in which goods exchange. If exchange is an equation of labour-time (costs of production being expressed as labour-times) where does profit come from? If exchange ratios are determined by the labour-times necessary for the production of a commodity then 'profit' must be *represented in labour-time* (it cannot arise in exchange, for beggaring one's neighbour through sharp dealing in no way increases the total labour-time). *Capital*, in conceiving exchange as the equation of labour-times, thus sets up the condition for discovering the origin of *profit* in labour-time. Marx argues that profit depends on a prior exchange which is in form an equation (labour-power = wages) but which has effects different from other exchange equations (i.e. identity of the commodities exchanged). Profit results not from the unequal exchange of wages for labour-power, but from the 'exploitation' of the labourers who produce the goods—the value which is equal to their labour-power (wages) is less than that which they produce with their labour (labour-time embodied in the product). Central in this conception is that exchange is an equation, *an identity of labour-times*. Central also is the notion that the socially necessary labour-time contributions of the producers determine the ratios in which commodities exchange, that the product can be represented as (measured as) a totality of labour-times. For this measurement to work labour must be social (production for exchange) and take this social form in exchange.

Marx's theory of value supposes, therefore, a number of conditions:

1 exchange is conceived as an *equation*;

2 the ratios in which goods exchange (1 cwt iron = 1 ton coal = 1 bushel of wheat) are necessary ones and have general determinants;

3 these determinants are found in the need to distribute labour in quantities appropriate to the different quantities of product required by society;

4 this distribution, where there is a division of labour and production based on private property, equates labour-times through the exchange ratios of the products.

These conditions make 'value' the measure of the ratios of exchange between products, the measure which makes these exchanges (ratios) possible (commensurable). This defines the *form* of the value-standard (measure). These conditions also explain the *foundation* of this measure, why it and it alone is necessarily the measure. This form and this foundation enable Marx to define the problem of the determinants of profit in such a way as to ascribe it to an origin in the labour contributions of the producers to the product. We have seen that to conceive exchange as an equation involves definite theoretical conditions. Once these conditions are problematised all the concepts dependent on this conception of exchange are also threatened. Without this measure in which the labour contributions of the agents are expressed there can be no effective theory of surplus value. In this chapter we will argue that conceiving exchange as an equation is necessary if one seeks a specific type of explanation of the determinants of profits, one which links profit to the labour contributions of the agents. If one does not seek a single general determinant of profits—rejecting both Marxist and orthodox general accounts of their origin and accepting that the profits capitalist enterprises actually make have no single 'origin' (that they cannot be ascribed to any one category of agents or factors in the production process, and are the product of many determinations)—then there is no *a priori* reason to conceive exchange in this way. The ratios in which goods can be expressed one to another (through the medium of money) would in consequence not be necessary ratios. Abandoning a single general determinant of profits also entails abandoning a single general determinant of prices or exchange ratios.

In this part of the book we will challenge the notion that 'value' is such a general determinant. We will question the notions of the pertinence of labour-time to the determination of the quantity of the product and its distribution that underlie it. This is not a challenge to the technical *functioning* of the concept 'value' as a measure, it is a challenge to its function as *measure*. This challenge is not made on the basis of some alternative general theory of profits or of exchange-values, it in no way involves adherence to the marginalist or any other theory of prices. Within the circle of contest between Marxist and 'bourgeois' economic theory Marxism always has an answer, this is because it is contesting on a common terrain of problems. It can attempt to justify its general theory of profit against others, and also its general theory of exchange-values and prices against others. Our critique does not start from a place within that terrain but questions the space of contest itself.

Value in the classics and *Capital*

Histories of political economy written by Marxists often place Marx in the position of 'solving' an already given problem of value. Marx is conceived of as giving a coherent answer to problems the classics have been able to pose, however incompletely.

In a sense there is no rigorous theory of value before Marx. It is Marx who gives the problem of value and labour-time as the measure of its magnitude a central place in political economy. This centrality of value in Marx changes the significance of the positions on value in such writers as Ricardo and Smith. Value is heretofore secondary to the problem of *wealth* (*richesse*), political economy is concerned with economic policy and the management of national economies. Questions of distribution between the classes who form the nation are the mode in which the nature and source of profit arises as a problem. Marx's theory displaces these problems of national economy—hitherto, questions of trade policy, taxes, the regulation of the poor and of wages have a more central place in the discourse of political economy than they do in *Capital*. Smith and Ricardo are discussed here in so far as they give answers to questions which become pertinent in a new way in Marx, which have a new discursive place. Marx's *Capital* transforms the history of political economy, reordering political economy's discourses and problems as a means of producing and as an effect of producing its own. The problem of value in the classics is considered here not *à la lettre* but as it is pertinent to *Capital*. *Capital* is both continuous with political economy (offering solutions to its problems) and constitutive of the tradition it claims to inherit (transforming its problems and giving them a new place in a new discursive order).

It is no accident that in the classics the problem of value is common to both barter and commodity exchange. In Smith and Ricardo (although neither has a theory of value like Marx's—all three accord a different status to labour or labour-time) equivalence in exchange is conceived as a relationship between *products of labour*. Money, in so far as it is considered, merely mediates such exchanges of products of labour and reflects the corrrespondences of those products. The problem of the necessity of labour or labour-time as the measure of 'value' is therefore posed by all three (although each has a different conception of measurement) in terms of why goods exchange in particular ratios against each other.

One way of posing the problem of the necessity of the exchange of equivalents (Smith, equivalent *efforts*, Ricardo, labour-times) is to suppose a simple division of labour between independent individual producers who directly exchange their products one with another. Smith and Ricardo refer to this imaginary economy; neither of them elaborates the argument it makes possible for the necessity of equivalence and yet neither of them could contradict it.* According to this argument, if certain producers receive less for their labour-time than the equivalent labour-time in other goods (an elephant, the product of a week's hunting, is exchanged for a rat, which can be caught by the hour) then the division of labour on which this exchange system is based is supposed to become problematic. Individuals are supposed to be unable to subsist on the products which are given in exchange for the fruits of their present occupations and may withdraw into subsistence production or may switch to other lines of production (elephant-hunters become rat-catchers). The differentiation of products by means of social specialisation is thus considered to be threatened if equivalents (in some sense) are not exchanged. This is the only answer that could be given to the form of the question: 'given a social division of labour, why is it that the exchanges which link its parts together must take the form of the equivalence of the labour-times (efforts) of the producers?' Equivalent exchanges preserve the division of labour; this answer is made necessary by the primacy of independent and yet interdependent labours in the question. This answer, which is never given by Smith or Ricardo, is basic to the problem of value as equivalence or equation. Smith, Ricardo, and Marx all use (albeit with differences) this economy of independent/interdependent labours mediated by exchange to consider the question of value, to consider the problem of why there are general and necessary ratios in which goods (products of labour) exchange against one another. Marx will develop and transform this answer which is never (explicitly) given to say that the equation of labour times through exchange, a condition

* It should be noted that Smith never asks the question posed here, although he answers it. The division of labour is not threatened in his discourse with such a question because its status as a concept answers it, it is providential. The division of labour justifies itself because it so increases the productivity of labour that it is not in men's interest to undo it and it could not be undone without general impoverishment.

imposed by these independent/interdependent labours, is one form of a universal social necessity: the allocation of labour-times to produce a social product corresponding to need.

Smith's explanation of the necessity of value is to be found in *The Wealth of Nations*. Smith explains exchange as motivated by self-interest:

> . . . man has almost constant occasion for the help of his brethren, and it is in vain for him to expect it from their benevolence only. He will be more likely to prevail if he can interest their self love in his favour, and shew them that it is for their own advantage to do for him what he requires of them. Whoever offers to another a bargain of any kind, proposes to do this: Give me that which I want, and you shall have this which you want, is the meaning of every such offer; and it is in this manner that we obtain from one another the far greater part of the good offices which we stand in need of. It is not from the benevolence of the butcher, the brewer, or the baker, that we expect our dinner, but from their regard to their own interest. (Smith, *Works*, vol. 2, pp. 21–2)

Exchange is the self-interested mutual satisfaction of distinct wants through the means of the objects exchanged. The division of labour arises from this self-interested mutual assistance:

> As it is by treaty, by barter, and by purchase, that we obtain from one another the greater part of those mutual good offices we stand in need of, so it is this same trucking disposition which originally gives occasion to the division of labour. (*ibid*., vol. 2, p. 22)

Smith says: 'Labour, therefore, is the real measure of the exchangeable value of all things' (*ibid*., vol. 2, p. 44). This is because men, acting on the principle of self-interest, regard their labour as a cost and therefore value the time and effort which the production of the good to be exchanged involves:

> *The real price of every thing, what every thing really costs to the man who wants to acquire it, is the toil and trouble of acquiring it*. What every thing is really worth to the man who has acquired it, and who wants to dispose of it or exchange it for something else, is the toil and trouble which it can save to himself, and which it can impose on other people. What is bought with money

> or with goods is purchased by labour, as much as what we acquire by the toil of our own body. That money or those goods save us this toil. They contain the value of a certain quantity of labour which we exchange for what is *supposed* at the time to contain the value of an equal quantity. ***Labour was the first price, the original purchase-money that was paid for all things.*** It was not by gold or silver, but by labour, that all the wealth of the world was originally purchased. . . . (*ibid.*, vol. 2, p. 44—our emphasis)

Robinson paid the money of effort on his island. Labour, as effort, has a value relative to our needs. The decision to produce goods and the basis on which they are exchanged is equated by a rigorous subjectivism. The price of effort to satisfy oneself and the price of alienating goods to satisfy wants through other's goods are equated. Value depends on men's estimating the time and trouble each has taken, measuring against their self-interest (against their desire for value-in-use) the cost of acquisition. Labours are equated in exchange because otherwise it would not be *worth the trouble* of onc of the parties to exchange. Labours are equated through *supposition*—labour as measure of value includes the estimation of effort, difficulty, and skill. Labour is a subjective and conventional measure, an estimate of value agreeable to both parties. The Smithian 'law of value' (a law realised through calculation) preserves the division of labour through men's mutual self-interest; through the habitual intersection of their wants, and the gradual realisation that the division of labour saves effort. This effort can only be saved if 'equivalent' toils are equally rewarded. Otherwise, the self-interest of the disadvantaged would lead them to withdraw from their specialisms. Smith comments:

> In that early and rude state of society which proceeds both the accumulation of stock and the appropriation of land, the proportion between the quantities of labour necessary for acquiring different objects seems to be the only circumstance which can afford any rule for exchanging them for one another. If among a nation of hunters, for example, it usually costs twice the labour to kill a beaver which it does to kill a deer, one beaver should naturally exchange for or be worth two deer. It is natural that what is usually the produce of two days' or two hours' labour, should be worth double what is usually the produce of one day's or one hour's labour. (*ibid.*, vol. 2, pp. 70–1)

Ricardo eliminates the ambiguities of Smith's labour theory of value, reducing exchange proportionality strictly to labour-time. Ricardo decisively rejects Smith's position that value (to the purchaser) also includes what one receives in return for one's labour-time, that is, the goods obtained and one's esteem of them. This 'confusion' in Smith's theory of value, between value as determined by labour-time and by esteem (utility) of the participants in exchange, is discursively possible for Smith because both are united by a rigorous subjectivism. Both sources of value are conceived in subjective terms. Labour and 'effort' are identified. Labours are equated through the *supposition* of what is reasonably equivalent. Exchange, like all human intercourse, involves the faculty of judgment and questions of interest. Hence one's desire for a good will affect one's estimation of its value and one's preparedness to part with the proceeds of effort to obtain it. Smith's 'confusion' on value is no confusion at all, it is a slide which is inevitable in the calculations of the human subjects on which Smith bases his theory of exchange. Smith's economics is founded on the moral sciences.

Ricardo ignores this subjectivism: he does not (he could not) explicitly criticise and reject it. Instead, he bases the exchange of equivalents on equal magnitudes of the same objective substance, labour-time. Equivalence, for Ricardo, has an objective existence, it is not the product of supposition. Ricardo denies that utility has any role in determining the magnitude of value: 'Utility then is not the measure of exchangeable value, although it is absolutely essential to it' (Ricardo, *Principles of Political Economy and Taxation* (ed. Sraffa), p. 1). Ricardo criticises Smith's restriction of the strict law of labour proportionality to 'that early . . . state of society which proceeds the accumulation of stock and the appropriation of land'. Profit on capital and rent of land do not affect the relative value of commodities independent of the labour necessary for their production. The law of value operates 'in all stages of society' (Ricardo to James Mill, cited by Sraffa, *Principles*, p. xxxvii). Capital enters into the value of the product in terms of the labour-time necessary for its production and the rate at which it is consumed (*ibid*., ch. 1, sections iii and iv).

The necessity of proportional exchange attained by correspondence in labour-time terms is not justified by Ricardo by reference to 'effort', to estimation or to the threat to the division of labour posed by its dependence on mutual self-interest. Ricardo does not justify the law of value as such. He merely performs certain analytic exclusions (utility cannot be the foundation of value) and removes Smith's 'incoherences'. For Ricardo value logically involves the proportionality of labour-times, and labour is, logically, the sole and objective 'substance' of value. Ricardo, unlike Smith, refuses to found the law of value on an anthropological/moral necessity. Labour-time offers a logically coherent solution to the problem of equivalence in exchange. Utility does not do so, nor do certain apparently privileged commodities (corn, gold, etc.). Ricardo argues (following Smith) that whilst nature may produce use-values only labour can produce exchangeable-value (*ibid.*, pp. 285–6). With the exception of land, all the elements which enter into production are themselves obtained by or are the products of labour (raw materials, tools, machines, etc.) and exchange according to their labour-times of production. Labour is, therefore, the basic element in social production. All commodities have the common property of being products of labour. Labour is a possible equivalent because it is universal, and is negatively privileged as equivalent because it has no competitor. This is as near a justification for the law of value as can be reconstructed from the *Principles*. But it does not explain, all this being true, *why* labour should prevail as the substance underlying exchangeable-value, *why* goods should exchange according to the labour times embodied in them, and what would happen if they did not? Smith's anthropological answer is ignored, but no substitute is proffered. Smith's account has the advantage that it provides a *mechanism* (however dubious or implausible) which sustains the law of value: human subjects, through calculation and interaction, respect a certain 'rule' (equate efforts—as well as you can suppose them) in order to sustain a division of labour and through it their own self-interest.

Marx recognises the analytic rigour which is at the same time the theoretical weakness in Ricardo's position when he argues that Ricardo concentrates exhaustively on the *magnitude* of value and ignores the question of why the distribution of the product takes this *form*. This criticism, expressed in a famous passage in *Capital*, vol. 1, is further developed in *Theories of Surplus Value*:

> Ricardo's method is as follows: He begins with the determination of the magnitude of the value of the commodity by labour time and then *examines* whether the economic

> relations and categories *contradict* this determination or to what extent they modify it. . . . Ricardo starts out from the determination of the relative values (or exchangeable values) of commodities by the *quantity of labour*. . . . The character of this 'labour' is not further examined. . . . But *Ricardo does not examine* the form—the peculiar characteristic of labour that creates exchange values or manifests itself in exchange values—the *nature* of this labour. Hence he does not grasp the connection of *this* labour with *money* or that it must assume the form of *money*. (*Theories of Surplus Value*, vol. 2, p. 164—modified, emphasis in original)

Ricardo equates exchange-value and value as categories, for him labour as such is the substance of value. He does not explain *why* the exchange of goods in ratios proportional to the labour-times necessary for their production should be the form of regulation of the distribution of the social product.

Marx will seek to explain the *form* of value (value-in-exchange) as a consequence of certain social relations (those of commodity production) but in the context of a general law of value which applies to all forms of production. In vol. 1 of *Capital* Marx begins with the analysis of the commodity as object of exchange and with the problem of how it is possible for there to be equivalent exchanges of such objects. He poses this problem in the form of a third term (distinct from and applicable to both objects) in which both objects can be expressed as equal (identical in the third term). That term is labour-time: this is because only human labour in the abstract, devoid of qualities, independent of the use-values it produces, can serve as a universal and quantifiable standard of value. Exchange-value is the phenomenal form (x object A = y object B) of a relation of identity (of labour-times). So far Marx's argument is negative, concerning the relative merits of labour-time as a measure against others. He follows Ricardo's line of argument (with the difference that he has defined the exchange explicitly as an equation-identity of labour-times). But why do the products of labour take this form (equivalence in exchange) and why do they do so in the form of labour-time? Marx answers the first question by making the *form* of value conditional on certain social relations, and he answers the second through the general category of 'value', by explaining that the apportionment and distribution of labour is a primary and essential economic function whatever its social form.

Marx explains the necessity of the 'law of value' in section 4 of chapter 1 of *Capital* on 'The fetishism of commodities'. Marx opposes any rationalistic account of exchange in terms of the calculations of advantage of human subjects:

> Men do not therefore bring the products of their labour into relation with each other as values because they see these objects as the material integuments of homogeneous human labour. The reverse is true: by equating their different products to each other in exchange as values, they equate their different kinds of labour as human labour. (*Capital*, vol. 1, Penguin edn, p. 166)

Value is a 'social hieroglyphic': its foundation in abstract labour is glimpsed at by Smith and this labour is mistakenly universalised by him into an essential human attribute. For Smith the value-form is present at the rude beginnings of society; he creates an imaginary scene in which private property and the divided labour characteristic of commodity production are presupposed as simple extensions or consequences of basic human motives and attributes. Marx argues that, on the contrary: 'The value character of the products of human labour becomes firmly established only when they act as magnitudes of value (*ibid.*, p. 167), that is, when they function as the means of linking divided labours and of equating them.

But why should labours need linking in the form of equation? Marx criticises Smith for erecting, in his rude deer- and beaver-hunters, an economic 'state of nature', for essentialising forms which are specific to commodity production. What Marx does *not* criticise is what is at stake in this scene, the exchange of *equivalents* (although Marx's and Smith's conceptions of that equivalence are different). Marx does not criticise the problem of the interrelation of divided labours involved in this equivalence, merely the de-historicised (or rather, historical-imaginary) mode of its posing and the form of the equivalence itself (it becomes an objective equation rather than a subjective equity). In *Capital* the form of value (value-in-exchange) is one particular type of solution to a universal economic problem, the allocation of social labour in proportions necessary for a certain composition of the product. The equation of labour-times is necessary in order that this allocation be possible in an unplanned division of labour between independent producers (without equivalence it is supposed that this alloeation will not work out 'right').

In order to explain the economic necessity of the distribution of labour-time Marx provocatively returns to the imaginary scene:

> As political economists are fond of Robinson Crusoe stories, let us look first at Robinson on his island. Undemanding though he is by nature, he still has needs to satisfy, and must therefore perform useful labours of various kinds. . . . Despite the diversity of his productive functions, he knows that they are only different forms of one and the same Robinson, hence only different modes of human labour. Necessity itself compels him to divide his time with precision between his different functions. Whether one function occupies a greater space in his total activity than another depends on the magnitude of the difficulties to be overcome in attaining the useful objects aimed at. . . . His stock-book contains a catalogue of the useful objects he possesses, of the various operations necessary for their production, and finally of the labour time that specific quantities of these products have on average cost him. (*Capital*, vol. 1, Penguin edn, p. 170)

This example serves to present the pertinence of value as a general category: 'All the relations between Robinson and these objects contain all the essential determinants of value' (*ibid.*).* Value is the message of the stock-books all societies keep, although these books are written in different languages. All societies apportion labour between the different tasks to be performed and objects to be produced. Whether it be Robinson, a peasant household or a society of associated producers, they must apportion the labour necessary to the reproduction of society and its members correctly.

As Marx reminded the bemused Kugelmann:

> All this palaver about the necessity of proving the concept of value comes from complete ignorance both of the subject dealt with and of scientific method. Every child knows that a nation which ceased to work, I will not say for a year, but even for a few weeks, would perish. Every child knows, too, that the

---

* Marx is exaggerating here. There is a real difference between the way this problem occurs in commodity and non-commodity forms of production. Robinson's allocation is a direct distribution of *time*. In a commodity system it is *products* which are distributed and the allocation of social labour-time is regulated through the ratios in which products exchange one with another.

> masses of products corresponding to the different needs require different and quantitatively determined masses of the total labour of society. That this *necessity* of the *distribution* of social labour in definite proportions cannot possibly be done away with by a *particular form* of social production but can only change the *mode* of its *appearance*, is self-evident. No natural laws can be done away with. (Marx to Kugelmann—11 July 1868)

Exchange-value is the stock-book of commodity production. In exchanging the products of their labour as equivalents in labour-time independent producers, blindly and unknowingly, are supposed to reproduce the proportions of social labour objectively necessary for a certain composition and scale of production. Marx clearly has no truck with Smith's subjectivism, with his equation of labour-times through the calculating principles of economy of effort and self-interest. Marx does, however, explain the necessity of equivalent exchange in terms of its reproducing the division of labour. Equivalent exchange is conceived as a 'particular form' of a universal 'natural law'. To breach the law of value is to problematise the division of society's labour and in turn the existence of society itself.

Further, for Marx equivalent exchange (identity of labour-times) is the form of manifestation of the general law of value in only one type of economy, simple commodity production. Smith's deer- and beaver-hunters are given an historically specific form by Marx: a society characterised by a division of labour between independent petty producers who are the possessors of their own labour products. These products are exchanged according to the labour-times necessary for their production. In this society exchange is conducted, Marx insists, through the medium of money rather than simple barter. Money is a means of payment, but only because it is a commodity with a value that serves as the measure of value. The general value-form is the 'social expression' (*Capital*, vol. 1, Penguin edn, p. 160) or 'résumé' (Aveling and Moore) of the world of commodities and money, because it takes the place of the general form, functions as a 'résumé' of all other commodities, as the measure of value. Money can serve this function only because it is itself a commodity, the product of labour and has a value: 'The measure of values measures commodities considered as values . . . But gold can serve as a measure of value only because it is itself a product of labour and therefore potentially variable in value' (*Capital*, vol. 1, Penguin edn, p. 192). Money is the medium of the exchange of equivalents. Money-relations are value-relations. Here the structure of social production is preserved by the exchange of equal quanta of labour-time.

Capitalism entails a different form of manifestation of the universal law. Exchange is conducted not in terms of equal quanta of labour-time but through (fluctuations excepted) prices of production. *Profits not values are equated*: commodities cannot exchange according to the labour embodied in them if surplus value is to be redistributed across capitals to ensure an equal average rate of profit. Capitalist economies distribute ('redistribute') social labour in a forced and approximate way through competition and crises. The 'law of value' no longer takes the form of exchange of equivalents. The methodical Robinson of Defoe is replaced by Tournier's all-too-human Robinson who built his boat and forgot about the necessity of launching it. Marx analyses in the case of capitalism social relations which, contrary to the knowledge of 'every child', do not distribute labour with the exactness and parsimony of Crusoe the Puritan, but with the largesse and disorder of a Pantagruel—and still survive.

Why, in fact, should the question of the distribution of labour-time dominate the analysis of exchange? Why should the question of the distribution of labour assume the form of proportionality? It is merely an assumption that the equation of labour-times of the producers is either necessary or sufficient for their reproduction (indeed, certain producers might not be able to subsist even given the labour-time equivalents of their products). The notion of a 'maldistribution' of social labour and its consequences supposes that labour-time has a central pertinence in determining the product. This can be disputed and, even if it were not, it could be argued that substantial deviations from identity of labour-times in exchange would not destroy the division of labour.

Labour-times are equated in exchange only in certain specific social relations of production. In simple commodity production the (necessary) labour-time contributions of the agents determine the distribution of the product, determine the ratios in which goods exchange against one another. In capitalism the producing agents are not the possessors of the product and it is sold by enterprises in exchanges which do not equalise labour-times. Exchange-value and value do not directly correspond in capitalism. However, the analysis of surplus value requires that the conceptions pertinent to one set of social relations be extended to the other. For the production of the concept of surplus-value wages and the product of labour must be expressed as and compared *as values*, they must be measurable in a term common to both (labour-time) and shown to represent discrepant quantities of that term. It must also be assumed that the labour-time contributions of the agents are a pertinent measure of the distribution of the product. The product can then be ascribed to labour, first as its producer, and second, in the relation of the value of wages (necessary labour) and the value of the product (necessary + surplus labour). If this assumption were not pertinent then there would be no reason to relate the one to the other. This relating of wages and the product of labour also assumes that labour-time equivalent exchanges are pertinent (they make the whole problem of 'surplus labour' possible): the wage = 'necessary labour' (equivalent exchange), the remainder of the working day is 'surplus' labour which arises from the fact of propertylessness (selling one's labour power) and which is given for no equivalent. Thus necessary to pose the concept of surplus value are: (1) exchanges as equations of labour-time; (2) the pertinence of the labour contributions of the agents; (3) the assumption on that basis that the product of labour is the measure of its reward.

Why in fact should the problem of 'revenues' be conceived in terms of the labour contributions of the agents? Given the assumption of proportionality and the law of value one can see why it should follow in the system of simple commodity production. But these assumptions are not necessary ones and their conditions are modified in capitalism. The *Critique of the Gotha Programme* raises a quite different way of conceiving the distribution of the product and the question of the 'revenues' of the agents. In the *Critique* Marx argues that the proportionality of rewards to labour-time expended and of equal reward for equivalent labours is a bourgeois principle. Its retention in the first phase of socialism is a necessary continuation of the ideology of bourgeois right. This is due to the fact that socialism involves a period of transition from capitalism; social productivity is still limited. It is a system without capitalist wage labour, but distributes the product nevertheless through money wages and is compelled to ration the means of consumption produced. Here the bourgeois principle of equivalence must be retained, formally equal labours (identical labour-times) are equally rewarded. This principle, however, rules *only for the distribution of means of consumption among workers*: the division of the product into means of production and means of consumption, and the allocation of means of consumption to those unable to work is determined on a different basis. Moreover, it ensures merely a formal equality between workers (labour-*times* not labours are equally rewarded). In this form of society the product is only partially distributed according to the labour contributions of the agents, in other forms it is not distributed on this basis at all. Marx's ideal is a society which inscribes upon its banner 'from each according to his ability, to each according to his needs' (an admirable principle, the necessary cornerstone of socialist ideology, but one which squares ill with the 'natural law' advanced in *Capital*).

In the *Critique* Marx argues *that for all systems of social production it is the form of distribution of the means of production between the agents which determines the distribution of the social product among them and not the labour contributions of these agents to that product.* In Marx's concept of simple commodity production the mode of distribution follows from the possession of the means of production by independent direct producers who are linked in a social division of labour. Equal right corresponds to autonomous private possession of the elements of this division of labour. Capitalism converts equal right into an *ideology*—class relations shatter the independent/interdependent exchange/association between members of society. As Marx says in the *Critique* the distribution of the product in capitalism follows from the distribution of the means of production between possessors and non-possessors.

May we not, therefore, dispense with the problem of distribution according to the labour contributions of the agents in the analysis of capitalist economies? Following the position taken in the *Critique* might we not take the view that workers obtain what money wages they can command for their labour power and capitalists obtain what money (and level of profits) accrues from the sale of the product? This distribution follows from the distribution of the means of production and no reference need be made to the labour contributions of the agents to the product. *Only the system of simple commodity production bases the distribution of the product on the labour contributions of the agents and in the form of exchanges between them.*

It is the problem of the origin of profit in the roles played by the different categories of agents which makes the consideration of labour contributions and the continued use of value terms necessary in the discourse of *Capital. Capital* cannot accept this reference to another text, to the *Critique*. For the concept of surplus value it is necessary that social production be conceived of in terms derived from and applicable to exchanges of equal labour-times (however much this 'assumption' may be modified later in the discourse, it cannot be abandoned at the point of production of this concept) and that the contributions of the different classes of agents to the product be considered (the product as a totality of value must be ascribed to the direct producers, the capitalist is a non-labourer).

The phenomenal form of the wage contract is that of an equal exchange. In Marx's terms the value of the labour-power (labour-time equivalent of the commodities needed to reproduce it) and the value of the wages received for it are equal. However, it is the worker's *capacity* to labour which is bought, not labour sufficient to produce the equivalent of the wage. The worker does not receive in the value of the wage the totality of values produced by him, the value represented by the labour he actually expends. The capitalist obtains through the wage form the right to utilise a value-creating power, a right the worker cannot exercise because of his non-possession of the means of production. The capitalist possesses and sells the totality of value thus produced and receives the money equivalent for it (an equivalent modified for the individual capitalist by the effects of averaging). This totality which is sold includes a portion of which no equivalent was given in the purchase of labour-power. Surplus value does not arise as such in either of the commodity transactions which precede or follow its production. As a consequence the product of the workers' 'unpaid' labour serves to exploit them in the future in the form of capital. This critique of the inner essence of capitalist production is only possible if the exchange of equivalents is supposed to be the ruling social form and if it takes the form of exchanges of equal quanta of labour-time.

If we adopt for capitalism the position taken in the *Critique* on the relationship between possession of the means of production and the distribution of the product, that is, the labour contribution of the agents is *not* the basis of distribution, then this contribution and the notion of 'unpaid' labour has no pertinence. Workers receive wages as a consequence of their separation from (non-possession of) the means of production. What role the labourer plays in production is irrelevant to the *form* of distribution. The notion of 'unpaid' labour can only appear by supposing the pertinence of different conditions of distribution—applying the principle of the proportionality of rewards to actual labour contributions. Then the questions of what the workers produce with their labour and of the status of that labour (whether it is constitutive of value) do become pertinent to the distribution question. The contribution of the agents to the product becomes pertinent only if it is assumed that the ruling relations of distribution can be conceived as ones in which the product is circulated as commodities in the form of equivalent quanta of labour-time. It can then be shown that capitalist possession of the means of production contradicts these relations of circulation: it does so because the form of exchange involving labour-power and variable capital makes possible the creation of 'unpaid' labour, labour-time given for no equivalent. The concept of 'unpaid' or 'surplus' labour means work beyond the labour-time necessary to produce the value equivalent to the wage. This concept involves the assumption that equivalence is the general form of exchange with this one (crucial) exception—if it is not the general form why should this divergence (incalculable in any case, since value would not be a *social* standard) be more significant than any other?

The concept 'value' (labour-time) and the assumption that value-relations govern the exchange of commodities enables Marx to explain the origin and nature of profit. It enables him to ascribe it to a definite category of agents who produce it and do not possess it. It enables him to resolve the concrete forms of distribution (profits, rents, wages) into divisions of a totality of value produced by the workers, the product of paid and unpaid labour-time. On this assumption *surplus value equals profit* (under prices of production the totality of surplus value and the totality of capitalist's profits correspond). At the risk of repetition, surplus value arises in the difference between the value of labour-power and the value of the product created by the labour actually expended. This analysis of the two quantities cannot work unless value-terms in labour-time are supposed and form the basis of calculation. In order for it to be shown that the two sums are not equal (value of wages—value created by labour) it is necessary that comparable terms be present on both sides (wages and the product can be expressed as quanta of the same measure). *When the assumption that labour-time is the 'substance of value' is abandoned then the two sides of the equation become incommensurable. This is not a technical matter of calculation in price-terms versus value-terms, but a question of the theoretical conditions of existence of calculation. The linking of the two sides of the equation depends on the concept of the value-creating power of labour.* With this concept the analysis of exploitation could be done where prices and values deviate in an ordered way (value-relations govern price-relations). Remove the assumptions of the value-creating power of labour and the pertinence of equivalent exchange and the result is that the analysis cannot be done. There is no reason to ascribe profit to an origin in labour, as the product of 'unpaid' labour.

Value analysis can analyse the exploitation in capitalist production because of the concept of the value-creating power of labour and the assumption that commodities despite divergence 'represent' values. This means that for the purpose of analysis of exploitation the differences between production and circulation are obliterated, or rather, that categories of exchange are interiorised within production. The value of the product exists independently of market fluctuations—exploitation can be calculated at the level of production once the values of necessary labour and constant capital are known. Failure to sell the product or to sell at an appropriate price is a failure to *realise* surplus value in the form of profit (realisation is a complexity which is introduced at a later stage in the exposition). Realisation is a question distinct from exploitation and does not change it in Marx's analysis, nor does the redistribution of surplus value which takes place through the averaging of the rate of profit.

It might be argued as a form of defence of the category, that 'value' is *merely* a means of calculating exploitation. It might be considered as a necessary abstraction in order to make visible a phenomenon which would otherwise remain invisible. This position is untenable if it is to be articulated with the other concepts of *Capital*. It radically contradicts *Capital*'s theory of measurement and its concept of value as measure. That theory conceives value as a theoretical category (a form existing in abstraction) but not as an *abstraction from reality*. Like the other concepts in *Capital* it is part of an abstract process of reasoning which appropriates reality in thought. Value-relations are not visible, are not phenomenal forms, but they are *real*, they are a fundamental condition of production and are operative through the intersection of production and exchange. Value is a concept which represents (in thought) a real effectivity, the determination of socially necessary labour-time. Value-relations are calculable because they are real (technical calculation is, however, quite secondary to Marx's argument, he is quite happy to use arbitrarily assigned numbers for purposes of theoretical exposition). If these relations existed merely as assigned values (labour-times assigned thus could only be 'necessary' for the theoretical purposes in question not *socially* necessary) then they could not causally *govern* social relations. *Capital*'s conception of value as measure does suppose this. The assumption that value prevails socially as a real measure (that commodities are directly or indirectly determined in the ratios in which they exchange by their socially necessary labour-times, and are calculable in their labour-time equivalents) is necessary both for Marx's theory of exchange-relations and his theory of surplus value. This assumption depends on another, that only human labour is a value-creating power and that human labour takes the form of value under definite social relations. This theory of value and value-creating power is posed in *Capital* on the basis of the social relations of simple commodity production and then extended to capitalism.

We know that *Capital* argues that value-relations underlie the system of prices of production which determine exchange-relations in capitalism; social production is still regulated by the labour-times necessary for the production of commodities. We also know that the theory of value supposes that labour-times are equated through the ratios in which commodities exchange (even though they make those ratios possible). Marx must therefore establish a connection between the forms of exchange, production and value in capitalism if his theory of exploitation and accumulation is to be possible in it. This theory depends on a category (value in the form of value) which is elaborated on the basis of social relations of exchange which are different from those of capitalism.

Exchanges in capitalism are not the equation of labour-times. In the subsequent chapters of this part, on Hilferding and Rubin, we will consider in more detail how Marx attempts to link exchange-relations and their value-determinants in capitalism.

Here we will merely make the point that this problem is not an imaginary one created by 'bourgeois' critics. Even if one accepts the general 'law of value' proposed in certain sections of *Capital* (all societies must have a mechanism to ensure the distribution of labour-time so as to produce a certain composition of the product) it is not at all clear why the operation of this 'law' should ever require the exchange of *equal* quanta of labour-time. Marx attempts to argue this for a system of divided/interdependent labours, but why this interrelation should collapse or be impossible with discrepancies of a considerable order from equality is not shown. Even if capitalist production were regulated in the long run by changes in the productivity of labour, this regulator (a form of the general law of value) can operate with exchanges of radically discrepant quanta of labour-time. Maldistributions of social labour (obsolete methods of production) are ultimately supposed to be penalised in crises and through competition: labour-time operates through discrepancy from equality. The theory of surplus value does suppose, however, that exchange-equation terms are applicable to capitalism; labour-time identities are exchanged in relations of ordered deviation. We are pointing out that this form of measure is applicable with these modifications only if its *foundation* is a pertinent one. We cannot see why the 'law of value' in its general form (whatever the merits of that conception) should ever necessitate value in the form of value, exchange-values as labour-time identities or as ordered modifications of them.

The positing of the *form* of value is a brilliant device whereby Marx avoids a labour-substance theory of value (which would universalise the form). The insistence that value and exchange-value are distinct in capitalism and the theory of prices of production enables Marx to avoid the difficulties of a simple labour theory of price under capitalist conditions. This analysis displaces the value-form as the immediate form of the process of exchange. The combination of value analysis and the analysis of capitalistic circulation is a problematic one. The retention of value analysis must reduce the capitalist circulation relations to a mere phenomenal form or expression of value-relations, or, the 'phenomena' must problematise the conditions of exchange-equivalence necessary for the 'essence'. We will argue in Volume Two that the value-concept has constituted an obstacle to the analysis of circulation and money in capitalism.

Labour and labour-power, constant and variable capital

The labour/labour-power distinction is the basis of the argument that the wage-form does not in its effects represent an exchange of equivalents. This is because of the dual nature of the commodity involved in the wage-form (labour-power) as an exchange-value and as a use-value. Labour-power is consumed as concrete labour.

But all commodities involve a difference between their exchange-values and their usefulness.

What is it that makes the commodity labour-power unique? Here we come up against not merely the *form* of the measure of equivalence but also its *foundation*; what it is that necessitates the form and its uniqueness as the sole standard of value. The distinction between constant and variable capital is based on the proposition that the commodity involved in the wage-form has a dual nature as exchange-value and use-value which is different from all other commodities. There is a general discrepancy between values (universal and equivalent in form—representing quanta of a single standard) and use-value (heterogeneous, non-equivalent, useful *because* of their distinct and use-specific forms). The use-value of the commodity labour-power is unlike all others because it becomes on consumption the substance of value itself (labour-time) and is capable therefore of being represented as value. Marx argues that means of production and machines are *constant* capital because, being sold at their values, they can only have the value embodied in them (x past labour) transferred to the product by the newly applied labour engaged in the process of production in which they function as means. Machines are merely 'dead labour' and have no value-creating power: 'Machinery, like every other component of constant capital, creates no new value, but yields up its own value to the product it serves to beget' (*Capital*, vol. 1, Penguin edn, p. 509).

The distinction between constant and variable capital rests on the rejection of all other elements of the production process than labour-time being pertinent to the theory of value. Why is labour-power a unique commodity? Because labour-time is the *substance* of value. This 'substance' is not an ontological attribute of labour *as such*, it is a function of labour which produces commodities. The value-form of labour-time is a function of the fact that the products of labour enter a social process of exchange. Marx cannot explain the dominance of the value standard by reference to the nature of human labour in general. It is not because human labour is constitutive of the product that it is the substance of value.

Marx differentiates between the *productivity* of labour and its *value-creating power*. The productivity of labour, the mass of use-values produced by a number of hours of labour, is a function of the means of production which it employs. Marx defines the productivity of labour thus:

> By an increase in the productivity of labour, we mean an alteration in the labour process of such a kind as to shorten the labour time socially necessary for the production of a commodity, and to endow a given quantity of labour with the power of producing a greater quantity of use value. (*ibid.*, p. 431)

The mass of *use-values* measures the productivity of labour. The *value* of labour-time is distributed over this mass, and as this mass rises so the value of each of the units composing it falls. Marx says: 'The value of commodities stands in inverse ratio to the productivity of labour' (*ibid.*, p. 436). The means of production determine the productivity of labour. The value of the means of production and the value per unit of the products produced by them depend on the units of labour-time entailed in the production of those means and in the production of each unit of the product.

Marx therefore recognises that the means of production and the forms of organisation of production (division of labour, co-operation) are the source of changes in the productivity of labour. Marx treats the productive power of machines, their capacity of work, like a force of nature. The difference between the cost of a machine and that machine's capacity for work is the 'gratuitous service' the machine performs. Marx says:

> Both in the case of the machine and the tool, we find that after allowing for their average daily cost, that is for the value they transmit to the product by their average wear and tear . . . they do their work for nothing, like the natural forces which are already available without the intervention of human labour. The greater the productive effectiveness of machinery compared with that of the tool, the greater is the extent of this gratuitous service. Only in large-scale industry has man succeeded in making the product of his past labour, labour which has already

> been objectified, perform gratuitous service on a large scale, like a force of nature. (*ibid.*, p. 510)

For Marx this difference of machine cost and machine capacity means that the product cannot be ascribed to labour as an origin: human labour is no longer the primary determinant of the transformation of raw materials into a product. The productive power of a machine is determined by its technical characteristics and not by the labour that we needed to make it (that labour determines its *value*). The value embodied in the machine (its cost to its productive consumer) is transmitted piecemeal to the products it creates during its normal working life; the mass of those products is not determined by that value.

The productive capacity of technique acts on value-relations in the following ways:

1 The productivity of a process of production determines the value component per unit of product; the capacity of the process determines the number of units of product over which the totality of labour-time involved must be distributed. Productivity, therefore, affects the relative value per unit of product of different ways of making the same or a similar commodity. Productivity acts on value-relations by reducing the labour-time component per unit of the product, 'cheapening' it (in value-terms).

2 It is labour-time which bestows value on the product. For any given process a certain number of hours of labour-time is necessary for a certain quantity of the product. Productivity increases act to reduce this total. If the quantity of the product produced does not increase proportionately not only does the value-component per unit fall but the absolute value-total (hours of labour) falls.

It follows that were human labour to be excluded from the process of production or be reduced to an infinitesimal quantity then, according to the theory of value, the products of that process would be like fruits of nature, use-values but without a value. In the *Grundrisse* Marx considered this possibility. Automatic machinery subordinates the worker to the process of production, reducing him to a mere conscious moment (supervision) in an objective mechanism created by scientific knowledge and the combined power of co-operative social labour. The term 'labour process' has become a misnomer: 'In no way does the machine appear as the individual worker's means of labour. . . . The production process has ceased to be a process dominated by labour as its governing unity' (*Grundrisse*, notebook vi, pp. 692–3). Capitalism, in creating in the automatic mechanism the objective form of domination over the worker appropriate to its existence as capital, as dead labour, creates the conditions of its own dissolution. The labourer and labour-time become insignificant in relation to the combined productive power of society represented in capital:

> To the degree that labour time—the mere quantity of labour—is posited by capital as the sole determinant element, to that degree does direct labour and its quantity disappear as the determinant principle of production—of the creation of use values—and is reduced both quantitatively, to a smaller proportion, and qualitatively, as an, of course, indispensable but subordinate moment, compared to general scientific labour, technological application of the natural sciences, on the one side, and to the general productive force arising from social combination in total production on the other side—a combination which appears as the natural fruit of social labour (although it is a historic product). Capital thus works towards its own dissolution as the form dominating production. (*ibid*., note book vii, p. 700)

Value-relations (relations based on labour-time) become irrelevant to this combined productive mechanism. The social product is less due to the direct labours of men than to the associated scientific knowledge and technical application of humanity. Value-relations are threatened with irrelevance by the indeterminacy of direct labour-time to social production. The combined and co-operative, socialised nature of production makes the capitalist property form irrelevant because it makes the division of society into separate private producers irrelevant. Capitalism, through the forces of competition, displaces labour from the production process, cheapening the product and, ultimately, displacing itself. It would appear from Marx's position in the *Grundrisse* that socialism could dispense with the law of value in *both* the senses used in *Capital*, as a law of proportionality in exchange and as a law of distribution of social labour.

We have seen that Marx rejects any simple labour-substance theory of value. However, whilst value-in-exchange is a form produced by certain social relations and is effective *through* relations of exchange, value takes labour-time as its standard because of the central role of labour-time in determining what is produced and in what quantities. Why must the products of independent units of production exchange in ratios directly determined (simple commodity production) or indirectly determined (capitalism) by the labour-times necessary for their production? Because labour-time *is* the determinant of what can be produced. The social product must be expressed in labour-time terms because the labour of transformation is its primary condition of existence. The law of value as a general law of distribution of social labour must assign this status to labour—the form of value is a modality of representation of this determinance made necessary by private and socially divided production.

The product can be made a function of labour-time only if the elements in the process of its production can be reduced to and expressed in labour-time terms. The action of the direct labourer determines the rate of working of each of these elements, these elements are themselves products of previous labour processes, and, in consequence, the product of the process can be ascribed in its magnitude to the duration and intensity of labour. The effects of machinery, production organisation (division of labour, co-operation, methods of working) and joint production mean that this relation no longer holds. What and how much is produced is no longer a function of labour-time, but of the technical productivity of the process in question. Labour power is reduced to a 'factor' in the process, an element which may be necessary but ancillary, which does not determine its productive capacity. The law of value operates (as the example of Robinson shows) to ensure a certain composition of the total product. Under conditions where labour power is merely a 'factor' it is the distribution and organisation of the *means* of production which determines a certain size and composition of the total product.

Even if it were assumed that the radical effects of production organisation and technique were confined to industrial capitalism it would still follow that the basis for the law of value (as a law of distribution of social labour) is rendered irrelevant by this system of production. Not only would capitalism modify the *form* of value (exchange of equivalents) but it also undercuts the foundation on which that form (and all other manifestations of the general law) are based.

To justify the law of value as a law of exchange-proportions Marx argues that exchange takes the form of an equation measured as such in a third term. It might be argued that the status of labour in the production process is irrelevant and that the theory of value rests on the fact that labour-times can be equated because they can be given an abstract quantitative form whereas use-values cannot. This defence undercuts the law of value as a general law of distribution of social labour. There are two arguments against this line of defence of the value form. The first is the possibility of a utility theory of exchange-proportions—we will consider this in more detail when we discuss Böhm-Bawerk. The second is that this defence supposes the necessity of exchange taking the form of an identity of labour-times. This necessity returns us to the general law of value (undercut by this defence). The one possible argument for this supposition is that unless 'equivalents' are exchanged the distribution of social labour will problematise the social division of labour. We have encountered this argument above and will consider it again in its usage by Hilferding and Rubin. Here we will merely repeat that it in no way follows that social production needs must collapse if equivalents are not exchanged or labour is 'maldistributed'. The threat of collapse, further, cannot necessitate the conditions which remove that threat except by means of a teleological mechanism or the postulation of a 'human nature'.

Marx's explanation of the centrality of labour-time is not based on a simple ontology of human labour. It does entail the primacy of direct labour in the labour process, but, as we have seen, in both the *Grundrisse* and *Capital* Marx argues that this primacy is displaced in capitalism. Many contemporary justifications of the law of value are at bottom philosophical/anthropological. They entail the conception of human labour in the *1844 Manuscripts*. They refer us back to the conception of labour as human self-creation, to the notion of man as his own product, and to labour as an activity which is ontologically unique as a power derived from nature but which acts upon it and is transformative of it. Labour as constitutive of product is a position which is plausible only if all machines and techniques are conceived as extensions of the handicraft tool, and the labourers who work with machines as the direct agents of transformation of the product.

Yet, in the fifteenth chapter of *Capital* 'Machinery and Modern Industry', Marx goes beyond this ideology of *homo faber*, he argues that as capitalist production develops the labourers are reduced to the role of agents of the process (this is often conceived as the 'alienation' of man in machine production—an 'alienation' that Marx does not resolutely refuse—'alienation' here reveals the extent to which man is considered as the subject or origin of the process of production). Once the limits of value theory are removed then it becomes possible to correct and develop Marx's analysis of the factory as a complex and collective process of production. If it is recognised that the agency of transformation of the *raw* material is the complex *process* (including each of its necessary elements, machines, the collective labourer, techniques and knowledges) then the resulting product can be ascribed only to the process itself (and to all its effectivities in combination) and not to labour or labour-time alone. Such a conception makes possible the investigation of the distinct forms of such processes, the differential effectivity of methods of working, and so on. These analyses have not been done, they have been submerged by the concentration on the direct labourer and on the production of relative surplus value (e.g. Braverman's *Labour and Monopoly Capital*).

The capacity of the *process* to produce products of composition and quality which are distinct from the raw materials does not provide the foundation for a new theory of value. Once value-terms are removed the question of how the relative efficiency of processes of production is evaluated becomes a serious one. This difficulty is, however, hardly sufficient reason to retain this problematic concept.

The distinction between constant and variable capital ultimately depends on the theory of value and the notion of the value-creating power of labour. This distinction and that between labour and labour-power are distinct, and they have different fates. Labour/labour-power is a mode of stating the relation between wages and the production process; it has some point even if value-terms are abandoned. Labour-power, the commodity sold for wages, is determined by the cost of production of the labourer (which can be expressed in non-value-terms) and other factors. The determinants of the wage level (price of labour-power) have no direct relation to the labourer's contribution to the product. This difference of the determinants of wages and of the labourer's role in the production process is a necessary effect of the separation of the phases of circulation (sale/purchase of labour-power) and production (productive consumption of labour-power as a means of production) involved in the wage-form; it expresses the separation of the labourers from the means of production. When value-terms are abandoned this distinction of labour and labour-power becomes a mode of stating the relations of production involved in the wage-form under capitalism. It is no longer, however, the means of demonstrating 'unequal' exchange and therefore the source of profit. When value-terms are abandoned, as we have seen, the relation of 'necessary' and 'surplus' labour becomes incalculable.

As a consequence of this incommensurability of wages and the worker's contribution to the product the notion of 'exploitation' becomes untenable. The notion of 'surplus value' or 'unpaid' labour in *Capital* does not entail the Proudhonist notion that it should therefore actually be *paid*—it could not be 'paid' without abolishing the wage-form, and, as the *Critique* shows, even under socialist forms the worker's contribution does not belong 'undiminished' to him. It does, however, entail the position that the 'unpaid' portion is *calculable* and the unit of calculation is a social standard of measurement (value-terms make wages and the product of labour commensurable as sums of that standard). If this standard of measurement does not prevail then the concepts of 'exploitation' and 'surplus value' lose their theoretical foundations. Their place in discourse is problematised because they are not moral or political-polemical terms but theoretical categories of political economy. They depend for their importance on appropriating an objective phenomenon with a real measure.

'Exploitation' and classes

It may be considered that if 'exploitation' becomes incalculable (in terms of a socially prevailing measure represented in theoretical concepts) then the whole basis of the capitalist system of class relations becomes problematic. There is no reason for this fear. Classes of economic agents are defined by their relation to the means and conditions of production (as possessors and non-possessors) and not by the portion of the product they are supposed to contribute.

Capitalist relations of production entail the separation of the workers from the means of production, the wage-form, and the distribution of the product (including the means of production) through commodity exchange. This combination of separation (non-possession) and the wage-form creates a *working class*, in the sense of agents compelled to sell their labour-power in order to obtain the means of subsistence. The different branches of production, the technical forms of production and the forms of production organisation differentiate this class of wage workers into distinct economic functions and specialisms: co-ordinators, technical functionaries, 'skilled' workers, machine attendants, handicraftsmen, etc. The forms of circulation and the existence of non-industrial commodities also generate specialisms. The social form of this distribution of the working class into distinct levels is variable.

Capitalist relations of production entail the separation of the workers from the means of production by a property form, but they do not, in general, entail a *class* of capitalists in the sense of agents who own the means of production as their private property and draw their consumption funds from the profits derived from this property. Under conditions of the socialisation of capital (capital funds result from the centralisation of deposits and the sale of financial commodities by finance capitalist enterprises) and of capitalist enterprises as trusts (supra-individual property) then no such class, conceived as a group of human agents, need exist. Instead paid functionaries effect the combination of these means of production with labour power, and they operate as agents necessitated by the structure of separation, serving the form of exclusive possession for which they work. *Capitals* (not capital*ists*) are the agents of possession necessary to capitalist relations of production (depending on the economic and political/legal context, they may take the form of human or non-human economic subjects).

Removing the notion of 'exploitation' as an economic category does not remove the economic foundations of the division of agents into classes. It does not eliminate capitalist relations of production. First, let us again insist that for Marx 'exploitation' is a category of political economy which represents an inner connection of the system of capitalist production and not a phenomenal form which is represented to the agents (otherwise there would be a royal expressway to science). Exploitation is hidden by the wage form (here it is a *form*), concealed as an exchange of equivalents. If it is not so represented it cannot, *as a category*, be effective as a cause of the class struggle—and Marx does not make the class struggle dependent on *consciousness* of exploitation. As an inner connection it is effective through its effects; now these 'effects' exist whether or not 'exploitation' exists or is calculable. Economic class struggle in capitalism arises from the 'antagonistic' nature of the separation of labour-power and the means of production ('antagonism' is here used in the sense defined in Hindess and Hirst, *Pre-Capitalist Modes of Production*). Let us consider the elements of this separation:

1 the worker's conditions of existence depend on his combination with the means of production, this combination is not in his power and depends on anarchic conditions of commodity exchange;
2 the 'anarchy' of capitalist production (the relation of production and circulation) necessarily produces unemployment and other changes which the workers (considered solely as agents) cannot control;
3 capitalist production is not governed by criteria of social usefulness;
4 the level of wages is not given but is the subject of struggle.

These conditions explain the existence of the economic class struggle. They also explain the reason why, in order for the effects of anarchy and the denial of socially necessary priorities in production to be overcome, capitalist relations of production must be superseded. These conditions affect all wage workers in varying degrees. The notion of 'exploitation' does not apply to all wage workers (for example, 'unproductive' workers do not produce surplus value and cannot be exploited). Further, in its vulgar applications it forms the basis for an essentialist ideology of the working class centring in 'productive' (exploited) labour.

This position poses an important problem for analysis: the determinants of the differentiation of the 'working class' (defined by the wage form) into distinct economic specialisms and social fractions, in particular the existence of what are conventionally called 'petty bourgeois' strata of specialists and functionaries. The notion of 'exploitation' has not resolved this problem. Indeed, 'exploitation' theory has generated essentialism and sociologism attempting to resolve social forces and politically divergent occupations into immediate effects of the relations of production. 'Exploitation' theory essentialises classes as social and political forces determined at the economic level. This essentialism and sociologism can be seen all too clearly in current attempts to differentiate classes utilising the concepts of productive and unproductive labour.

Production and circulation

It remains to consider the relation of production and circulation once value-terms are displaced.

Before we proceed let us be clear that there are two levels of analysis of the production/distribution (circulation) question in *Capital*. The first level, which involves the theory of value and exploitation, has two sources: first, the *theoretical*, the contestation of the problems of the exchange of equivalents and the source of profits as they are developed in classical political economy; second, the *ideological*, the contestation of vulgar economy (and the vulgarity of the classics) which represents directly (according to Marx) the illusions of the phenomenal forms, commodity exchange as equal exchange and profit as the 'reward' of capital. The esoteric and the vulgar are settled in a single answer by Marx, he both 'solves' the theoretical problem and destroys the illusions by moving to relations necessitated by production (surplus value, accumulation). This removes the classical distributional problem and at the same time the absurdities of vulgarity. The second level of analysis has nothing to do with the classical distributional problem of the 'revenues' of the classes and their sources. It concerns the structure of capitalist production; production and circulation (distribution) are considered as combined and contradictory elements of a complex process. Whereas at the first level of analysis production is privileged (it is the level of reality itself, the site of explication of error), at the second level it is no more determinant of the outcome of the process (a distinct cycle of circulation, production, circulation) than circulation, which is coupled with it.

Having argued that the distribution (circulation) of the product does not correspond to the contributions of the agents, that 'exploitation' is incalculable and that surplus value is not *the* source of profit, one has passed a long way from *Capital*. It may be objected that this means that there is now no basis for differentiating between capitalist and non-capitalist (e.g. socialist) forms. Does not the *Critique* explicitly concern itself with the relation of production and distribution under socialism? Certainly, the capitalist mode of production needs to be reconceptualised if these theoretical changes and omissions are made. We will, for purposes of illustration, demarcate capitalist and socialist economies in a very provisional way.

Capitalism may be defined as follows:

1 it entails the separation of the workers from the means of production (in the form of legal property and effective possession by the agency of ownership);
2 it entails the combination of the workers with the means of production through the wage-form;
3 these two conditions entail the distribution of the means of reproduction of labour-power in the form of commodities;
4 the ownership of the means of production is separated into distinct 'capitals' and the existence of distinct forms of combination of the means of production and labour-power, 'enterprises';
5 the relation between production and distribution therefore takes the form of commodity circulation between the separate capitals and between wage workers and capitals, the distribution of the means of production and consumption takes place through commodity circulation (in so far as capitals do not produce their own means of production).

The process of construction of socialist relations of production must entail the transformation of this double separation, of workers from the means of production and of enterprises one from another. These two separations are mutually conditional. Separation of the workers from the means of production at the level of the enterprise (through wage labour) strengthens commodity forms (wage labour as commodity—purchase of commodities with wages). The separation of enterprises one from another limits their practical possession by the collectivity. This possession can only take the form of the unification of the enterprises through their effective direction by means of planning. Possession, of the means of production employed by enterprises, as co-operative property or at the level of day-to-day decision-making, by the personnel directly employed in factories does not confer control of an increasingly co-operative and co-ordinated system of social production. Such possession further excludes those workers whose place in the division of labour is outside of such units of production (teachers, nurses, administrative functionaries, etc.). Planning, if it is to be the agency of effective possession (direction of the means of production) by the organs of the collectivity and yet serve the people, must be democratic in form and content. It must be an activity of the State in which the people and their wishes are effectively represented: a strategic direction of the economy which follows the broad lines of popular needs. Such representation requires participation. Charles Bettelheim has struggled hard to establish a similar conception of socialist possession and socialist planning. Although *Economic Calculation and Forms of Property* retains value categories it draws the consequences of the two separations all too clearly. Bettelheim's conception of the USSR as a *State capitalist* country is not shared by us. However, his analysis of the two separations makes all too clear the political and economic consequences of the mockery and debasement of popular democracy in that country: its very name, a union of *soviet* republics, has become a basis for criticism of the current regime. We will return to and develop these points in Part III, Chapter 13

Chapter 2

Böhm-Bawerk and Hilferding

Böhm-Bawerk's *Karl Marx and the Close of his System* is unique in the literature on the theory of value for the anger and contempt it has provoked from Marxists. No one could expect a fundamental theoretical challenge from a leading representative of the 'psychological school', who was finance minister of Austria-Hungary, to be well received. But the response is symptomatic of something else. Marxist economists of the stature of Hilferding and Bukharin felt the need to reply. The nature of the response stems from the fact that there are elements in Böhm-Bawerk's critique which cannot be answered or exorcised.

This only becomes clear if one reads the text outside of the party struggle it has generated, and independently of certain of its own claims. The discourse of this text must be subjected to careful analysis in order to see the unanswerable questions it raises. Marxist critics consider the text as an emanation of a 'position' in economic theory and concentrate on the defects of that position and the misperception of Marx which it produces. Böhm-Bawerk does have a position, and this produces a conception of the practice of 'critique' appropriate to works in economics. *Capital* is conceived as a 'system', a logical structure of concepts which attempts to account for the appearances of capitalist economies and, therefore, particularly for the nature of exchange relations. Criticism has two main weapons, analysis of logical consistency (which is useful but secondary, *Karl Marx and the Close of his System*, p. 64) and correspondence with the facts of experience. Marx's explanation is inconsistent with the facts of experience and becomes inconsistent in his attempts to reconcile explanation and reality. Marx's theory of value is conceived as analogous to and in competition with economic theories; it must produce a consistent account of the facts of exchange: 'What then, we ask, is the chief object of the "law of value"? It is nothing else than the elucidation of the exchange relations of commodities as they actually appear to us, (*ibid*., p. 34).

Marxists have no difficulty in replying to this conception of a 'critique'. Marx's object is not the 'elucidation of exchange relations . . . as they appear to us', it is an analysis of capitalist social relations of production and their effects. Hilferding does this clearly and competently. He also denies the pertinence of positivist epistemology, which, in restricting the criterion of validation to experience, condemns analysis to remain permanently at the level of the forms of appearance of capitalism and to fail to penetrate to the inner determinations of these forms. Epistemological debate is open and uncloseable here. Böhm-Bawerk can deny the pertinence of the form/inner determination distinction, insisting that all that exists is present to experience. Such a contest is interminable.

The contest does take place on common ground, however. Hilferding accepts Böhm-Bawerk's conception of *Capital* as a 'system' and the theory of value as its core. He, therefore, constantly equates showing that exchange cannot explain capitalist social relations, pointing to the theory of the structure of the capitalist mode of production as a theory of the social conditions of existence of capitalist commodity exchange, with a defence of the theory of value. Hilferding also treats Böhm-Bawerk's text as part of a 'system', considering his critique of Marx as an emanation of the positions of his own theory. Thus, he argues, Böhm-Bawerk fails to see the difference between value and price. For Böhm-Bawerk's own theory of exchange there is, indeed, no difference. But Böhm-Bawerk recognises that there is for Marx a difference—he examines in detail the attempt in *Capital* to relate them.

Two points follow from this double identification of Hilferding's. The theory of value and the theory of the capitalist mode of production in *Capital* are inseparable. The substance of Böhm-Bawerk's criticism is identical with his conception of 'critique'. It is this double identification which makes the debate unavoidable and of critical importance for Marxists. We propose to challenge both parts of this identification. In this way it is possible to recognise that there are serious critical points in Böhm-Bawerk's text, that they do challenge the theory of value, but that they do not mean an end to Marx's 'system'. *Capital* is not a system; it is not the coherent presence in discourse of a single and unitary logical order of concepts, it is the co-presence of often very different questions, concepts, and answers. The theory of value is closely implicated with much of the exposition of *Capital*, many concepts and problems must be rejected along with it but not all. We have contended that the structure of capitalist social relations not only can be analysed without the theory of value, but that this theory is actually an *obstacle* to their analysis. As Marxists we have no fear in accepting the critical challenge Böhm-Bawerk presents. Again, to accept certain of Böhm-Bawerk's criticisms is not to accept his 'critique'. These criticisms are not emanations of the conception of how a critique should be conducted. They are products of the critical theoretical work Böhm-Bawerk did on *Capital*. They cannot be reduced to effects of his epistemological position or to his own theory of value. The questions Böhm-Bawerk asks which generate serious problems for the theory of value in *Capital* are 'invisible' to Marxist critics because they share Hilferding's double identification. This makes the relation to Böhm-Bawerk antagonistic, for 'invisible' or not these questions will not go away. Identifying *Capital* and the theory of value, and Böhm-Bawerk's criticisms with his own conception of 'critique' completely closes the possibility of recognising these questions and facing up to them.

Value and price

Böhm-Bawerk *is* right to argue that the theory of value is a theory which must account for the exchange relations that actually pertain in capitalism. If the necessities of the distribution of social labour govern all forms of distribution then they must explain capitalist circulation. The concept of 'value' is posed by Marx, in relation to the problem of the *exchange of equivalents*. It explains how it is possible for there to be exchanges by conceiving them as equations (identities of labour-time). If these exchange-relations are not exchanges of equivalent quanta of the value-standard then the relation of this standard to exchange and, therefore, its whole pertinence becomes problematic. Value-relations must underlie or govern price relations in some systematic way in capitalism if the theory of value is to have any pertinence to it. Böhm-Bawerk questions the conditions of correspondence of the categories of values and prices, surplus value and profit, and asks how can the former *govern* the latter. This is not some problem of his making, but a problem which is central to the way *Capital* is written.

Marx says: 'Total profit and total surplus value are identical amounts' (*Capital*, vol. 3, Kerr edn, p. 204). They are equal in value-terms (as totalities of labour-time) but different in form (one is a phenomenal form the other is not). This difference of values and prices raises a serious question about the status of value. It is not raised as such by Böhm-Bawerk, but it is a question which makes the problems of correspondence he raises vital and explosive. If commodities exchange according to production prices then the processes of exchange and circulation in capitalism are not conducted in value-equivalent terms. Commodities are exchanged in ratios which reflect discrepant quanta of the value-standard which do not directly equate labour-times. Value is not, therefore, directly determined through the exchange of the *products of labour*. Value-relations are now outside the sphere of circulation (at best they *govern* it). The conditions of production of surplus value determine its differential distribution among capitals; this differential distribution is then redistributed across the capitals as an equal average rate of profit. Value is here threatened with a loss of *value form*—the value form determines the abstract labour ratios of goods through the exchange proportions of their products. Labours take a value form through the effects of the exchange process. If the process of exchange does not correspond to value terms (measured in labour-time) and value categories govern exchange then value (abstract labour) must be determined in the labour process. Labour in the labour process in capitalism already has the form of abstract labour and is commensurable with other labours (in units of the same measure, labour-time). Circulation merely redistributes as profit the surplus value produced elsewhere as *value*. This means either abstract labour exists at the level of production (the effects of circulation govern the process of production, becoming necessities of productivity which govern the process of circulation and, ultimately, determine it), or, labour must be a substance which in itself represents value. Marx insists that labours are equated through the exchange of their products in definite proportions:

> Men do not therefore bring the products of their labour into relation with each other as values because they see these objects merely as the material integuments of homogeneous human

> labour. The reverse is true: by equating their different products to each other as values, they equate their different kinds of labour as human labour (*Capital*, vol. 1, Penguin edn, p. 166)

Labour in the production process can only be counted as abstract social labour by applying to it the (past or anticipated) results of the social process of exchange.

It may be argued that labour time regulates production and through it ultimately the proportions in which goods exchange. The law of value in exchange is modified in capitalism (its concepts hold strictly only for simple commodity production). But *how* does labour-time regulate production and through it exchange? Through changes in the productivity of labour. Given that exchanges are not conducted in value-terms then productivity must affect exchange-relations through changes in *costs*. Wages per unit of product, overheads per unit and so on fall. But the labour which produces these changes in cost structure can also be considered simply as *concrete labour*. If the time to produce a yard of cotton is quartered by some technical invention then so many hours less of spinning or weaving are necessary per unit, so many hours less of the wages of spinners or weavers per unit. Changes in productivity and their effect on prices could be explained without the theory of value. One need not suppose labour-time is constitutive of value to explain changes in costs induced by technical innovation.

If the social process of exchange does not mark labour with the form of value then labour must possess that form through the articulation of circulation and the labour process. The effects of this articulation (changes in costs and prices) can be explained without the theory of value. As we have seen, value-terms are essential for the theory of exploitation. The discrepancy of values and prices, the expulsion of value (exchange of equivalents in the value-standard) from a direct place in the process of exchange, creates serious problems for retaining the theory to analyse capitalist production. Böhm-Bawerk's attention to the discrepancy touches on a sore spot in value theory.

To return directly to Böhm-Bawerk. He considers in some detail the four arguments which *he* considers Marx to advance to explain the correspondence of values and prices. Whether they do indeed function in *Capital* as 'arguments' is in certain cases most dubious. We will consider them in turn.

1 The sum total of all prices corresponds to that of all values.

> In the same proportion in which one part of the commodities is sold above its value another part will be sold under its value. (*Capital*, vol. 3, Kerr edn, p. 185)
>
> . . . by as much as there is too much surplus value in one commodity there is too little in another, and therefore the *deviations from value* which lurk in the prices of production reciprocally cancel each other. In capitalist production as a whole '*the general law maintains itself as the governing tendency*', only in a very complex and approximate manner as the constantly changing average of perpetual fluctuations. (*ibid.*, p. 90)

Böhm-Bawerk is scathing about this 'argument'.* First, it simply presumes value-terms. The issue is how do prices and values correspond or relate in *exchange-relations*. If value-relations *govern* prices, they must regulate their distribution and have some definite relation to them. The correspondence of the two totalities or universes (itself notional) says nothing about distribution:

> As soon, however, as one looks at all commodities *as a whole* and sums up the prices one must studiously and of necessity avoid looking at the relations existing inside of this whole. . . . In any case, when we ask for information regarding the exchange of commodities in political economy it is no answer to our question to be told the total price which they bring when taken altogether. (*Karl Marx and the Close of his System*, p. 35)

Marx's position on averaging gets equally short shrift. Böhm-Bawerk says: 'Here Marx confounds two very different things: an *average of fluctuations*, and an average between permanently and fundamentally unequal quantities, (*ibid.*, p. 37) Averaging merely explains how profits can be 'cancelled-out' to correspond to value-terms. This arithmetical exercise cannot show how value-relations govern prices and profits. As Böhm-Bawerk says, there is no 'fluctuation' between value and price, no question of deviation, there is *difference*. This difference is systematic and needs to be explained by a *mechanism*.

---

* Hilferding claims it is *not* an argument but merely a logical consequence of the theory of value. Hence as a logical consequence it cannot do other than 'presume' value-terms.

2 (This is Böhm-Bawerk's fourth point but is included here as it follows on from the first).

> The average rate of profit which determines the price of production must, however, always be approximately equal to the amount of surplus-value which falls to a given capital as an aliquot part of the total social capital. . . . Now, as the total value of commodities governs the total surplus value, and this again determines the amount of the average profit and consequently the general rate of profit—as a general law or a law governing fluctuation—the law of value regulates the price of production. (*Capital*, vol. 3, Kerr edn, pp. 211–12)

The total value of commodities is claimed to govern the total surplus value as follows:

It determines the value of the means of subsistence and therefore of the total necessary labour (once the portion of constant capital entering into the value of the products is deducted), it is the total from which that necessary labour is deducted to give the total surplus value. Total surplus value = total profit: it therefore determines the *amount* of profit to be distributed between the capitals (and through its effect on this magnitude the rate of profit). These correspondences only exist if value-terms are supposed: they do not explain *how* value-relations pertain or how they can be pertinent if they are not established directly in the process of exchange through the proportions in which products exchange. This is again a logical consequence of the theory of value and not a mechanism by which it governs the capitalist process of circulation.

3 The law of value operates in simple commodity production and in the period of the formation of capitalism but is displaced in developed capitalism. Böhm-Bawerk produces an elaborate argument against this thesis, which Hilferding successfully counters in his reply. The point, however, is that it would be irrelevant as an 'argument'. It does nothing to explain the relation of value and price in capitalism.

4 (This is the argument Böhm-Bawerk cites second): This is the one example of a possible mechanism in the four 'arguments' cited by Böhm-Bawerk. In general it is the only strong argument there could be and we have alluded to it above.

The law of value governs production prices since changes in the labour-time necessary for production causes the price of a commodity to fall relative to others. Böhm-Bawerk argues that it is not labour-time alone which does this. Changes in the working period also reduce the portion of constant capital per unit of the product, reduce overhead costs and therefore prices. It may be objected that Marx is not trying to explain *all* changes in prices, merely to state the effect of labour productivity (as Hilferding does). But this misses the point. Böhm-Bawerk's example points to the fact that it is possible to deal with changes in prices (at this level) in terms of changes in the costs of production. Labour-time (concrete labour-time) is one source of costs at par with others. To deny it is at par, one has to produce other arguments than the above—which explains why only labour-time is the measure of value and only labour constitutive of value. Constant capital can then ultimately be reduced to labour-terms, to 'dead labour'. Savings in constant capital merely reduce the portion of value stored in it which is transferred to the product. This returns us to the central basic debate and does not close it.

Labour-time and utility as foundations of theories of value

Marx's concept of 'value' arises in relation to the problem of an exchange of equivalents. Marx must consider exchange as an *equation*. Marx seeks the third term in which two commodities dissimilar in substance and quality can be said to 'equal' one another, which makes possible their exchange as equivalents. Böhm-Bawerk challenges the exhaustiveness of Marx's search for this third term: 'Why then . . . may not the principle of value reside in any one of these common properties as well as in the property of being products of labour?' (*Karl Marx and the Close of his System*, p. 75). Marx excludes all physical qualities of goods which lead them to be use-values because they are heterogeneous and incommensurable. But Böhm-Bawerk says use-values are not merely specific, one can abstract from their specific physical forms and consider all use-values as unified by the fact they have utility (they are objects of need or desire). Again: 'Is not the property of being scarce in proportion to demand common to all exchangeable goods?' (*ibid.*, p. 75). Use-values, Marx argues, are specific, discrepant, and non-quantifiable. But, says Böhm-Bawerk, both labour and utility have their qualitative and quantitative sides. Labour is hours of weaving, sewing, etc., as well as hours of abstract labour-time. Similarly, utility can be quantified. The desire of certain or all consumers is *greater* for this good than for

that, or for another. Utility is measured in the goods which consumers are willing to part with to obtain another good (money is a general expression of utilities). Utility and scarcity could explain the exchange proportions of goods. Why are they inferior to labour? Marx does not answer. He merely dismisses the question of use-value in determining the physical form of goods.
Hilferding's response to this misses the point. He argues:

> It is a precondition to the exchangeability of commodities that they should possess utility for others, but since for me they are devoid of utility, the use value of my commodities is in no sense a *measure* even of my individual estimate of value, and still less is it a measure of any objective estimate of value. It avails nothing to say that the use-value consists of the capacity of these commodities to be exchanged for other commodities for that would imply that the extent of the 'use-value' is now determined by the extent of the exchange-value, not the extent of the exchange-value by the extent of the use-value. (Hilferding, *Böhm-Bawerk's Criticism of Marx* (ed. Sweezy), p. 126; published with Böhm-Bawerk, *Karl Marx and the Close of his System*.)

According to Hilferding commodities are devoid of utility to their producer (they have no use-value for him, he has no measure of their utility independent of exchange). Utility does not explain exchange proportions because these are essential in establishing what utilities are (utility and exchange are implicated in a vacuous circle). This criticism misrecognises the nature and status of a utility theory of exchange. Value in utility theory is 'subjective'. In contrast, says Hilferding: 'Labour is . . . an objective magnitude, inherent in the commodities and determined by the degree of development of social productivity' (*Karl Marx/Böhm-Bawerk's Criticism*, p. 186). Hilferding's couple subjective-objective shows us the difference of the criteria a value theory can be called on to meet. Hilferding measures utility theory against the standard of the labour theory of value and finds it wanting. But the notion that a theory of value must establish the third term (in which commodities are equivalent) independent of the results of specific exchanges is one imposed by Hilferding. It does not criticise a utility theory of exchange-value as such (it merely tells us it is not a theory of value like Marx's).

Clearly, exchanges are necessary to a utility theory of value—it is, as Hilferding recognises, a theory of exchange-value only. Exchange involves the interaction of two objects capable of being utilities and two estimators of the value (utility) of these objects. Each utility is measured in the other—exchanges always entail a willingness to part with something in order to obtain something else. It is true that both utilities are measured in the objects for which they are exchanges—they depend upon exchange as their measure (commodities do have a utility to their possessors—this utility is measured in other goods of a nature-quality or quantity for which they will *not* exchange them). Utility must be relative to exchanges as a theory of exchange-value—it explains exchanges as an interaction of wants. Ultimately, exchange proportions are determined by the respective desires for the respective utilities.

Hilferding's objection is in essence epistemological—it concerns the *status* of the explanation (its 'subjectivism') and the problem explained (exchange-values). He does not criticise a utility theory of exchange as such. Although, of course, it can be criticised, and devastatingly. We do not challenge Hilferding's response in the interests of such a theory. However, Hilferding's critique is thoroughly disingenuous. It fails to deal with the status of the concept *use-value* in Marx's theory of value. We shall see in our discussion of Rubin that Marx cannot dispense with the category of use-value as a critical part of the theory of value as a law of distribution of social labour.

To explain the pertinence of labour-time as the third term, Marx would have to explain why the distribution of the product takes the form of a law of distribution of social labour. In vol. 1, as we have seen, he asserts the necessity and primacy of this law but fails to justify its necessity.

Supply and demand

Böhm-Bawerk rightly charges Marx with inconsistency on the question of supply and demand. On the one hand, Marx criticises the explanatory value of this concept, and on the other, he makes use of it at central places in his theory.

Marx denies the general pertinence of supply and demand to the explanation of prices. He says:

> If demand and supply balance one another *they cease to act*. If two forms act equally and in opposite directions they cancel each

> other—they produce no result, and phenomena occurring under these conditions *must be explained by some other agency than either of these forces*. If supply and demand cancel each other then *they cease to explain anything, they do not affect the market value*, and they leave us altogether in the dark as to the reasons why the market value should express itself in this and no other sum of money. (*Capital*, vol. 3, Kerr edn, pp. 223–4)

Böhm-Bawerk has no trouble in demolishing this argument. First, supply always equates demand at a given price:

> It is quite true that when a commodity sells at its usual market value, supply and demand must in a certain sense balance each other; that is to say, at this price just the same quantity of a commodity is effectively demanded as is offered. But this is not only the case when commodities are sold at a normal market value, but at whatever market value they are sold, even when this is a varying irregular one. (*Karl Marx/Böhm-Bawerk's Criticism*, p. 94)

Secondly, the notion that when supply and demand are equal they cease to act is specific to a definite theory of prices and their functions. Böhm-Bawerk has a different general theory of the functions of prices, in it the general function assigned to prices is that of equating supply and demand. For him supply and demand are elastic quantities, determined directly or indirectly by utilities. Effective supply and demand are not given but are formed in exchange relations; effective supply and demand equate at a price. Such a condition (supply = demand) is an effect of supply–demand movements (and their determinants). Price is determined by the *relation* of supply and demand—such an 'equilibrium' is an effect of the forces acting one on another and not a suspension of those forces.

Böhm-Bawerk says:

> Assuming that it is only the successful part of supply and demand, being in quantitative equilibrium, that affects the fixing of a price, it is quite erroneous and unscientific to assume that forces which hold each other in equilibrium 'cease to act'. On the contrary, the state of equilibrium is precisely the result of their action and when an explanation has to be given of this state of equilibrium with all its details—one of the most prominent of

> which is the height of the level in which the equilibrium was found—it certainly cannot be given in some other way than by the agency of the two forces. (*ibid.*, p. 95)

Böhm-Bawerk does not believe that supply and demand are self-explanatory forces. They have their *determinants* (these are predominantly psychological for him): 'It is by no means my opinion that a really complete and satisfying explanation of the fixing of permanent prices is contained in the reference to the formula of supply and demand' (*ibid.*, p. 97).

Two different conceptions of the pertinence of prices confront one another here. For Marx the primary function of prices in capitalism is to equate the rates of profit in different branches of production and between capitals of different organic compositions. This function is indeed performed when supply and demand equal one another (supply and demand being considered as objective quantities corresponding to a certain composition of the social product). This function being attained prices cease to act for Marx. Marx's position on the role of prices in his own system cannot serve as the basis for a critique of other and different theories of prices or values. He does try to use it as such. In rejecting Marx's argument there is no reason to commit oneself to Böhm-Bawerk's or any other general theory of price.

Competition is central to Marx's theory of value and to the theory of production prices. In simple commodity production the competition of producers in the same branch *socialises* the effects of exchange—forcing producers to adapt to the labour-time established as necessary through the quanta of other products they receive in exchange for their own. In our discussion of Rubin we will see that socially necessary demand imposes the conditions of competition on producers by defining 'overproduction' and 'underproduction'. Competition must be relative to the market conditions established by the demand-supply relation. Similarly, competition between capitals leads to the formation of an equal average rate of profit. Capital moves freely to equate profit rates by entering high-profit sectors and leaving low ones. The supply of and the effective demand for capital is relative to the expected rate of return on the capital. Marx, like Böhm-Bawerk, postulates a rational economic subject (the capitalist investor) who maximises the return on his capital. Böhm-Bawerk is correct to argue that Marx does not rigorously theorise 'competition' as a market process, but tends to use the theory of supply and demand in an assumed and unrigorous way.

Labour reduction

Böhm-Bawerk problematises Marx's reduction of skilled labour to 'simple average labour'. He argues that different concrete forms of labour receive different rewards. Marx's labour reduction actually work on wage rates—it treats 'skilled' labour as a multiple of unskilled. This is possible because 'skilled' labour earns a certain proportion more than unskilled and is therefore held to represent so much more simple average labour. Böhm-Bawerk objects: 'Marx certainly says that skilled labour "counts" as multiplied unskilled labour, but to "count as" is not "to be" and the theory deals with the being of things' (*Karl Marx/Böhm-Bawerk's Criticism*, p. 82). The different labours are related through their rewards and their rewards are taken from the prevailing conditions of exchange:

> . . . the standard of reduction is determined solely *by the* actual exchange relations themselves. . . . Under these circumstances what is the meaning of the appeal to 'value' and 'the social process' as determining factors of the standard of reduction. Apart from anything else it simply means that Marx is arguing in a complete circle. (*ibid.*, p. 83)

Skilled wages are divided by the unskilled—one wage is divided by another. This is possible arithmetically but it does not prove skilled labour is simply so much 'concentrated' unskilled labour, it proves merely that wages differ by that amount.

Hilferding replies to Böhm-Bawerk's arguments as follows. First, he correctly maintains that there is no necessary relation between the value of a labour-power (wages) and the value created by the expenditure of that labour-power. We cannot as Böhm-Bawerk tries to do make the wage of the skilled labourer an effect of his superior value-creating power. This objection of Hilferding's is true in terms of the labour theory of value but, assuming a utility theory of value and dealing with artisans who sell the products of their labour, Böhm-Bawerk *can* argue that the labour of a Cellini creates objects of greater utility (aesthetic value to *cognoscenti*) than the labour of an ordinary goldsmith and in consequence receives a greater reward (the *cognoscenti* are willing to part with more utilities to obtain the Cellini than they are for the common work). This would not mean that a wage-labouring Cellini would receive the full superior value of his product. Skilled and unskilled labour differ, Hilferding argues, in terms of the costs of their reproduction. So much more unskilled labour goes into the creation of a skilled labourer than an unskilled one—this labour cost of production is reflected in the wage. This supposes labour-reduction terms operate, that we can treat skilled labour-power as so much unskilled labour invested in it. Second, Hilferding argues that Böhm-Bawerk has a positivist theory of measurement. Böhm-Bawerk demands that Marx prove his position by reference to given wage rates—but Marx is not actually interested in such immediate differences of wages. His object is to show that in the long run wages do obey the theory of value, that skilled labour-power changes in value with the costs of its production and that labour-powers change in value as a function of changes in productivity, and new labour processes 'de-skill' the worker and reduce the value of his labour-power.

To say that Böhm-Bawerk because of his positivism ignores the effect of value-relations on wages is also of necessity to hold that an account can be given of that effect. Wages have value-determinants and must in the long run conform to them. Labour-power is a commodity and must be governed by the law of value. Marx holds that labour-power has a value (the value of its means of reproduction), that this value is socially determined (by the productivity of labour itself and by historical/cultural circumstances) and that simple average labour has an objective social form (it corresponds to the realities of labour mobility in capitalism). Wages can therefore be analysed in and reduced to value-terms. To argue this two equivalences must be created: the first between unskilled wage rates and the prevailing historical minimum means of subsistence; the second between unskilled labour and simple average labour.

The first equivalence supposes that unskilled wage rates reflect the value of labour-power; they do correspond to the costs of reproduction of the labourer (historical subsistence minimum). Thus averaging out the effects of changes in the demand for labour over a period will give the prevailing wage level. This supposes that relative surplus population and competition in the labour market keep the rate at the necessary historical minimum (this is a dubious assumption, it implies that population and labour demand are determined by economic laws): otherwise unskilled labour-power would be sold consistently above its 'value'.

The second equivalence is crucial however to any calculable (not merely a positivist) labour reduction. It makes possible the comparison of determinate labour—unskilled labour *counts as* simple average labour. Making this assumption, and assuming that skilled labour differs from unskilled (in the long run) according to the cost of its reproduction, then wage differences do serve as the standard of reduction: the one can be divided by the other. Wages do reflect the social process. But can unskilled labour be *counted as* simple average labour? Is not 'unskilled' labour simply a classificatory category for different kinds of *concrete labours*? Builders' labouring, dishwashing, general handling, are all 'unskilled', yet these different concrete forms of labouring are not interchangeable. They have different labour markets; different conditions of entry and labour supply. The difference is not simply a difference of material form of the labour. These occupations form distinct divisions of the labour market and the labour force, and in consequence 'unskilled' wage rates differ widely. 'Unskilled' labour exists as a unitary category only relative to that of 'skilled' labour. The labours grouped under it are non-homogeneous concrete labours not homogeneous, interchangeable simple average labour. Böhm-Bawerk does not make this point directly. It undermines the calculability of the labour reduction in principle. Böhm-Bawerk raises the issue that the labour theory of value requires an undifferentiated unit as its measure, and that labours are, however, distinct in form and remuneration. Marx effects the reduction of certain of these labours to a supposed base, but this reduction is in fact the using of one type of labour ('unskilled') and its wages to serve as the multiple of another.

'Skilled' labour, it can be argued, derives its wage advantage not from its greater cost of reproduction but from (in general) a superior bargaining position. The issue of the determination of the value of labour-power cannot be considered solely in relation to the theory of vaue. It raises issues about the nature of the labour market, of the industrial reserve army and the determinants of wages. These issues cannot be settled at the level of the general concept of the capitalist mode of production as *Capital* attempts to do (see Part II).

We have concentrated on the criticisms in Böhm-Bawerk's text which must be taken seriously. There are numerous erroneous criticisms in addition—these have been picked over endlessly and there is no need to add to the remarks of Hilferding on this score. We have used Böhm-Bawerk's questions to raise difficulties about the theory of value in a way which is rather different from his own—they serve as a point of departure in relation to certain problems. Böhm-Bawerk could provide no alternative to *Capital*. Hilferding is correct to argue that he has no conception of Marx's analysis of the structure of the capitalist mode of production. He confines his analysis to the critique of value as an 'economic' theory. Only Marxists* can make a *constructive* exercise out of the rejection of Marx's theory of value because only they can expand and develop, as a consequence, Marx's theory of capitalist social relations. They will not do so if they fail to recognise and merely reject what is serious in the, negative, criticism of opponents like Böhm-Bawerk.

Hilferding's reply

We will not review Hilferding's reply to Böhm-Bawerk here; reference to certain of his points has been made above and certain others will be dealt with in greater detail in our discussion of Rubin. Here we will concentrate on Hilferding's conception of the critical struggle he is engaged in and the relation this establishes between Marx's theory and Böhm-Bawerk's intervention in his text.

Hilferding begins by establishing the place of the critic in modern economic science—explaining why a critique of Marx should be important for Böhm-Bawerk. Vulgar bourgeois economics either ignores Marx or confines itself to simple ideological abuse. It has abandoned any attempt to explain the totality of economic relations rigorously and theoretically. The psychological school is

---

* We mean this in no exclusive and sectarian sense—we mean only that those who have understood Marx's theoretical positions and are willing to do theoretical work in relation to them can produce any real advances in this area. Sectarian loyalism cannot but hinder the open, honest and critical practice needed for theoretical advance. This involves taking critics who are serious seriously. Böhm-Bawerk took *Capital* seriously—his reading of those parts of it he considered relevant to 'economic' theory (vol. 1, pt 1 and vol. 3, pts 1–3) is meticulous and follows Marx's discourse closely. Hilferding recognised this and paid him due respect (*Karl Marx/Böhm-Bawerk's Criticism*, p. 122)—for many modern Marxists he is worse than a dead dog.

the notable exception to this degeneration:

> The adherents of this school resemble the classical economists and the Marxists in that they endeavour to apprehend economic phenomena from a unitary outlook. Opposing Marxism with a circumscribed theory, their criticism is systematic in character, and their critical attitude is forced upon them because they have started from totally different premises. (*Karl Marx/Böhm-Bawerk's Criticism,* p, 122)

The character of both critique and counter-critique is outlined. The critique challenges Marx from a position; it recognises him through the refracting and distorting lens of its 'totally different premises'. The counter-critique will essentially be a mapping of this difference of premises, drawing lines between the opposed positions, and showing the misperceptions which result from the standpoint of the opposed premises. Hilferding's answer is essentially an attempt to reduce Böhm-Bawerk's criticisms to a series of conditioned misperceptions, non-recognitions of central aspects of Marx's theory and misrecognitions of others. To counter Böhm-Bawerk is to state Marx's theory itself, from its own premises, and to carry the war to the other camp, to challenge the premises of the 'psychological school' and their theoretical effects.

The terrain of the confrontation is that of the utility versus labour theories of value. Hilferding begins by attempting to assign utility its place in Marxism. Utility has, in its Marxist equivalent (use-value), no real place in social science:

> The commodity is a unity of use-value and of value, but we can regard that unity from two different aspects. As a natural thing, it is the object of natural science; as a social thing, it is the object of a social science, the object of political economy. The object of political economy is the social aspect of the commodity, of the good, in so far as it is a symbol of social intercommunication. On the other hand, the natural aspect of the commodity, its use-value, lies outside of the domain of political economy. (*ibid.*, p. 130)

We have here an opposition between the social/symbolic form (object of political economy) and the natural properties of the thing (object of natural science). Use-value is excluded from economic theory. It is made something incidental, material and technical to the social/symbolic process of exchange. Hilferding commits himself to the radical position that political economy has as its object the *form* of social intercommunication, not the *content* of this process (*Stoffswechsel*). By this position content would be excluded from economics and with it any account of why certain commodities are produced, the quantities in which they are produced and the determinants of the consumption of the commodities. Hilferding does not and could not consistently hold to this position.

For Hilferding use-values are individual rather than social: 'A use-value is an individual relationship between a thing and a human being . . . solely in its individuality can a use-value be a measure of any personal estimate of value' (*ibid.*, p. 131). As such it is ahistorical and asocial, and any theory of value based upon it must share these attributes:

> Every theory of value which starts from use-value, that is to say from the natural qualities of a thing . . . starts from the individual relationship between a thing and a human being instead of starting from the social relationships of human beings one with another. (*ibid.*, pp. 132–3)

This rests on the couples individual-social, natural-social. Use-value derives from the natural attributes of things and exists only for individuals. In Hilferding's own position this is absurd and contradictory; for him a certain distribution of labour *and therefore of its products* is socially necessary and in every society the producers are always associated producers, whatever the mode of their association. Use-values can only be socially useful to social individuals. Whence then comes the stigma of naturalness? It appears because demand and utility must be declared non-pertinent. Utility cannot be given a place in social relations without making demand a determinant of what is consumed and, therefore, ultimately of what is produced (as we shall see in our discussion of Rubin).

This characterisation of use-value as natural/individual can be easily refuted by utility theorists. Utility theory necessarily supposes a range of utilities, the calculation of values and priorities between things. As an exchange theory it supposes (as we have seen) the definition of utilities in the objects for which a good will be exchanged. Utilities are relative to the social process of exchange and are measured in other utilities. Utility theory supposes a universal subject, the calculating subject of desire and need.

Economising and maximising the satisfaction of utilities, distributing scarce resources according to priorities, is a universal human attribute. But if utility is ahistorical and eternal, is not labour also?

How does Hilferding explain the general pertinence of the theory of value? By asserting labour is the *constitutive* element in human society: 'Marx . . . starts from labour in its significance as the *constitutive* element in human society, as the element whose development determines in the final analysis the development of society' (*ibid*., p. 133). He continues:

> . . . in the principle of value he grasps the factor (labour) . . . by whose organisation and productive energy, social life is causally controlled. The fundamental economic idea is consequently identical with the fundamental idea of the materialist conception of history. (*ibid*., p. 133)

An asocial naturalism is countered by a social/historical materialism. But what are the foundations of this materialism? Labour is the constitutive element in society: men, lacking a given nature and depending on means of subsistence to live, make themselves in producing their means of subsistence. In Hilferding's case this constitutivity is founded on an Engelian/neo-Darwinian anthropology rather than an Hegelian one. It nevertheless makes labour a trans-historical anthropological necessity. Labour is constitutive because of man's nature (materialism-naturalism) and is so throughout history (it is a trans-historical, eternal, necessity). The eternal/natural couple can be imposed upon Marxism too.

At this level of 'premises' one anthropology confronts another: *homo economicus* v. *homo faber*. Hilferding attempts to give Marxism a privileged status through the couples natural-social, individual-social, eternal-historical. These couples are problematic, no privilege is possible on the terrain where one essentialism (of the subject) confronts another (humanity as labouring subjects). Hilferding, convinced of the 'objectivity' of his position, cannot recognise that there can be no privileged *metaphysics* of political economy. Essentialisms can only *rival* one another.

Value-as-symbol appears in definite social conditions. It reflects the social atomisation of production which is produced by private property and private production. Value-as-symbol is the way in which the social necessity of a certain division of labour, a distribution of labour in definite proportions is imposed on the producers. The symbolic order of value represents what is manifest and immediately comprehensible in socialised production:

> *Society has, as it were, assigned to each of its members the quota of social labour necessary to society; has specified to each individual how much labour he must expend.* And these individuals have forgotten what their quota was and rediscover it only in the process of social life. (*ibid.*, p. 134)

The symbolism of value recalls to the atomised producers the memory that they are members of society, it imposes society's demands upon them. Value is the mechanism which, providentially, gives atomised production the effect of socialised production: it enforces a necessary social division of labour. We will consider this teleological law of value in greater detail when we discuss the work of Rubin and will then show that it requires a concept not at all alien to marginalism, 'equilibrium'.

This providential law of value governs capitalist social relations. It leads to a providential system of production prices. Hilferding argues that supply and demand are epiphenomena. Supply and demand equal one another at a certain price level because of certain necessities of capitalist production.

> In order that the capitalist may continue to produce, he must be able to sell the commodity at a price which is equal to its cost price plus average profit. If he is unable to realise this price . . . the process of reproduction is arrested, and the supply is reduced to a point at which the relationship between supply and demand renders it possible to realise this price. Thus the relationship between supply and demand ceases to be a mere matter of chance; we perceive that it is regulated by the price of production, which constitutes the centre around which market prices fluctuate. . . . Thus the price of production is a condition of the supply, of the reproduction, of commodities . . . for then only can the course of the capitalist mode of production continue undisturbed, then only can occur the perpetual reproduction through the very course of the process of circulation, of the social preconditions of a mode of production whose motive force is the need of capital for the creation of surplus value. (*ibid.*, pp. 194–5)

Production prices are 'equilibrium prices' for the capitalist mode of production. Only through such a price structure can capitalist *relations of production* be preserved: only 'equilibrium prices' yield an equal average rate of profit such that all sectors of capital can reproduce themselves (and they are interdependent). In the concept of 'equilibrium' we see the economistic hope of an end to capitalist relations of production. 'Equilibrium', the state of capitalism's vitality, is also the threat of its death.

Should equilibrium conditions be threatened, systematic non-reproduction is possible, a systematic non-reproduction which undermines the relations of production. This fantasy is the dark side of a functionalism—the death that awaits the organism if its vital mechanisms are inhibited. It rests on an organic interdependence, the necessity of a certain division of labour. But capitalism has consistently shed branches of production and created new ones. Whole groups of industries have suffered below-average rates of profit and losses for decades at a time. The composition of the division of social labour changes constantly and sometimes massively. If capitalist economies survive, is it because new 'equilibriums' are constantly restored? But if this is so, no 'equilibrium structure' of the division of labour is necessary. Hilferding's position on production prices reveals his economistic conception of the conditions of existence of capitalist relations of production. These relations are not dependent on some 'state' of the economy. They operate (with varying effects) at all states of the economy. These relations can only be superseded by practices (economic and political) which construct *other* relations of production. The functionalism and economism entailed in the 'law of value' are all too glaringly exposed in this passage of Hilferding's.

Chapter 3

I. I. Rubin—'Essays on Marx's Theory of Value'

Rubin's text is arguably the most serious and systematic attempt to present and defend Marx's theory of value other than *Capital* itself. Rubin takes the same position as Hilferding on the theoretical status of the problem of 'value'. This problem is not exclusively the concern of a special and independent science of 'economics', the object of which is to explain or to account for the phenomena which occur in the process of exchange. Value is a problem which concerns the effectivity of specific social relations of production. It is part of the theory of historical materialism which, unlike 'economics', raises the conditions of existence of and the effects of social relations as a *problem*. Theoretical political economy is a science subordinate to historical materialism, it is concerned like 'economics' with one type of system of social production only—the commodity/capitalist economy. Historical materialism provides political economy with the basis for a *critical* analysis of commodity/capitalist social relations, unlike bourgeois political economy or 'economics' which takes these relations as an unreflected point of departure.

Critics like Böhm-Bawerk fail to recognise the theoretical form in which Marx poses the problem of value. Marx's object is mistaken by these critics—generating misplaced objections. Böhm-Bawerk criticises Marx for the contradictions inherent in a labour-value theory of price—equating Marx's object with his own. Rubin challenges Böhm-Bawerk's contention that Marx *deduces* labour-value from the problem of the exchange of equivalents. Marx's *presentation* of the problem and his method of analysis are different—the process of analysis cannot be equated with that of exposition. Böhm-Bawerk equates analysis and exposition because he conceives Marx's method as logical deduction. Marx does not arrive at his results by simple logical abstraction, but by the penetration of the essence of the social relations of capitalism. This penetration requires the dialectical method which alone is capable of respecting the complexities and contradictions in reality itself. In analysis (unlike exposition) Marx does not start with exchange: exchange-relations are effects of definite social relations of production: 'The labour theory of value is not based on an analysis of exchange transactions as such in their material form but on an analysis of those social production relations expressed in the transactions' (*Essays on Marx's Theory of Value*, p. 62). Marx cannot take exchange-relations as a problem in themselves because they are effects, only the analysis of production in its definite social forms makes possible a proper presentation of the problem of value.

Böhm-Bawerk challenges the Marxist theory of value because labour-time does not explain the prices at which certain commodities (works of art, parcels of land) exchange. But the labour theory of value is not concerned to establish labour as the 'substance' which makes possible and explains all exchanges. Money is the material form in which the exchange of equivalents takes place in commodity/capitalist society. This form is not without effects: 'The Material form has its own logic and can include other phenomena which it expresses in a given economic formation' (*ibid.*, p. 46). Hence money can be used to buy paintings at prices which have no relation to the labour-time embodied in them or commodities like land, products of nature which have no value. These exchanges are derived effects of the material form of exchange in a definite type of society. The theory of value is concerned with these social relations, with the exchange of products of *labour*. The category of 'value' is a part of the law of distribution of social labour and not simply a means of accounting for the exchangeability of all commodities:

> . . . Marx analyses the act of exchange only to the extent that it plays a specific role in the process of reproduction and is closely connected with that process. Marx's theory of value does not analyse every exchange of things, but only that exchange which takes place: (1) in a *commodity society*, (2) among autonomous *commodity producers*, (3) when it is connected with the *process of reproduction* in a determined way, thus representing one of

> the phases of the process of reproduction. The interconnection of the processes of exchange and distribution of labour in production leads us . . . to concentrate on the value of products of labour (as opposed to natural goods which have a price . . .), and then only on those products which can be reproduced. (*ibid.*, pp. 100–1)

The centrality of *reproducible products of labour* is no 'exclusion' or 'limitation' of Marx's theory, it is its strength: Marx explains through the theory of value the articulation of production and distribution, the centrality of the distribution of social labour to the process of reproduction.

Marx's method does not only differ from that of Böhm-Bawerk, the representative of neo-classical 'economics', but also from that of the classical economist. Marx's theory of value is different from the classical theories, even their most sophisticated representative David Ricardo. Marx investigates the social conditions of existence of and social forms of economic relations:

> Marx's economic theory deals precisely with the 'differences in form' (social economic forms, production relations) which actually develop on the basis of certain material-technical conditions, but which must not be confused with them. It is precisely this which represents the completely *new methodological formulation* of economic problems which is Marx's great service. . . . The attention of (the) Classical Economists was directed to discovering the material-technical basis of social forms which they took as given and not subject to further analysis. (*ibid.*, p. 42)

Classical political economy performs the analytic operation of reducing forms to their content. Thus it recognises labour as the 'substance' of exchangeability. It reduces value to being labour. It ignores the problem of the *form* of value, and fails to ask why this content ('labour') takes this form (the proportionate exchange of products of labour). Labour is conceived as a 'substance' which explains exchange and prices by providing the determinant of exchange proportions as quanta of that substance. This ignores the fact that labour is not *as such* value. Classical economics fails to differentiate between abstract and concrete labour—it conceives 'value' as a labour substance present in the commodity as an effect of the process of labouring. This is not Marx's position says Rubin.

Not only does Marx not have a labour-value theory of price in capitalism, but he does not have a labour-substance theory of value. Analytic method reduces form to content, social relations (which it takes as givens) to technique. Marx says:

> Political Economy has indeed analysed, however incompletely, value and its magnitude, and has discovered what lies beneath these forms. But it has never once asked the question why labour is represented in the value of its product and labour-time by the magnitude of that value. (*Capital*, vol. 1, Kerr edn, p. 80)

Only historical materialism and the dialectical method can answer these questions.

Fetishism

The concept of the fetishism of commodities is Rubin's starting point in his analysis of the theory of value. Rubin is strongly committed to the Hegelian elements in *Capital* and sees its method as dialectics. The theory of fetishism is not concerned with *illusions* generated in the experience of subjects by capitalist social relations. Fetishism is not an appearance of things, a misleading illusion, it corresponds to real properties of their essence. Commodity fetishism is based on the objective necessities of the existence of commodity/capitalist social relations. Under conditions of private property and commodity exchange independent producers are linked with one another merely through sales and purchases. 'Private' labour becomes *social* labour (relates to the labours and products of other producers) only through exchange. The exchange/equalisation of *the products of labour* is the form in which the labour of men takes a social form in a commodity economy. The social division of labour is mediated and realised through the market whereas in a non-commodity economy labour is directly social, its form the product of conscious social decisions and expressed needs. In a commodity economy relations between 'things' (commodities—the equalisation of things as proportions in exchange) is the form taken by relations between men—'relations among *people* acquire the form of equalisation among *things*' (*Essays*, p. 16). Connections between producers are established by the transfer and equalisation of their products (social life is mediated by what Marx calls the *Stoffswechsel*, the exchange of matter). Men confront one another as economic subjects, as possessors of things, as buyers and sellers:

> in commodity-capitalist society separate individuals are related directly to each other by determined production relations, not as members of society, not as persons who occupy a place in the social process of production, but as owners of determined things, as 'social representatives' of different factions of production. This 'personification', in which critics of Marx saw something incomprehensible and even mystical, indicated a very real phenomenon: the dependence of production relations among people on the social form of things (factors of production) which belong to them, and which are personified by them. (*ibid.*, p. 21)

The 'reification' of production-relations between people in experience has an objective basis, it reflects the complex nature of reality itself. 'Reification' is not a mere *appearance*, it is the actual material form of social interaction made necessary by determinate production relations.

Production-relations among people determine the *social form of things*, but this form, once established, imposes its necessity on individuals; relations between individuals are possible only through the social forms of things. 'Reification' exists because only the material/social form is visible and the production-relations among people which produce it are only visible as this form, in their effects: 'only the . . . personification of things . . . lies on the surface of economic life and can be directly observed. . . . This side of the process is related directly to the psyche of individuals and can be directly observed' (*Essays*, p. 25). Rubin recognises that the theory of fetishism requires that observable forms of things be generated by reality itself and given to the experience of subjects. 'Fetishism' is an essential experience-form. This position requires the subject/object structure of the empiricist process of knowledge: a subject with a given capacity for 'experience' who internalises what is given to it by the object. The presence of this subject of experience signals the presence of the subject in another sense. The theory of fetishism depends on the oppositions social/material, thing/person. Why should commodities be conceived as 'things'?

The place of the subject in the theory of fetishism emerges when we consider the questions how and why do production relations between people come to take on the form of relations between *things*? Rubin says:

> This side of the process, i.e. the 'reification' of production relations among people, is the heterogeneous result of a mass of transactions, of human actions which are deposited on top of each other. It is the result of a social process which is carried on 'behind their backs', i.e. a result which was not set in advance as a goal. (*ibid.*, p. 25)

Relations have their conditions of formation:

> When the given type of production relations among people is still rare and exceptional in a given society, it cannot impose a different and permanent social character on the products of labour which exist in it. . . . These relations are frequently repeated, become common and spread in a given social environment. This 'crystallisation' of production relations among people leads to the 'crystallisation' of the corresponding social forms among things. (*ibid.*, p. 23)

We see here the foundation of the whole 'reification' problem and the thing/person opposition which is central to it, the concept of spontaneous or unmediated social interaction. Spontaneous human interactions become regularised and 'crystallised', 'behind men's backs' they take as the unplanned consequence of their actions forms they cannot control. This doctrine of 'alienation' is central to the concept of 'reification'—it supposes the possibility of the presence of the subject's essence to itself, its products and interactions then taking an unmediated form. Contrasted to 'reified' social relations are those in which social life is pure intersubjectivity—the social division of labour is the product of conscious communal decision. Social relations of production vanish into the collective subject.

The opposition thing/person is a *critical* opposition ('critical' in the sense of its use in left-Hegelian critical philosophy). It supposes that 'things' exist because their social/human form is not manifest, their form as products of labour, as social labour. It supposes that forms of pure intersubjectivity form the basis for the criticism of 'reified' forms. Why, however, should we consider commodities as 'things' rather than as parts of a social process of exchange? Why, however, should we suppose that the social division of labour and the social forms of the products of labour do not take on definite forms in socialist and communist societies (forms which are 'independent of the will' of the producers)? The social relations of production and the forms of communal decision-making in a communist society will have an objective social existence, the social division of labour will impose itself on individuals through forms of necessity. Why should these social forms not be considered 'thinglike' and opposed to persons?

The theory of reification/alienation supposes an essential subject, persons/collectives, who are potentially the unmediated authors of their acts. These essential or constitutive subjects are the origin of social relations and are unquestionable as origin. Persons are essential and irreducible, 'things' are secondary effects and must be recognised as the alienated products of persons. Persons have a privileged ontological status: hence the *critical* force of the *thing/person* distinction. If persons were not constitutive subjects and 'things' were not the reified form of their products then the distinction person/thing could not be privileged *theoretically* but only ethically. Persons are then merely preferable to things. The distinction requires that persons be constitutive subjects, ontologically unique as the creators of their products. Things are not constitutive, they do not create persons rather persons create (in the alienated form) things. This distinction refers us back to an ontological uniqueness we have encountered before: Man-as-origin, *homo faber*.

Rubin does not develop these implications of the concepts. He uses the thing/person, material/social distinctions as *critical* categories without going into their critical-philosophical foundations. These implications were wisely left undeveloped—his work as it was provoked the charge of 'Menshevising Idealism'. (It should be noted that Rubin, like Abram Deborin and many others, was vilified by the vulgar materialist sectarians in Soviet intellectual life. As strongly as we reject the categories Rubin uses we must praise his seriousness, rigour, and courage. He was another of the countless able Marxists who met an untimely and unjustifiable death at the hands of Stalin and the NKVD. He was arrested to implicate his patron David Raisanov, with whom Stalin had old scores to settle: see R. Medvedev, *Let History Judge*, pp. 132–6.)

The material/social distinction makes possible Rubin's dispersion content (social)—form (material), technical (presupposition)—social (articulation of presupposition). Social objects are assigned places in this system. Why should money be considered the 'material' form of a social relation? Why is it not social? Likewise, the difference between a painting and land is reduced to a *material* difference, a difference in natural form rather than a difference of social usefulness. Again, technology is considered as material/ technical, articulated with social relations of production as their 'presupposition' rather than as part of them. This material/social distinction enables elements of social relations (money, technology) to be placed outside social relations or assigned a secondary status as their material forms of expression. In the case of money, the space of the 'social' is reserved for what underlies the relations of money-exchange value. The material/technical distinction enables Rubin to counter certain of the effects of vulgar Marxism, consigning technique to the status of a 'presupposition' of certain social relations rather than a direct and primary cause. Technique has to develop to a certain level to make certain social relations possible. It is, however, the social relations of production which determine these social forms.

Technology underlies and affects the law of value-technology by changing the productivity of labour affects the conditions of exchange and the proportions in which goods exchange. It does not determine the form in which they become social nor does it directly determine the process of exchange itself. Rubin thus avoids a pure exchange-proportionality theory of value whilst retaining the autonomy of the processes of the social relations of production from direct determination by production technique. In effect these categories restrict the social to the social relations of production (to 'relations between men') and to the essence of these relations rather than to their material forms of expression. These categories indicate the privilege granted to the level at which the theory of value is operative. Technique and material forms of exchange are assigned a secondary status in advance by these categories (the vulgar Marxists and economists like Böhm-Bawerk miss the essence of social relations)—the essence of social relations is the way the labours of man become social, become linked with one another. The law of value is concerned essentially with the distribution of social labour—exchanges, money and prices are merely the material expression-forms this distribution takes in commodity/capitalist society. Rubin's starting point, the theory of fetishism and its central category, thing/person is therefore no accident.

Rubin's presentation of the role of the theory of fetishism in *Capital* is by and large an accurate one. The attempt in *Reading Capital* to eliminate or 'write-out' this concept from the discourse of *Capital* is problematic to say the least. First, fetishism is conceived as an ideological excrescence in an otherwise scientific problematic. Its exclusion rests upon a general epistemological division of knowledges into ideological and scientific ones. Central in this division is the conception of the place of the subject within knowledge; concepts which accord an actually or potentially constitutive role to the subject are ideological. Fetishism is such a concept. Secondly, fetishism can only be rejected on the basis of accentuating other concepts of the relation of the process to the agents which are to be found combined with it in *Capital*.

Fetishism is made possible as a concept in *Capital* by the way that the problem of value-in-exchange is set up. The divided labours of socially atomised but interdependent producers are united by means of the equation of the *products* of their labours. Relations between men take the form of relations between things. Althusser conceives fetishism as an ideological residue. Rejecting fetishism involves a mutation in the discourse. It involves generalising the position taken in *Capital* on the representation of the process to the agents. This is conceived as part of an anti-humanist structural causality, operative in all modes of production, which secures in its effects on the agents the conditions of operation of the structure (the agents functioning as supports). The rejection involves preventing any counterposition in the discourse of the position of these supports with the position of subjects in a society subject to conscious collective direction. In the discourse of *Capital* the space of this counterposition is not suppressed. The empty subject necessary for the capitalist process of representation can be conceived as a subject emptied of its potential by alienation, an alienation which is the condition of existence of this process. The empty (passive) subjects necessary to commodity production and capitalism will be replaced in socialism by the full constitutive subject, the members of humanity linked in conscious collectivity.

Althusser rejects this conception. Anti-humanist structural causality accentuates the conception of the totality, as an entity which secures its own conditions of existence, entailed in the concept of fetishism. It denies the notion of a different kind of totality and causality which is necessary for fetishism to function as a *critical* concept. In Part II of this volume we challenge this concept of totality which the theories of fetishism and structural causality share—a totality which necessarily (in its concept) secures its own conditions of existence. Althusser's 'writing-out' of fetishism from the discourse of *Capital* is only possible because of his retention of the concept of the representation of the process to the agents. We reject both the concept of fetishism and *Capital*'s general conception of the representation of the process to the agents. This is because of the problems generated by the conceptions of totality and causality necessary for both of these positions.

Value and equilibrium

'Value' is a concept of Marxist political economy and it expresses 'social relations among people'. Rubin sets out his object:

> If we approach the theory of value from this point of view, then we face the task of demonstrating that value: (1) is a social relation among *people*, (2) which assumes a material *form* and (3) is related to the process of production. (*Essays on Marx's Theory of Value*, p. 63)

Marx begins *Capital* with an exercise in abstraction. He considers commodity exchanges prior to and independent of capitalist production. He uses the concept of simple commodity production to outline his theory of value. By conceiving an economy of producers who are separate and formally independent from one another Marx is able to consider the effects of the commodity form of relation between them as producers without the complexities introduced by the wage labour/capital relation. The producers are separated from one another and independent, how is it then that their labourers can take a social and useful form? A commodity economy raises the social division of labour and its proportional composition as a problem:

> Every system of *divided* labour is at the same time a system of *distributed* labour. . . . In a commodity economy, no one controls the distribution of labour among the individual branches of production and the individual enterprises. . . . Commodity production is a system of constantly disturbed equilibrium. . . . *But if this is so, then how does the commodity economy continue to exist as a totality of different branches of production which complement each other*? (Our emphasis) (*ibid*., p. 64)

Rubin's answer to this question is a teleological-functionalist law of value based on the concept of an 'equilibrium' proportionality of socially necessary labours. Value relations directly express this proportionality in exchange relations, in average prices:

> In conditions of a simple commodity economy the average prices of products are proportional to their labour value. In other words, value represents that average price level around which market prices fluctuate and with which the prices would coincide if *social labour* were proportionally divided among the various branches of production. Thus a state of equilibrium would be established among the branches of production. (*ibid*., p. 64)

The proportions in which commodities exchange are the mode in which society adjusts the amounts of labour expended on various goods to its needs for those goods: 'The quantitative proportions in which things exchange are expressions of the law of proportional distribution of social labour' (*ibid*., p. 105). Equilibrium between the amounts of labour expended in production is established through exchange. In exchange society expresses its judgment on the existing distribution of labour. Anarchy is the form of order in commodity production. Disturbed equilibrium is the mechanism of restoration of equilibrium:

> The tendency to reestablish equilibrium is brought about by means of the market mechanism and market prices. . . . The deviation of market prices from values is the mechanism by means of which the overproduction and underproduction is removed and the tendency toward the reestablishment of equilibrium among the given branches of the national economy is set up. (*ibid*., pp. 64–5)

This mechanism is self-regulating, deviations are self-compensating and engender correcting deviations in the other direction which tend to restore balance:

> If every deviation tended to develop uninterruptedly, then the continuation of production would not be possible; the social economy, based on a division of labour, would break down. In reality every deviation of production, whether up or down, provokes forces which put a stop to the deviation in the given direction and give birth to movements in the opposite direction. . . . The fluctuations of market prices are in reality a barometer, an indicator of the process of distribution of social labour which

> takes place in the depths of the social economy. *But it is a very unusual barometer; a barometer which not only indicates the weather but corrects it.* (Our emphasis) (*ibid.*, pp. 77–8)

The central concept of Rubin's theory of value is the concept of 'equilibrium'. This concept amounts to a proportional distribution of the labour of society so as to produce exactly the right quantities of the right range of goods. It is a 'theoretically defined state', the centre around which all fluctuations move:

> Market-value corresponds to the theoretically defined state of equilibrium among the different branches of production. If commodities are sold according to market-values then the state of equilibrium is maintained, i.e. the production of a given branch does not expand or contract at the expense of other branches. *Equilibrium among the different branches of production, the correspondence of social production with social needs* and the coincidence of market prices with market-values—all these factors are closely related and concomitant. (Our emphasis) (*ibid.*, p. 178)

Rubin's position gets him into the difficulty that value appears to depend on demand, social needs appear to determine the proportions in which goods exchange. He attempts to argue on the contrary that the equilibrium depends on the relative productivity between branches of production and between enterprises within branches: 'equilibrium depends . . . on the level of development of the productive forces' (*ibid.*, p. 179). The 'value of social needs or demand' has an objective form but the level of demand depends on the development of the productive forces and these in turn depend upon technique:

> The state of technology determines the *value* of the product, and value in turn determines the normal *value of demand* and the corresponding *normal quantity of supply*, if we suppose a given level of needs and a given level of income of the population. (*ibid.*, p. 190)

Income and needs both depend on the productive forces. Rubin argues that: '*equilibrium between demand and supply* takes place if there is equilibrium between the various branches of production'. Rubin's attempt to deny the dependence of value on demand and the social process of exchange is clearly an attempt to counter the charge of 'idealism': as we shall see his conception of value does make value-proportions dependent on exchange-relations (that is its great strength).

Despite Rubin's attempt to avoid certain consequences of his position the concept of equilibrium he uses does suppose that a certain composition of the social product is necessary. Whether or not there is an independent 'demand function', certain goods in certain quantities are conceived to be necessary and this proportional composition regulates the actual composition, punishing overproduction with unfavourable terms of exchange relative to other goods and stimulating underproduction with favourable terms of exchange. In the form of Rubin's argument this proportional composition imposes itself as a necessary demand schedule; proportionality is regulated through the effects of sales and purchases in the market. This schedule can only be a structure of needs 'spontaneously' realised as the objective resultant or sum of individuals' choices: otherwise 'needs' would realise themselves without a mechanism. This demand schedule is not truly independent but has social determinants. 'Spontaneity' is an effect of basic social causes. These choices and this demand depend upon men's income and needs: both of them are ultimately determined by the productive forces and at any given time they correspond broadly to the actual composition of production. Demand and needs change as productivity and products change. This means that potentially *any* composition of the social product is possible (products and techniques are not given—production has no given necessary structure) and *every* composition is at a given moment necessary. Rubin's position appears to involve the concomitant that production determines consumption. This would mean that whatever is produced is consumed, which is not only patently false but would contradict his argument. *Any composition would be proportional*. Value and demand would not adjust production to 'need'.

We return to the autonomy of need. Either this must take the form of an autonomous 'demand', or, it must somehow shape the development of the productive forces themselves. This means that certain compositions of production are necessary; production *does* have a necessary structure of composition imposed on it, a structure selected from all the possibilities of development. As products and techniques develop they must be shaped by human needs: not all possible products and techniques are created or introduced. In the long run the productive forces develop in such a way as to develop the capacities and needs of humanity; this is because the agent of their development is humanity itself. Technique does not develop randomly. Human needs exercise a natural selection process over the composition of production. But this argument does not get Rubin out of his difficulty. These needs cannot, except in a system of socialised production, directly determine the products and the quantities of these products produced. In a market economy this process of selection must take place through the market. Like it or not, Rubin must invoke the autonomy of demand. Only in this way can a certain composition be *necessary* and play the role of an equilibrium composition. Like it or not Rubin's position entails a *norm* which regulates the goods and quantities produced through its form as demand expressed in the market. Only in this way can the exchange-proportions of the products be conceived as effecting (through fluctuations) a necessary distribution of social labour ('necessary' here refers to the necessity of a certain composition of the product produced by that labour). The problem of the source or determinants of this demand remains. We have seen that it cannot come directly from production without any composition becoming as proportional as any other. It can only be the unconscious providential 'hidden hand' whereby humanity chooses in the market what is good for it.

The concept of 'equilibrium' used by Rubin (and Hilferding) is not some importation, a borrowing from bourgeois economics alien to Marxism. We have seen that Marx conceives the law of value as a law of distribution of social labour in part 1 of volume 1. In volume 3 Marx expands on this position (part 6, ch. XXVII): here, like Rubin, Marx relates the concept of proportionality to the concept of use-value.

> The same is true for all division of labour within society as a whole. . . . It is the labour necessary for the production of particular articles, for the satisfaction of some particular need of society for these articles. If this division is proportional, then the products of various groups are sold at their values (at a later stage of development they are sold at their prices of production). It is indeed the effect of the law of value, not with reference to individual commodities or articles, but to each total product of the particular social spheres of production made independent by the division of labour; so that not only is no more than the

> necessary labour-time used up for each specific commodity, but only the necessary proportional quantity of the total labour-time is used up in the various groups. For the condition remains that the commodity represents use-value. But if the use-value of individual commodities depends on whether they satisfy a particular need then the use-value of the mass of the social product depends on whether it satisfies the quantitatively definite social need for each particular kind of product in an adequate manner, and whether the labour is therefore proportionately distributed among the different spheres in keeping with these social needs. . . . *The social need, that is, use-value as a social scale appears here as the determining factor for the amount of total social labour-time which is expended in the various spheres of production.* (*Capital*, vol. 3, Moscow edn, pp. 620–1)

Earlier (in Chapter 1), in discussing the exchange of equivalents, we considered a functionalist law of value as a law of exchange-proportions related to labour-time. Elephants and rats exchanged in certain proportions in order to keep their respective hunters in their place in the division of labour. Disproportionality of labour-times problematised the division of labour. The necessity of the composition of the division of labour was taken for granted there. Here we see Rubin and Marx expressing a functionalist law from the other side. Certain qualities of certain goods are required, and given the labour-times necessary to produce these goods certain quantities of labour must be distributed. Exchange-ratios are determined by the labour-times necessary for the production of the goods and the demand for these goods. Goods have no value if they are not demanded: Marx says, '*Only just so much of . . . [a good] is required for the satisfaction of social needs. The limitation occurring here is due to the use-value*' (*Capital*, vol. 3, p. 621).

Marx's use of the concept of use-value is here equivalent to *demand*. Marx gives no rigorous account of the concept use-value. However, the 'usefulness' of goods must be their use to the agents who purchase them. The quantities desired will depend upon their utility to the agent and the conditions of acquisition. Demand regulates the composition of the product and the quantities (at any given stage of social productivity) demanded. Demand/utility has a crucial and hidden place in the theory of value. '*Use-value*' is the equivalent of the classical bourgeois concept of 'utility' in that it is circular. What is demanded has a use-value and it has it to the extent that certain quantities are required. This merely amounts to saying that what is purchased is wanted and that the quantities in which it is wanted affect prices. When production and consumption are equivalent to one another value-proportionality prevails (supply and demand explain nothing here). Marx's analysis of demand is far less systematic than that of neo-classical economics, since whatever marginalism's limits and absurdities, it does attempt to produce a theory of preference.

Marx, like Rubin, has no position on why a certain composition (products and quantities) is necessary other than that it is wanted and that market fluctuations attempt to establish it. But *any* composition is then necessary. Value proportionality centres on the average of price fluctuations. Marx retreats to a generalisation about averages in attempting to state the relation of prices and values (*Capital*, vol. 3, p. 90). The theory of value rests on a certain composition being necessary, but in effect any working economy is supposed to express such a composition as its core, a composition constantly sought and restored through deviations. The circularity of the Marxist theory of demand ('use-value') enables us to argue any composition to be a necessary one. It can be argued to exist through the fluctuations and to be revealed when they are 'averaged out'. This means that this variant of the Marxist theory of value posits a functionalism (a certain composition is necessary in an economy, this composition regulates production) and then makes *any* working economy exhibit this functionality (it must have a composition structure since production *must* be regulated—these goods would not be bought if they were not use-values). 'Equilibrium' is a concept which in its strong formulations involves teleology: it is a definite 'state' of the economy (conceived as necessary for its existence or as having certain desirable effects) which is sought or attained (in teleological formulations) by certain necessary mechanisms (e.g. demand/market fluctuations). In Marxism this state of 'equilibrium' is an empty one—short of terminal crises all economies are always in the process of adjusting production to the proportions necessitated by society's requirement for use-values. Rubin did us a great service by emphasising what is secondary in the discourse of *Capital* and giving this position the appropriate concept from neo-classical theory.

There are other objections to this proportional-composition theory of value. If taken rigorously it purports to explain why certain goods are produced in certain proportions one to another, it also purports to explain changes in the exchange-ratios between them as a function of restoration of proportionality. Demand therefore directly affects exchange-ratios by attempting to return production to a certain composition. Society is indifferent to the techniques by which a given composition of the product is produced. If goods are produced in the 'right' proportions then there will be no tendency for demand to produce changes in the exchange-ratios of goods. It will be quite obvious that certain quantities of certain goods can be produced by different methods of production involving different numbers of labourers and different totals of hours of labour. So far as society is concerned, provided x chairs, y boots and z cans of dog food are produced the techniques and labour-times involved are irrelevant—the demand structure will not shift because production has changed its relative labour-times between goods. *Demand is indifferent to changes in the distribution of labour if these different distributions still continue to produce the same composition of the product.* Demand only restores a given composition with given techniques. How can we then consider composition part of a law of 'distribution' of social labour? The *distribution* is not determined by the composition.

It is a truism that certain numbers of workers are needed to produce certain goods in certain quantities with a given intensity of labour and given techniques. So much 'concrete labour' is required: so many hours of hunting and so many hunters. This distribution is no necessary function of the composition of the product, it can be produced with quite different totals of the labour force and quite different distributions of workers between branches. Composition does not regulate the choice of technique (and therefore the distribution of labour). Techniques do not determine themselves.

The problems for the theory of value as a law of 'distribution' of social labour are the following: what is the relation between the abstract-labour ratios established in the process of exchange and the distribution of production, and what is the relation of these two to the composition of the product expressed in demand?

To answer these questions one must consider the concepts of abstract labour and the form of value.

Abstract labour and the form of value

We have seen that Rubin argues that the law of value acts to correct excesses in the labour distributed to the production of certain goods by changes in the exchange-relations of these goods with others. The equation of commodities one with another (x commodities a = y commodities b) is a means of distribution of labour. Labours (incommensurable in concrete form) are equalised *through exchange*: '[Labour] becomes social only because it is equalised with some other labour, and this equalisation is carried out by means of exchange' (*Essays on Marx's Theory of Value*, p. 66). Equalisation takes place through the quantities in which the products of different kinds of labour exchange: different kinds of labour are socialised through the relation of their products one with another.

It is *abstract labour* which forms the basis of Marx's theory of value. Marx rejects a simple labour-substance theory of value: 'Labour does not, in itself, give value to the product, but only that *labour* which is organised in a determined social *form* (in the form of a commodity economy)' (*ibid.*, p. 68). Value does not inhere in things, it is not a substance planted 'in' them by the concrete labour of making them, rather value is the product of a complex social process. Labour in itself, as concrete labour, is not the *substance* of value: the concrete activity of labouring can never bestow value on the product. It is only in the process of exchange and through the *products of labour* exchanged with one another that the labour which produces these products is given the form of value-creating labour. The equation of the products of labour (x commodities a = y commodities b) establishes a relation of equivalence between the labours which produce them:

> We can see that the first property of abstract labour consists in the fact that it becomes *social* only if it is *equal*. Its second property consists in the fact that the equalisation of labour is carried out through the equalisation of *things*. (*ibid.*, p. 98)

The *form of value*, value-in-exchange, is the mode of existence of labour as social labour; labour-times are related through the exchange-relations of their products:

> In such a 'commodity' form of economy, social labour necessary for the production of a given product is not expressed directly in working units, but indirectly, in the 'form of value', in the form

of products which are exchanged for the given product. (*ibid.*, p. 115)

Value-in-exchange is not, however, arbitrary. When arbitrary fluctuations are averaged out it will be seen that goods do exchange in definite proportions. For example, one chair and one pair of boots exchange one with another. Why? Value-in-exchange gives a social form to (expresses through the exchange-ratios of the products) the realities of the process of production and the division of labour. Concrete labours cannot be equated as such, an hour of shoemaking has nothing in common with an hour of carpentry. If one chair and one pair of boots exchange, it is because they cost their producers one day of labour-time to make them. Labour-time becomes an abstraction independent of its labour-form. Abstract labour is possible (can be formed in exchange-products) because the producers are *equal* and because a society of commodity producers makes labour an abstraction (men can enter different crafts, change their labour-form). These two facts make possible and threaten the division of labour. Men must remain equal for the system of value-exchange to work, and as they can quit any branch of production the division of labour can be problematised.

Our discussion of a functionalist law of value in Chapter 1, 'Value, Exploitation, and Profit', will be recalled. A boot and a chair exchange with one another because both entail one day of labour-time. If it now takes ten minutes to make a chair as against one day still to make a boot then the ratios of exchange of boots and chairs must change. The realities of labour-time are expressed in the form of value. Otherwise the division of labour is threatened—our bootmaker must work like a dog to furnish his dining room whilst our carpenter enjoys the luxury of leisure. If exchange-ratios do not change as labour-times of the production of goods change then certain producers must suffer (our unlucky elephant-hunters will be recalled), and their place in production is threatened.

Why should that matter? We return again to another part of the functionalism of the law of value-proportional composition. The division of labour reflects a certain necessary composition of the product—it cannot be problematised. Society will adjust through its need for boots and chairs the exchange-ratio between boots and chairs. This shows, however, that demand affects value. There is more at stake here. Suppose a technique is introduced which reduces the production-time of a chair to seconds. How will chairs and boots exchange? This depends *primarily upon demand.* We know that labour in itself has no value—even though a good takes many months of labouring to produce it may still be worthless since it does not have a 'use-value'. But what does it mean to say something has a 'use-value'? Marx tends to use the concept as if it had a non-comparative and non-quantitative sense—as if something only has a use-value in itself (not relative to other things) and as if there could not be more of it or less of it required according to circumstances. In Rubin's account of Marx's theory, however, it does not in fact function in this way. For in fact there must be degrees of social usefulness or utility of a good relative to supply and of utility between one good and another. To return to our chairs. If society's demand for chairs has up till now exceeded supply then an increase in the supply will mean that its production structure has hitherto been 'disproportional'. The exchange-ratio with boots will now depend on the demand for boots—suppose this is proportional to need. The exchange-ratio of chairs to boots will fall (otherwise boot-production is threatened). If it is not 'proportional' (boots are 'over' or 'under' produced) then boots will rise or fall relative to demand in *some ratio* with the labour-times expended. If boots are overproduced boots and chairs will exchange on such terms as reduces the number of bootmakers to a level where the division of labour is threatened and demand for boots changes the exchange-ratios again. In all this supply and demand are the crucial determinants and the exchange-ratios (good-for-good) depend upon them and not specifically on labour-time. Labour-time enters as a determinant only in that if it is flagrantly contradicted supply will fall and the division of labour will be threatened.

It would be possible to conduct this analysis entirely in demand/supply terms and in terms of exchange-ratios between goods relative to the needs of their producers, without reference to labour-time terms. Equilibrium concepts are compatible with either a marginalist or a labour-time theory of value. It should be clear that marginalism can attempt to 'explain' the composition of the product in terms of supply and demand and that the labour theory of value cannot dispense with demand as one of its crucial (and hidden) determinants.

The classic critical response to what we have argued is that it concerns *changes* in supply and demand. What happens if supply and demand are *equal*, if an equilibrium condition is attained? Why do goods then exchange between themselves in definite proportions? Surely it is relative to the labour-time necessary to produce them? Is it? Aside from the argument of Böhm-Bawerk considered above, the combination of value-proportionality and a necessary composition of the product generates special problems. This position leaves out of account the aggregate *quantities* demanded and their relation to production techniques. If society requires 1,000,000 boots (one day per boot), 1,000,000 chairs (half a day per chair) and 1,000,000 cans of dog food (one-tenth of a day per can) how will these commodities be distributed? Only 100 thousand boots can exchange for the cans, only 500 thousand boots exchange against the chairs—what happens to the 400 thousand boots? Society must spend 1,000,000 days making boots, 500,000 making chairs and 100,000 making dog food because these are the *quantities* needed and at a given point only the techniques involved are available. In fact exchange-ratios cannot correspond to times per unit in production if the mass of utilities required by the composition is to be respected. The composition of the product (necessary 'use-values') determines the relative proportions of goods in that it determines the quantities of them wanted. If labours are related through their *products* then it is the conditions of demand and exchange which determine the exchange-ratios of these products. Commodities would not exchange 'at their values' (in quantities strictly relative to the labour-times involved) *even in simple commodity production*. Labour-time would affect exchange only if it affected supply relative to demand, producing over or underproduction, altering the *scarcity* of goods. The role of labour-time would itself depend upon *changes* in supply relative to demand—if bootmakers are driven out of production this makes boots scarce and therefore causes their exchange-ratios with other commodities to rise.

There is no way the Marxist theory of value can eliminate the central role of supply and demand (Böhm-Bawerk was correct to note Marx's dependence upon 'competition' to explain various tendencies and effects of the capitalist mode of production). We have seen that demand cannot be made a simple function of production. If demand (need for use-values) corresponded with production, then what was produced would be consumed. Similarly, 'income' cannot be made a function of production, *since 'income' is a function* of the ratios in which products exchange (income involves the realisation of products in others: all products, Marx admits, do not have value).

To return to the question we asked on p. 88 above. There is no necessary relation between the proportions of goods exchanged one with another and the number of hours of labour needed to produce them. The demand structure (composition of the product) actually subverts any consistent relationship between times of production per unit and the number of units of one good that are obtained for another.

To recapitulate the point, let us consider the concept of *socially necessary labour-time*. Rubin says, revealingly:

> two labour expenditures are recognised as equal if they create *equal quantities of a given product*, even though in fact these labour expenditures can be very different from each other in terms of length of labour-time, intensity, and so on. (*Essays*, p. 157)

This concept explains that the producers in any given branch of production are related one to another by conditions of production imposed through the process of exchange. Exchange *socialises* production, forcing exchange-conditions of production upon producers. If one boot exchanges for 2 lb of grain and an incompetent bootmaker takes two weeks to make one then he must adjust his standard of living accordingly. Why one boot exchanges for 2 lb of grain is another question. We have seen that it is not simply relative to the number of units of labour involved in 2 lb of grain and one boot. The proportions in which goods exchange are determined primarily by demand (composition of the necessary product) and only to a limited extent by the labour-times involved (in so far as they affect scarcity). These arguments are not an attempt to substitute a marginalist theory of value for the Marxist labour theory. It will be clear from Chapter 1, that we regard the exchange of *equivalents* (identities of labour-time) as an unnecessary problem and one which involves the economy realising certain necessary states of affairs (preserving a certain social division of labour). Demand is not some problem alien to Marxist theory (it is raised in the concepts of composition and use-value). The labour theory of value, if it is not to be a simple labour-as-substance theory, must admit the crucial role of demand if it is (as it must be) combined with a notion of a necessary composition of the social product. It is true, however, that the role of demand is not the same as it is in marginalism.

Simple commodity production and capitalist production

Our discussion of Rubin's text has so far been confined to the theory of value in simple commodity production. How does this discussion relate to capitalism? Capitalism modifies the operation of the law of value. It is no longer an economy of independent producers who receive the value-form of their labour in other products of labour. The law of distribution of social labour no longer operates as it does when the producers possess their own means of production. Whereas values exchange with values in the simple commodity economy, products in capitalism are sold at *production prices* (costs of production plus average profit). Equal capitals have therefore equal rates of profit, their organic compositions notwithstanding: Rubin comments: 'Since both commodities were produced by equal capitals, they are equalised with each other on the market regardless of the fact that they were produced with unequal quantities of labour' (*Essays*, p. 231). The distribution of labour is effected through the distribution of capital. This distribution of capital is indirectly a function of the productivity of labour. Changes in the average rate of profit result from changes in the rate or mass of the total surplus value, these changes are 'brought about, in the last analysis, by changes in the *productivity of labour* and, consequently, by changes in the *value* of some goods' (*ibid.*, p. 249). Value or the productivity of labour still regulates the distribution of labour through capitalist social relations. Strict value-proportionality in exchange does not hold, but value-relations (productivity of labour) regulate the distribution of social labour nevertheless: 'If the law of *quantitative proportions* of exchange is modified in capitalist exchange, compared to simple commodity exchange, the qualitative side of exchange is the same in both economies' (*ibid.*, p. 93).

Rubin's attempt to save the 'qualitative' side of the theory of value in capitalism means that he must rely crucially on the two positions which form the basis of his argument:

1 that society requires a certain composition of the product and hence a certain distribution of labour;

2 that changes in the value of products are determined by changes in the productivity of labour.

His account of the role of value in capitalism merely displaces the direct exchange of equivalent quanta of labour-time in favour of a distribution of labour mediated through capitalist profits. It rests on the two propositions we have shown to be problematic.

Appendix

The Problem of 'Reproduction' in 'Capital'

What place does the problem of 'reproduction' occupy in the discursive order of *Capital*? What is its theoretical location as a problem; how does this location affect the form in which it is posed? 'Reproduction' is presented in vol. 2, *The Process of Circulation of Capital*, under the heading, 'The reproduction and circulation of the total social capital'. The problem appears because of the nature of capitalist relations of circulation. Its form is unique to capitalism and is not a universal 'necessity' of all economies (Marx does not consider reproduction in general except in the truistical sense that 'all societies must renew their means of production'). The problem concerns the effects of the forms of circulation at the level of the economy: the relation of classes and enterprises one to another considered as a totality. The forms of circulation, as *Capital*, vol. 1 and vol. 2, pt 1 show us, are the mode of existence of the relations of production, all relations existing in and effective through the form of sales and purchases. The problem involved in the analysiss of 'reproduction' is that of the effectivity of the relations of production/circulation at the level of the total social capital, it is nothing else than the analysis of the forms and effects of circulation itself.

Why should 'reproduction' appear as a problem specific to capitalism? Capitalist relations of production involve the following two elements: the separation of the workers from the means of production and their connection with them through the wage-form; and the separation of enterprises one from another and their connection through serial commodity exchanges. Capitalist economies have a definite structure, a division of social labour into distinct branches of production, but this structure exists through the mechanism of sales and purchases. Reproduction concerns the relations between the division of social labour, enterprises and classes effected through commodity exchange:

1 Separation of the workers from the means of production—how does that portion of money capital transferred to workers in the form of wages 'return' to the capitals in question through the system of commodity exchanges?

2 Separation of the enterprises one from another—how does this 'anarchy', the complex division of production into branches and enterprises, resolve itself through unplanned series of sales and purchases into a distribution of the product such that enterprises can renew their means of production?

Marx says:

> We cannot rest content any longer, as we did in the analysis of the value of the product of the individual capital, with the *assumption* that the individual capitalist can first convert the component parts of his capital into money by the sale of his commodities, and then reconvert them into productive capital by renewed purchases of the elements of product on the commodity-market. Inasmuch as those elements of production are by nature material, they represent as much a constituent of the social capital as the individual finished product, which is exchanged for them and replaced by them. Contrariwise the movement of that portion of the social commodity-product which is consumed by the labourer in expending his wages, and by the capitalist in expending his surplus-value, not only forms an integral part of the movement of the total product, but intermingles with the movements of the individual capitals, and therefore this process cannot be explained by merely assuming it. (*Capital*, vol. 2, p. 393)

'Reproduction' concerns the articulation of the generalised commodity production (GCP)/generalised commodity exchange (GCE) structure of capitalism. The 'reproduction schemas' are the discursive device by means of which Marx demonstrates the properties of capitalist relations of circulation. Marx supposes certain conditions as a means of demonstrating how the distribution of the means of production to enterprises and the circulation of the capital advanced in wages operates. The 'departments' and the classes are related in a 'closed' series of exchanges, a complete circulation of the total product within a definite time period (1 year). This enables a synoptic presentation of the properties of the GCP/GCE structure, each sector being simultaneously related to the next in a closed series of exchanges.

The familiar notion of a 'reproduction cycle' appears as a result of this device, that is, if it is supposed that the conditions of this synoptic resolution of the social product really do operate, and if it is supposed that there is a definite period of turnover or renewal of the total social capital. To rephrase Marx, this process cannot be assumed without explaining it. It would have to be demonstrated that such a cycle does operate (for example, the Physiocrats conceived social production to be based upon an annual cycle determined by the harvest). If not then there is no need to conceive of 'reproduction' as a special process, a 'renewal' of the economy. The concept of a cycle depends on imposing a time period on the process of circulation, imposing this period as a social necessity in which the commodity exchanges of the totality must 'sum'. Once this necessity is not supposed then at the end of any given period chosen as a measure there will always be workers with unexpended means of payment, enterprises with as yet uninvested money capitals, or with unsold products, or awaiting means of production. We would argue that there is no 'cycle' or period of reproduction for the total social capital (although enterprises do work on trading and investment cycles, these never 'sum' on a social scale). There is no reproduction process distinct from the continuous process of commodity circulation, the process which is the form of existence of the capitalist relations of production. Let us be clear, we are not denying the effectivity of the process of circulation at the level of the total social capital (that would amount to denying any effectivity to the relations of production on the economy, which *is* an absurdity), rather we are denying the notion that it takes the form of a periodic synoptic 'renewal' of production.

Certain economists (otherwise hostile to Marx, like Samuelson) have praised the reproduction schemas in *Capital*, vol. 2 because they see in them an 'equilibrium' state of the economy—a necessary proportionality of sectors. This position is as we have seen, taken by Marxists like Hilferding and Rubin. Nothing could be further from the truth:

> But inasmuch as only one-sided exchanges are made, a number of mere purchases on the one hand, a number of mere sales on

> the other . . . the balance can be maintained only on the assumption that in amount the value of the one-sided purchases and that of sales tally. The fact that the production of commodities is the general form of capitalist production implies the role which money is playing in it not only as a medium of circulation, but also as money-capital, and engenders certain conditions of normal exchange peculiar to this mode of production and therefore of the normal course of reproduction . . . conditions which change into so many conditions of abnormal movement, into so many possibilities of crises, since the balance is itself an accident owing to the spontaneous nature of this production. (*Capital*, vol. 2, pp. 494–5)

Although Marx uses the notion of a cycle, he ascribes no necessary outcomes or effects to the circulation process. Reproduction is not 'necessity' ensured by a providental mechanism which gives the desired result to the circulation process. Circulation may produce 'crises' (systematic discrepancies of sales and purchases); these crises imply no 'failure' of capitalist relations of production (no breakdown of capitalism), rather they register a specific modality of the effectivity of those relations. The structure of capitalist production (branches, enterprises, levels of employment) exists through commodity circulation; it, therefore, registers the effects of the circulation process. The 'proportions' 'necessary' for the reproduction of the existing structure of the means of production do not impose themselves as necessities on the process of circulation. Circulation involves money, and, as Marx recognises, it is a characteristic of monetary exchange that it does not involve the simultaneity of sale/purchase on both sides of the exchange (as in barter), sales need not be followed by purchases. Hence the possibility of discrepancies or crises.

Marx recognises that value-analysis does not provide the means to pose the problem of the production-circulation ('reproduction') relation:

> So long as we looked upon the production of value and the value of the product of capital individually, the bodily form of the commodities produced was wholly immaterial for the analysis. . . . This merely formal manner of presentation is no longer adequate in the study of the total social capital and of the value of its products. The reconversion of one portion of the value of

> the product into capital and the passing of another portion into the individual consumption of the capitalist as well as the working class form a movement within the value of the product itself in which the result of the aggregate capital finds expression; and this movement is not only a replacement of value, but also a replacement in material and is therefore as much bound up with the relative proportions of the value components of the total social product as with their use-value, their material shape. (*Capital*, vol. 2, p. 394)

Marx recognises here the problem of the *composition* of the total product, that it is differentiated into certain distinct products ('use-values') in certain proportions. He does not raise the question of the *determinants* of this composition and their relation to circulation. What he does appear to argue is, however, that there is a determinate relation between the reproduction of the proportionate value components of the total and the proportionate material components. This position, as we have seen, is taken up by Hilferding. Were such a 'law of value' to operate it would indeed represent an 'equilibrium' state of the economy: proportionality of values and use-values necessary for production, synchronic balance of all exchanges and their effects. Marx provides, however, the means to challenge such a 'law'.

Value-analysis cannot set the terms of the 'reproduction' problem Marx poses (the forms of articulation of production and circulation). The theory of value supposes that it is *equivalents* which are exchanged, all equivalent values are identical aliquot parts of the totality of values (total product). It is the *composition* of production, its division into quanta of distinct products, and its distribution which are at issue. It is the circulation of means of payment and the determinants of the 'return' of means adequate for capitals to purchase anew the conditions of production which are at issue. The characteristics and quantities of the products, money as a medium of exchange/means of payment, are central to the problem of 'reproduction'. Quanta of goods, sums of money, are necessary conditions of existence for enterprises, necessary *in this specific form* not as 'values'. Value-terms mask this problem, they concern *equivalents* (identities) independent of form, whilst the problem of 'reproduction' concerns *differences* in products and requires precisely the form of *money*. Only by assuming that the 'law of value' guarantees the distribution of the means of production and the means of their purchase, or that forms of distribution must respect strict value-proportions (which amounts to the same thing)—this involves a functionalist law of value—is it possible to reduce the determinants involved in 'reproduction' to value-terms. Nothing requires that 'values' produced be purchased or that 'value' in the form of money change its form. To deny this is to deny the specific effectivity of capitalist relations of production in the interests of an hypostatised 'law of value', a 'law' which must have mechanisms of effectivity independent of and which override these relations.

Part II

Capital and Laws of Tendency

A brief comment on the status of our discussion of 'laws of tendency' is necessary here. We are concerned in this portion of the text with the concept of 'law of tendency' as such, with its theoretical conditions of existence and effects. The objective of this section is to challenge the conception of social causality which is entailed in it and which makes possible the notion of 'law of tendency'. In particular we are concerned with the consequences this conception has for the analysis of social formations. In our critical discussion of the general concept particular 'laws of tendency' are included only for purposes of developing the argument against this concept and for illustration. We offer here no exhaustive review of the particular 'laws' of tendency, their conditions of operation and the debates surrounding them. Given the nature of our criticism of the general concept there is no pertinence in considering *in this context* all the instances of 'laws' which fall under it. Specific 'laws of tendency' are discussed in this volume and in the second when they are directly relevant to the argument being conducted.

One implication of this discussion must be highlighted in advance of the discussions and conclusions in the second volume. The rejection of the conception of causality entailed in the notion of 'laws of tendency' has very definite implications for attempts to periodise the capitalist system. Conceptions of a 'monopoly' or 'advanced industrial' *stage* of capitalism have generally depended on some thesis of the interlocking and the maturation of the effects of certain laws of tendency (e.g. concentration and centralisation, development of the forces of production) to produce a significant mutation in the structure of this mode of production. What is involved here is the idea that necessary effectivities postulated in a general concept of the capitalist mode of production can be, directly or indirectly, 'mapped' on to capitalist social formations. It is this notion of causality we criticise and reject. It follows from this rejection that there can be no necessary and general periodisation of capitalist social formations at the level of a concept of capitalist mode of production. In our conception periodisation would involve specifying changes in the conditions in which capitalist relations of production are secured in definite social formations and the nature of the effects of those changes on those relations. The nature of those changes cannot be specified without reference to those conditions and in consequence cannot be generalised into a 'monopoly' or any other type of stage.

Chapter 4

Epistemology, Causality, and Laws of Tendency

A Contribution to the Critique of Political Economy, the *Grundrisse*, and *Capital* all share in substance the same conception of scientific knowledge of social relations and the manner of proceeding in producing that knowledge. This conception can be considered as an epistemology, that is, a conception of a necessary and general relation between a knowledge process (however conceived) and an object external to it (however conceived), this relation being one in which the former corresponds to or assimilates the latter. This epistemology is elaborated for a definite knowledge, political economy, rather than as a general philosophical doctrine of knowledge. It serves to define and differentiate a conception of the 'method' of political economy: this 'method' is a necessary manner of proceeding in analysis and investigation such that economic knowledge does assimilate its object. This form of knowledge and the 'method' corresponding to it are prefigured in the '1857 Introduction' to *A Contribution*. Our object in this particular text will be to investigate the concept of 'law of tendency' in *Capital*. In order to do so it is necessary to consider the conception of a form of knowledge process in which such 'laws' can be considered as possible and necessary products of this process; it is for this reason we devote such attention to the 1857 text.

A word of caution is necessary here. Or, rather, many words, given the influence of Althusserian rationalism on conceptions and practices of reading. This caution is necessary because our treatment of the relation of the epistemological doctrine to the other concepts in *Capital* does not follow that of the rationalist conception of discourse. The discourse of *Capital* must not be conceived as the emanation of an epistemological doctrine, that doctrine forming the 'basic concepts' from which all others are logically derived. In the rationalist conception of discourse the entire 'logic' of *Capital* would be conceived as immanent in its 'basic concepts', and first among these concepts would be that of the knowledge-being relation. In our conception the discourse *written under the sign* of an epistemological doctrine is not 'logically bound' by it. In the rationalist conception 'discrepant' positions are interpreted as external interventions into the 'logical' order of effects of the basic concepts of other concepts and their effects (thus, for example, in Althusser's conception ideologies intervene in discourse to constitute obstacles to the logical effects of scientificity, these obstacles can be removed by a critique which recognises the externality of these concepts and in removing them removes their negative effects). Epistemological doctrines do not, in our conception, have *necessary* discursive effects.

But we have argued elsewhere (Hindess, 1977a, Hindess and Hirst, 1977) that epistemological doctrines have no necessary discursive effects. An epistemological concept of knowledge-being relation is necessarily a general one: it specifies the form of the relation between being (the general category of what is external to knowledge and known by it) and knowledge (the process of assimilation of being into the order of its recognition). Epistemological doctrines are conceptions of this general relation. As such they claim to establish the general form all being must take and they do so by specifying it as the form appropriate to a definite conception of the knowledge process. They do not constitute the particular entities about which other definite theoretical discourses speak. These latter entities are specified in quite distinct forms of discourse, by means of concepts and problems which are not epistemological and which are not derived from epistemological concepts and problems. The entities so conceived need not have an *epistemological* status, as objects external to discourse and to which it corresponds. These entities—relations of production, photons, etc., need be assimilated to no general category of *being*. Thus a problem like the tendency of the rate of profit to decline cannot be *derived* or *deduced* from the conception of the knowledge process adopted in the text in which it is posed. These particular entities are conceived in epistemological doctrines as variants or exemplars of the general concept of being; but this assimilation depends on accepting the enterprise of epistemology. *Capital* cannot be conceived as an extension of the epistemology in terms of which it is written, the whole tied together by a single logically coherent discourse. Epistemological concepts are not 'basic concepts' in the rationalist sense.

Thus radically to limit the discursive effects of epistemological concepts is not to eliminate them. Epistemological doctrines have no necessary, logical, effects on the texts written under their sign. The relation between these concepts and the other concepts in the text into which they are written is determined by the specific conditions of the writing and by no inherent logical properties in the concepts themselves. They do not ensure that the substantive discourse of the text conforms to the protocols laid down in its epistemological concepts. Hence, if we demonstrate a form of congruence between the following things, a conception of the relation of knowledge and being, a conception of the form of development of concepts and the posing of problems, and definite concepts and entities, this congruence must be understood as an effect of the discourse in which it is produced (which makes this combination, however 'contradictory' it may appear, possible). It is an effect of the conditions of discourse and the form of discourse as a whole and is neither a *necessary* effect (it is specific to those conditions and has no validity as such vouchsafed in a logic), nor an effect of any particular *level* of concepts in that discourse (there are no 'basic concepts' privileged against the discourse and other concepts, in terms of which the whole must be read). The concept of 'law of tendency' that is developed in *Capital* cannot be conceived as made necessary by the epistemology of *Capital*, even if there is a definite relation to it. Further, there is no simple and singular concept of 'law', but a range of possible positions determined by the texture of the discourse; this complexity becomes greater as the specific 'laws' are worked out in different portions of the text which have different statuses and objectives. In this complex of discourses certain 'logical' consequences of the epistemological doctrine generally adopted in *Capital* and of conceptions of the law of tendency are refused and negated. These refusals do not constitute 'obstacles' or 'intrusions', they are the way in which the discourse proceeds and produces its effects. These refusals are not privileged, simple negations of what they reject. The rejection of these possible consequences, the substitution of other positions does have real effects, and so, in their counteraction, these possible positions are of discursive significance.

What is the epistemological doctrine under the sign of which these three very different texts are written? It is the conception of knowledge familiar and notorious from its reconstruction in *For Marx* and *Reading Capital*, the 'appropriation of the concrete in thought'. Marx's outline of this doctrine in the '1857 Introduction' illustrates the conception of the knowledge-being relation and the method of working in political economy associated with it very well.

In that text the 'correct scientific method' (Marx, 1857 Introduction, p. 206) is conceived as abstractive/analytic. It involves the formation of general concepts by a process of reasoning (which takes place in abstraction from the concrete) and the concretisation of the concepts through their development and elaboration in this process of reasoning. The concrete is 'appropriated' by a method which leads 'from abstract definitions by way of reasoning to the reproduction of the concrete situation' (*ibid.*). A process which takes place in thought produces the concrete in the order of knowledge just as the processes which take place in reality produce the concrete in the order of its existence. Knowledge must be conceived as a process which produces an effect, this process is a form of reasoning and the effect is to reproduce the concrete within thought: 'the method of advancing from the abstract to the concrete is simply the way in which thinking assimilates the concrete and reproduces it as a concrete mental category' (*ibid.*). Knowledge is a process (reasoning), which has a definite ontological status (it takes place in a distinct realm called 'thought'), this process has an effect on an object with a different ontological status (the 'concrete'), and the effect is to 'assimilate' the latter object within the former realm, 'reproducing' the latter object (it is itself) but in the mode appropriate to the realm of 'thought', as a 'concrete mental category'.

The correspondence between knowledge and its object is the correspondence of the *products* of two ontologically distinct processes which produce their results in different ways: the evolution of concepts in abstraction, through reasoning, and the evolution of the concrete through definite chains of historical causality. It is the *products* which correspond and not the processes; the process of reasoning does not follow the actual order of formation of the concrete, it does not mirror the history of the concrete. The concrete thought appropriates is a totality, a totality whose current existence is different from the circumstances of its formation. The correspondence between the two orders, knowledge and the concrete, is possible, despite their different natures and modes of formation, because both share the common property of being *synthetic*. In *Capital* Marx defines a process as a 'synthesis of many determinations'. In the text of 1857 the product of the 'process of evolution of the concrete world itself' is conceived as such a synthesis, a social totality with an effectivity internal to it and distinct from the circumstances of its formation. Knowledge is similarly conceived as a synthetic process: 'The concrete concept is concrete because it is a synthesis of many definitions, thus representing the unity of diverse aspects' (Marx, 1857 Introduction, p. 206). The synthesis of definitions comprehends the synthesis of determinations, the correspondence is that of the order of one totality with another. If the concrete were not synthetic, formed into an ordered whole, it would not be accessible to representation in a rational totality of concepts. Being could not have an order appropriate to reason. Thought can proceed in its own realm, by its own laws, and *still* correspond to reality, because what is formed through the coalescence of diverse circumstances is not itself circumstantial. The totality is knowable as such.

One synthetic combination of elements corresponds to and represents another. Having synthesised the concrete synthesis, thought possesses the key to the circumstances of its existences. Comprehending the articulation of the elements into and by the totality, thought can see what it is that is pertinent in the circumstances which constitute the specific processes of formation of that totality in reality. Hence Marx's oft-quoted aphorism: 'The anatomy of man is the key to the anatomy of the ape.' Comprehending the hierarchy of determinations and its effects, thought can determine what is significant in any concrete situation in which the totality exists and is operative.

Marx, in specifying the method appropriate to political economy, also specifies the general nature of the *objects* with which this discipline should deal. The form of being assimilated and reproduced in thought is a system of social relations. That system is the significant object of political economy, providing in its systematicity what must be known about the process of its own formation and what must be known about the conditions in which it exists. This articulation of elements into a whole, which can be mirrored in thought, is what is significant about being. By implication it does not exhaust social being, the totality of past and present circumstances, but it is privileged within it. Further, thought assimilates the concrete, it reproduces being within itself. Thus Marx in 1857 conceives the 'correct scientific method' in political economy to be the development of concrete totalities of social relations (concrete in thought as they are in reality) by reasoning from abstract simple concepts. This conception of method is not displaced in *Capital. Capital* is written as a knowledge process, as the presentation of the reasoning whereby a definite object (totality) is assimilated, that is, the capitalist mode of production. This object is a real object, a system synthesised in concepts. It is an existence (complete with its determinations) which is capable of expression in reason. Capitalist social relations are a unitary *object* capable of existence in the forms specified by abstraction.

In order to draw out the significance of this latter point we must return to the general discussion of epistemology. Epistemologies posit some definite form of knowledge-being relation and, because they concern themselves with the problem of the validity of knowledge, an account of the adequacy (or inadequacy) of that relation and the reasons why it is a necessary one. A definite form of knowledge corresponds to an object external to it: the knowledge and the object must exist in forms appropriate to one another if the correspondence is to be possible. The object must have a status appropriate to the forms of knowledge of it. Thus inductivist variants of positivism tend to suppose the possibility of knowledge through the recognition of individual and discrete objects of sensation. Or, to take an example where the relation is one of *in*adequation, a relation determined by the nature of the object, Weber conceives knowledge of social relations as necessarily limited by the fact that they constitute a realm of human purposes. This latter example illustrates a property of epistemological doctrines, that in specifying the knowledge-being relation they specify the general form of the being known and close off in this way all existences that can be known. Thus even when the adequacy of a definite form of knowledge is denied or radically limited epistemological doctrines purport to specify what it is that cannot (adequately) be known and why it cannot be known. Being is a general category in epistemological discourse, it is as general as the forms of knowledge. For each form there are postulated entities which have a general and common status. In some epistemologies this necessary ontological reference can be bracketed or nominalised by saying that these entities exist to knowledge and that they can be known as such only through the possible forms of knowledge. However, these are attempts to qualify the relation necessarily involved in specifying any general form of knowledge, a process which appropriates or corresponds to entities existing external to it. Where this reference is bracketed then generally the correspondence effect is weakened or subjected to sceptical challenge. Paradoxically, this has the effect of disvaluing all possible definite knowledges and subordinating them to epistemological discourse itself (that discourse is the only one not weakened and negated in relation to *its* objects). In general, therefore, epistemological doctrines establish a definite concept of the nature and limits of the object that the knowledge specified in them can know.

The object of *Capital* is the capitalist mode of production. It is not some definite capitalist country, its population, trade, the laws which regulate its commerce, etc., but capitalism in general which is the object to be known. Capitalism is an economic system, a totality of social relations, which can be *assimilated* in abstraction. Capitalism is a concrete totality. '*De te fabula narratur*'; of you it is written because the thought object of *Capital*, the capitalist mode of production and its economic laws of motion, appropriates a reality, these laws being the form of concrete action of that reality. Capital*ism* is not confined to England, or to any of the definite circumstances of its concrete existence. England merely illustrates in a specific context the working out of the logic and the laws of motion of this system. This system has particular conditions of genesis in England, but what is important is the general effect of the constituted system. These are the same in Germany as in England and act to eliminate the effects of previous social systems and the circumstances of genesis. England is not what Marx offers as a future to the Germans but the effects of *capitalism in England*. The concrete synthesis, capitalism, has effects which are necessary to it, which stem from it as a system and which make it a system. Capital*ism*, a generality independent of the specific conditions in which it acts, is the concrete totality synthesised in thought. It is because the real object is *existence-in-generality* that it can be comprehended in general concepts (synthesised in abstraction).

Capital's concrete object is a generality, but it is a concrete generality, rational in form and in its effects, which can be assimilated in abstraction. The concept of capitalism assimilates the determinations and the effects of the concrete system. For knowledge of this kind to be possible as the result of a process of abstract reasoning these effects must be rational and necessary, they must follow from the system as logical consequences from a concept. The category of 'laws of motion' comprehends a certain class of these necessary effects, those which develop with accentuated effectivity as the system develops.

What these effects *are*, however, cannot be derived from this conception of the capitalist mode of production as object of a definite knowledge process. For them to be given in the concept of that process the whole discourse of *Capital* would have to form a coherent logical whole. The discourse of *Capital* is not such a whole, and cannot be comprehended on the basis of the rationalist assumptions of coherence and logical hierarchy. The effects of the 'laws of motion' and, indeed, the general concept of those laws, are neither unambiguously nor coherently developed in the discourse of *Capital*. A conception of effectivity is advanced which corresponds to the knowledge process as a process of reasoning, but this conception by no means hegemonises specific analyses of definite supposed effects.

In order to deal with the concept of effectivity which makes possible a notion of 'laws of motion' that can be apprehended in abstraction we will first consider a conception of the capitalist mode of production advanced in *Capital*. Later we will qualify its relation to the discourse as a whole, showing that it does not play the role of 'basic concept' governing all less 'general' portions of the discourse.

In this conception *Capital* appropriates the essence of capitalist social relations. All possible capitalist societies are merely the specific localisations or realisations of this economic system and its necessary effects. Even this conception of the general status of the object known cannot tell us what those effects are going to be. It does not, and cannot, determine whether those effects are the necessary evolution of the structure toward some end (be it stagnation, collapse, or supersession) or its self-reproduction. All this general ontology tells us is that the effects of the system necessarily follow from it and have the same general form, there being no other possible order of effects which can contradict them. Whatever the specific nature of the effects or tendencies they would necessarily be realised, they could be considered as simple actualisations of potentialities present in the unity of being in question (capitalism) and comprehended (in advance) in its concept. This conception of tendency as necessary effect immanent in the being of the object can be found in different and politically quite opposed conceptions of *Capital*. For a certain type of anti-Marxist sociology or economics Marx hazarded 'predictions', that is, a necessary course of events, immiseration, perpetual slump, class polarisation, etc., and these 'predictions' have been refuted by the non-appearance of these events. Marxists of a certain stamp have replied that these necessary events are merely deferred and that their time will come. This time is the time of the notorious 'negation of the negation': the immanent tendencies, present at last, annul their own effects, for their ultimate effectivity is their own self-dissolution. For this Marxism capitalism crashes as a result of the realisation of its tendencies: in the stagnation produced by the declining rate of profit, in the crises and slumps produced by immiseration and underconsumption capitalism renders itself impossible.

We shall consider in detail later the most famous of the passages which support this reading, vol. 1, ch. 32, 'The Historical Tendency of Capitalist Accumulation'. We will also consider the crucial mechanism of this transformative action of the tendencies, Marx's concept of the forces and relations of production coming into contradiction. It will be argued that neither of these conceptions sustain in discourse a developed conception of necessarily realised tendency, certainly not one leading to the dissolution of capitalist social relations.

We said above that the concept of necessarily realised effect involved in the concept of capitalism as a system synthesised in reason does not give the *form* of that effect. The form of effectivity essayed in vol. 1, ch. 32 is not the only form of necessary effect. Other effects of the system which are not evolutionary-tendential but synchronic-structural have the same status as effects immanent in the system and specified in its concept. Whereas the forms of effectivity supposed in the 'negation of the negation' are challenged or ignored in other portions of the discourse of *Capital*, certain of the synchronic effects are sustained through the three volumes with remarkable consistency.

In considering these synchronic effects let us note firstly that what is assimilated in thought is a system of *social relations*. This may seem obvious, but the object known (relations between men) affects the knowledge process by which it is known, and the conception of object in the knowledge process affects the relations between men that can be specified in that process. This double and reversed connection of knowledge process and concept of object is located around the concept of ideology. The general conception of object in the epistemology under the sign of which *Capital* is written is that of an entity the effects of which are given in its concept. The system actually to be known in *Capital* is the production and distribution system of a type of economy. This means that the effects of the economy must be present in its concept. Here, the epistemological conception of object is reinforced by a specific theory of causality, historical materialism. In this theory the economy is the primary determinant of social relations: 'The mode of production of material life conditions the social, political and intellectual life process in general.' This primacy means that the economic can be elaborated in the order of thought autonomously from the other social relations. Indeed, since the economic determines these other relations in the last instance, it must be conceptualised and its effectivity recognised before any scientific analysis of those other relations is possible. In such an order of analysis the causal order in the real is respected, and, at the same time, the effects of that order on knowledge are avoided. For, if the economic level conditions the intellectual elements in social reality, it can impose that conditioning on knowledge. Hence the necessity of an abstraction which reconstructs the causal order of the real in thought. The knowledge process and the causal process in the real are linked in definite ways: the primacy of the economic system and the necessity of its effects make a certain type of knowledge possible (synthesis of the concrete in abstraction), they also make that type of knowledge necessary (abstraction from immediacy of concrete—recognition/avoidance of causal order of concrete). The epistemological doctrine and historical materialism interact and reinforce one another in definite ways.

This reinforcement can be summed-up as follows: first, the economy generates certain necessary effects which provide (through its causal primacy) its non-economic conditions of existence, and second, a definite order of thought is made necessary by the order of the real, necessary in order to correspond to the real (primacy of economic) and necessary to avoid certain effects of the real interrupting the order of thought (hence the abstraction of thought, the autonomy of the two orders). Ideology is thus doubly significant to Marxist knowledge. It is one of the necessary effects of the system, making that system possible as social relations, and it is a possible effect on knowledge which imposes a certain form and order on (scientific) thought.

The system assimilated in thought is one of *relations between men*, social relations with intersubjective effects. The effects of the system are the ways in which men are connected one to another in work, in exchange, etc. Men partake of the order of thought. In order for capitalism to be a system of relations between men it must affect how those men perceive and act. That is, in theoretical terms, the economy must secure its ideological conditions of existence. It must do so because certain effects are necessary to it as a system and these effects take place through relations between men. Because capitalism is a *system*, certain definite acts are required of the men who live it, because its effects are necessary in its concept these acts must occur *independently* of the will of these men, and in consequence the conditioning of their will is necessary. Hence the theory of ideology is necessary to a concept of a system of social relations in which certain effects are necessary consequences of the system.

In *Capital* the structure of social relations requires definite and necessary forms of representation of the economic process to the human subjects who serve as its agents in their relations one with another. Definite forms of calculation are necessary to the capitalist as agent and to capitalism (e.g. the theory of cost price). Definite representations of social relations are necessary in order that they be possible relations, that their antagonistic essence be masked (the appearence of the wage form as an equal contract, etc.). *Capital* establishes the concept of *phenomenal forms*, forms of representation of the economic process which are a necessary effect of the system and a part of the system, a condition of its systematicity. These phenomenal forms create perceptions and social relationships which correspond to realities and produce real effects. These forms are not mere appearances, illusions, false in essence. What makes the experience gained through these forms of representation ideological is that these representations are elements of the system and determined by it but they are experienced in consciousness as reality in toto.

These effects are generated as *experience*. It follows that human subjects must be conceived in a manner which can support the category of experience. The experience in question has its contents specified in general (in abstraction) at the level of the concept of capitalist mode of production. These contents are specific in nature (the definite perceptions which support a mode of calculation) and universal (they occur in the same definite way in all capitalisms). The concept of capitalist mode of production therefore specifies its ideological conditions of existence as invariant concrete effects of the system. It does so in general, irrespective of the way specific men associate in a society and are brought-up as members of that society. For capitalism thus to impose itself in general *men* must be conceivable in general (subjects with attributes appropriate to it). A general concept of the social, with necessary effects, requires a general concept of the subject capable of supporting those effects. The subject postulated here is the subject open to the effects of experience, subjects with a capacity of recognition who can internalise the experiences which the system generates for them, empty subjects, who can make this experience the ground of and content of their action. Any subject placed appropriately in the system will experience appropriately and act appropriately. *Capital*, as a theory of the working of the economy, requires a definite anthropology.

Capitalism as a system is thus conceived as generating 'experience effects', representations of itself which are auto-intelligible as experience. These effects correspond to a system of 'places', that is, specific *loci* for agents of the system, *loci* which impose necessities for action independent of the will of those agents. Corresponding to those places are human subjects, each a *tabula rasa*, deriving from experience the consent and grounds for its action. It is through the process of representation that men enter into relations which are independent of their will, but this is because their will is dependent on those relations.

This auto-effectivity of the economy in providing its own intersubjective conditions of existence may be called *economism*. The primacy of the economic generates a necessarily subordinate concept of human subject—a receptacle appropriate to the effects of this causality. It also constitutes a *general* concept of subject, one universally ready to receive these necessary effects. As the content of the subject is interiorised within the system, so the concept of subject supporting it is general and empty. This is often recognised by humanist commentators as the alienation of man in capitalism, but it is an effect of Marx's conception of capitalism in discourse. It is an effect coincident with the conception of capitalism as a unity of being capable of expression in abstraction. This economism of the action of the system cannot be dispensed with if the effects of the system can be designated through a process of reasoning.

Capitalism thus involves certain universal and necessary effects, effects representing social relations to their agents and constituting forms of calculation. The existence of these effects conditions the theoretical method of working in political economy itself. *Capital* is conceived in the way it is written as following a necessary order of development of concepts. The reasoning which penetrates the object has a necessary theoretical form and a theorised order of presentation. Knowledge proceeds in a definite order to avoid the effects of the representation process created by the system it seeks to assimilate. Thus it is necessary to begin with abstract concepts ('value' as general concept) and with the simplest forms (for example, barter) and not with capitalist social relations as they are represented in the consciousness of the agents. Marx's conception of method is systematically anti-positivist, it contains a radical rejection of the validity of any knowledge which works through the forms given to experience.

We have considered synchronic-structural effects in order to pose more clearly what is involved in effects conceived as 'tendential', which form the 'laws of motion' of the structure. In order to understand the problem posed by these 'laws' we must consider what results from the following two circumstances in *Capital*: that the order of reasoning is theorised as the order of production of knowledge; and that the concrete forms of appearance are conceived as the last portions of the system to be known theoretically, they are known as the product of more general concepts which are their conditions of possibility as knowledge.

Capital is conceived as proceeding as a discourse by a double theoretical process. It proceeds through the development of conceptual forms from the simple to the complex; this development of forms is the process by which thought is concretised. This discursive process which makes the complex-concrete appear in the development of categories supports another. On this other process abstraction constructs the inner determinations of the system and proceeds to connect them in a determining way with the phenomenal forms encountered in experience. The sequence of forms, simple → complex, and the connection of the inner structure and the phenomenal forms are linked in a single logical process of discourse. This process of complexification-concretisation has a necessary logical form and order (dialectic). The effect of successive logical relations between concepts is the assimilation of the totality in its concreteness. Discursive order is part of a process of knowledge and logical consequences have the effect of assimilation. Thus in *Capital* one of the laws of tendency, that of the rate of profit to decline, occurs as a consequence of certain concepts, it is bound to a certain site in the discourse. The concepts which precede it and are necessary to its formulation ('organic composition of capital', etc.) are not in themselves epistemological concepts (and they have non-epistemological problems as their source). Nevertheless, they operate within a conception of discourse in which the 'logic' of concepts, their consequences when deployed in a certain manner, cannot be considered as inconsequential.

This notion of a tendency of the rate of profit to decline, a notion made possible by the deployment of certain concepts, is conceived in *Capital* as a process (of whatever nature, we will consider that later) occurring in reality. It is difficult within the conception of discourse as assimilation through dialectic to discount something as merely a possible consequence of deploying concepts in a certain way. To do so is to undercut the very conception of knowledge as a process of complexification-concretisation. This space for such a discounting does not exist in the method of producing knowledge, and this method is attempted in the discourse of *Capital*. We shall see that the discourse of *Capital* refuses the conception of this law as a *realised* tendency but that it does not discount it as a *real* tendency in the system. Thus the dominant conception of the knowledge process within which *Capital* is written does have definite possible effects on the 'laws of tendency' developed within the discourse, both on their form as laws (necessary effects of the system) and on the conditions of their appearance (conceptual effects are appropriation effects and cannot be discounted) in discourse.

We have seen that *Capital* presents a conception of knowledge in which:

1 knowledge assimilates a concrete system and its effects in a process of abstraction;

2 the system is an economic system whose effects ultimately

determine the course of social life;

3 the process of abstraction/assimilation has a definite theoretical order, the consequences of concepts being assimilation effects.

It follows from this that social effectivity in general must be given in the concept of the economic level. The concept of the capitalist mode of production would, therefore, if these theses were correct, be directly 'mappable' on to concrete capitalist social formations. These social formations would represent degrees of realisation of the possible effects of the system in concrete states of affairs. The degree of realisation would ultimately depend on the form of temporality of the process generating those effects. All capitalist social formations, depending on their 'maturity', must in the end produce the same states of affairs. We are familiar with this conception from vulgar versions of the Marxist theory of crises (underconsumptionist or profit-deficiency or suplus-profit theories). What it illustrates is the effects of the theoretical/causal privilege of the economic level being coupled with a conception of knowledge as existence-in-abstraction. Marxist knowledge assimilates the concrete in thought, the social totality complete with the determinants and effects of its systematicity. The concept of social totality is a general concept and so too are all concepts of definite economic systems. All social totalities are determined by their economic level in their form and in the primary effects. All capitalisms are likewise determined by the structure of the capitalist mode of production. This specification is possible because of the general ontological privilege accorded to the economic within the totality and to the totalities themselves. The significant objects encountered in social knowledge are totalities, definite unities of being, and these finite objects (which in their form transcend the concrete circumstances of their existence) are defined by a single general order of causes. The limits of these totalities can be specified in abstraction because they are *concrete generalities*. Abstraction gives us the essence of the concrete because its determinants are in their general form not dependent on circumstances localised in time and place.

The 'mapping' of the concept on to the concrete, reading off as necessities in existence the effects specified in the concept, is possible because the concept records an ontological privilege, that is, the necessary and universal primacy of a certain order of causes and form of organisation of matter over all the phenomena of its domain (in this case the social). Hence, within this conception of knowledge and its objects it must be possible to move (within thought) from the general concepts of certain types of social relations to certain definite states of affairs. Marx insists that this is a process of *knowing*, assimilating an object existing outside of thought into thought. In the '1857 Introduction' Marx insists that this process is not the generation of the real *by* thought. That is Hegel's cardinal illusion, the central difficulty in the Hegelian method which necessitates its 'inversion'. Reality can be summed up in abstraction and concepts mapped back on to the real, but it is produced by itself. Its summing up is possible because it produces itself in concrete generalities which can be given expression in thought. Hegel's method is viable when transformed by the inversion, thought assimilates a reality which is dialectical in form and evolution and, therefore, rational in its reality. Speculation is the interiorisation of existence within thought, as spirituality. Science is the reflection of the rationality of existence (a contradictory, dialectical rationality) in abstraction.

In the essay 'Contradiction and Overdetermination' Althusser attempted to show that the metaphor of the inversion must always produce an impossible continuity between Marx and Hegel. Impossible, that is, if Marx's method were to be radically separated from Hegelian idealism. For Althusserian rationalism discourse is the emanation of a problematic, and central in a problematic is the doctrine of method (this doctrine forming the level of basic concepts which determine the scientificity or otherwise of the discourse). Continuity of *method* would, therefore, be continuity of the discourse as a whole. Althusser is correct about the continuity of the 'inversion'. The method supposed to be produced by the 'inversion' (materialisation of dialectics) involves a change from spiritual to material entities as the objects of its knowledge, and the transformation of the knowledge process from a speculative generation of the object to a scientific assimilation of it. Nevertheless, this change is possible because of the *dialectical* nature of the object: the material entities consist of unities of being with a rational form governed by general laws.

It does not matter whether Marx really does or does not produce his method by 'inverting' Hegel, whether this is a metaphor, or whether Marx's Hegel is the 'real' Hegel or not. These questions *do* matter to the rationalist conception of discourse and to the history of ideas. The former conceives concepts as having necessary effects and forming a hierarchy. Any continuity must imply the full effects of the discourse continued, hence the need for Althusser's 'epistemological break' to be a radical separation. When Althusserians later attempt to establish a continuity between Marx and Hegel, then they are forced to suppose the scientificity of that method (this is classically illustrated in Lecourt's paper 'Lenin, Hegel, Marx'). The latter conceives 'ideas' as entities with a determinable meaning whose history as continuity or discontinuity can therefore be known. For us a possible relation between two sets of epistemological concepts implies nothing about the totality of the discourses from which those concepts are supposed to come. Epistemological concepts do not form a privileged level of discourse.

To return from this digression to the main line of the argument. For the operation of 'mapping' to take place the concept must have interiorised the limits of its concrete object and this object must have limits appropriate to a determinate abstraction. For the effects of social relations to be specified (limited) in their concept they must be given in the concrete totality conceptualised (as potentialities which are necessary effects-to-be). Capitalism, for example, is a totality the effects of which are contained within itself and are present as potentialities from the moment of its existence as a totality. This conception of totality is possible whatever the nature of the effects, providing they can take the form of immanent necessities. Such effects are ever always present in the totality, derivable from the concept of what it *is*. Hence it must be conceived as a completed being which contains itself within itself and reveals its nature as its effects.

The concept of the capitalist mode of production, if this logic were followed through and exhausted the discourse, would thus entail:

1 the necessary presence of certain states of affairs as consequences-to-be within the system;

2 that the nature and limits of the system are present in it (are its systematicity) from the moment of its constitution. The system must be as it is in its concept because that concept assimilates the concrete. Hence the possibility of specifying the *future concrete* from the concept of the totality.

If this logic were to be the substance of Marxist theoretical discourse then it would correspond to its caricatures: its *Marxist* caricatures in evolutionism and economism; its *anti-Marxist* caricatures in the reactionary critique of historicism as historical inevitability (Berlin, Popper). Completed being present in its concept would reveal and realise that completion in definite events. These positions are *caricatures* of Marxist discourse, but they are not impossible *travesties.* Why are they caricatures? Certainly not because the logic we have outlined above is not possible as a consequence of the positions taken in the '1857 Introduction', the '1859 Preface' and *Capital.* It is because these consequences do not exhaust the discourse, because they are refused, qualified and contradicted in it. These positions (which create the space for such a logic) are not a privileged level which imposes and realises its consequences in discourse, these consequences being necessary effects. Paradoxically, such a hierarchy would be merely a repetition of its basic concepts. These concepts are *not* the generative level rationalism conceives them to be and they cannot bind the other regions of discourse because they cannot produce them. These regions are not a logical extension of the epistemological doctrine and its ontological implications. The hegemony of the doctrine would signify their absence. Why are they not travesties? Because the refusals and contradictions do not eliminate these positions, they are combined with them in the discourse. The discourse is written as these positions *and* their qualification/evasion.

There is no single 'refusal' of these consequences. Such as there might be if an 'author' (the mythical constitutive subject of the text) drew back from the consequences of his doctrine, recognising that he had gone 'too far' in a certain direction, and, like an absolutist monarch, withdrew the 'letters patent' of the offending concepts. These refusals and contradictions, etc., occur at many distinct discursive sites. Equally, the position thus qualified recurs at other sites. The discourse of *Capital* is written through and as such presences and refusals. What determines them and the form of their combination can only be resolved by analysis of the discourse itself, of the questions it poses and attempts to answer, of the conditions of conceptualisation and connection of concepts thus produced. As discourse lacks the necessary form imposed by rationalism or the manifest 'meaning' of the empiricist history of 'ideas' this analysis cannot be terminated in a definitive 'conclusion'.

The 'logical' (the possible) consequences for Marxist discourse of the assimilation of the concrete in thought and the general causal primacy of the economic are denied, refused, qualified, and affirmed at various sites. Here, for purposes of illustration we will contrast certain statements from the corpus of Marx and Engels. The first contrast:

> 1 With the change of the economic foundation the entire immense superstructure is more or less rapidly transformed. . . . No social order ever perishes before all the productive forces for which there is room in it have developed. (1859 Preface)
>
> 2 The economic situation is the basis, but the various elements of the superstructure . . . also exercise their influence upon the course of historical struggles and in many cases preponderate in determining their *form*. There is an interaction of all these elements in which, amid the endless host of accidents . . . the economic movement finally asserts itself as necessary. Otherwise the application of the theory to any period of history would be easier than the solution of a simple equation to the first degree. (Engels to J. Bloch, 21–22 September 1890)

The second contrast:

> 1 *De te fabula nattatur*. . . . It is a question of these laws themselves, of these tendencies working with iron necessity towards inevitable results. The country which is more developed industrially only shows, to the less developed, the image of its own future. (Preface to First German edition of *Capital*, 1867)
>
> 2 But that is too little for my critic. He feels he absolutely must metamorphose my historical sketch of the genesis of capitalism in Western Europe into an historical-philosophic theory of the path every people is fated to tread, whatever the historical circumstances in which it finds itself. Thus events strikingly analogous but taking place in different surroundings led to totally different results. By studying each of these forms of evolution separately and then comparing them one can easily find the clue to this phenomenon, but one will never arrive there by using as one's master key a general historical-philosophical theory, the supreme virtue of which consists in being super-historical. (Marx to *Otechestvenniye Zapiski*, November 1877)

But what, one may ask of the Marx of 1877, is the theory of the primacy of the economic level (universal to all social formations) if it is not super-historical? Similarly, Engels's letter to Bloch merely qualifies and complicates whilst ultimately restoring this primacy of the economic. How could this primacy of the economic (a necessary primacy and no mere generalisation) be explained except beyond the history it makes possible (in its condition, the evolution of organised matter, and in the product of that evolution, the human species as a consumer of energy)?

Let us see what happens when other social levels or 'historical surroundings' are called in to qualify a general determinism of the economic which has the effect of reducing history to the analogue of school mathematics. First, these 'accidents', 'historical surroundings', and other social levels merely complicate the determinism of the economic which is exercised through them and against them. The states of affairs given in the concept of the economic level are indeed ultimately realised, but only after a delay imposed by movement in a resistant medium of circumstances and subsidiary causalities. But, paradoxically, the general ontological privilege of the economic emerges reinforced from this encounter. Second, these 'accidents', 'historical surroundings', and other levels in another case really do substantially negate or redirect the economic from producing the states of affairs given in its concept. How are we to explain this if we are at the same time to retain the concept of a determining economic system? With the old joke conventionally offered at the expense of schematic vulgar Marxists, 'reality proved more complex'? But in that case the concept becomes a *model*. The concept now becomes abstract to the concrete, the effects in the concept may be complicated and perhaps contradicted by the concrete. It proposes a possible course of events which may or may not be realised depending on the effects of 'concrete' conditions which are outside the concept.

This model may have two possible theoretical forms. The first is that of *generalisation*. This could be stated thus: 'Economic relations tend to determine events to a greater degree than do other social relations.' However, there is a corollary to this: 'Sometimes they do not.' There can be no general privilege to the economic in this position, its causal significance is at stake in every particular case. Any social relations or circumstance or any combination of them may be determinant in any concrete case. Generalisations cannot be the products of a conception of knowledge in which it assimilates the concrete in thought. Generalising knowledge merely *abstracts from what has happened.* The second would be that knowledge really does assimilate the concrete in thought, but only partially. Thus knowledge can assimilate in the categories of reason only systems and other social relations capable of expression in abstraction. Other, concrete, conditions are too particular, too conditioned by time and place, to be so expressed. These latter concrete conditions may sometimes prove decisive over the former.

What a strange confrontation is staged in this latter form. A confrontation between 'abstract' yet real tendencies or effects, the consequences of systems as apprehended in their concept, and 'concrete' conditions too specific to be abstracted. These 'abstract' tendencies of the model are *real* effects which would exist in the form in which they are theoretically recognised were it not for the action of 'concrete' counteracting forces outside of the model. In effect one type of concrete determination confronts another. If the counteracting forces do counteract then what they counteract cannot be privileged. It has no causal privilege in this case. Why then is it privileged? Because its concept specifies it as such. The concept purports to assimilate the concrete in thought, but it can produce determinate abstractions only for a portion of what exists; nevertheless, for that portion it must produce a necessary and general analysis of effectivity. The result is an unstable combination of privilege and its contradiction. The privileged entities assimilated have an absurd 'cadet' status as necessary effectivities in abstraction which may be negated in effect. The notion of assimilation is part of an epistemological doctrine which cannot easily introduce elements of provisionality or falsifiability into the relation it establishes between knowledge and the concrete.

This doctrine does specify a knowledge-being relation within which, given the rationality of the concept, there is no problem of its 'application' to the concrete. Reality will be as the concept gives it because it is in essence or *in potentia* already so. This knowledge-being relation can only be qualified at the expense of the epistemological incoherence of the doctrine. That coherence can be maintained only by sticking to the necessity of a certain set of effects as products of privileged causes. That coherence in definite discursive conditions cannot be sustained. It involves merely repeating the programmatic position of the doctrine, a repetition which abolishes the problems created by other forms of discourse, problems which require some other answer than that given by the postulation of a privileged causal level. For the coherence to be sustained definite non-epistemological concepts and problems in the discourse must be obliterated. The privilege of a certain knowledge-being relation in discourse and the privilege of a certain general doctrine of causality associated with it create this impasse. Because the doctrine conceives itself as privileged it cannot accommodate parallel discourses or causalities; either the discourse which incorporates this doctrine must sacrifice the privilege by qualifying it, or it must sacrifice what lies beyond the doctrine, regions of problems and concepts which are not purely epistemological.

COMMENTS

Is not what we have called the 'privilege' of the economic level the theoretical foundation of Marxism? Does not Marx single out as his significant and original scientific discovery the economic 'laws of motion' of capitalism? Does not the rejection of this 'privilege' lead to an eclectic pluralism in social causation, with a necessary slide toward the multi-factorial empiricism of sociology? In framing these questions in advance of their articulation by others we anticipate a scandal, the scandal of Marxists denying the general primacy of determination by the 'economic'.

Let us be clear that the terrain of the criticism of classical Marxism we are engaged in is not that of the debate between monism and pluralism. That debate is a contest of opposed but theoretically equivalent positions, both are general doctrines of causality. What we are challenging is *not merely* the economic monist causality of Marxism, *but the very pertinence of all such general categories of causality and the privilege they accord to certain orders of causes as against others.*

Consider what the notion of a general order of causes within a certain domain of explanation entails:

1 The category of 'cause' involves, despite the possibility of degrees of effectivity and of reciprocal action, one distinct entity acting upon another.

2 This separation is necessary in order that the forces acting can be identified and given a general form.

3 In consequence the entities in existence must be separated into distinct classes necessary to be identified as acting or being acted on, the order of being in question is divided into sub-orders which form the classes of the causal doctrine, e.g. economic, spiritual,

political, etc.

4 A certain hierarchy of relations can then be established in the relations between these classes; thus one class may be conceived as necessarily predominating over the others and as acting upon them (it is privileged and singular in this respect).

5 This privileged status may be conditional (it is a generalisation, it is shared with other entities) or general, a necessary and unalterable relation between the entities in question.

6 A necessary dominance of certain entities over others raises the problem of the foundation of that dominance (it must have conditions of that necessity), the source of this dominance may be grounded on some other order of causes (e.g. nature) outside of the order in question (the social) or it may be asserted that this source is unknown or unknowable.

A number of points can be made here: (a) such doctrines of causality are conceived as applicable to and binding on all discourses in their domain; (b) these doctrines specify the entities which can be encountered, the classes into which these entities are distributed, and the relations between them within their domain of application; (c) the relation of the domain of the doctrine to other domains is raised as a question by the problem of grounding; (d) also raised as a question is the intersection of the causalities operating in these distinct domains (e.g. the relation of nature and the social). A doctrine of causality which involves a general and necessary connection between entities (whatever its form) thus has definite ontological implications and imposes ontological protocols on the nature and limits of the entities which can be encountered in knowledge. Such a doctrine is a general theory of causality. It establishes the forms of connection *possible* in a domain in general and is not the determinate analysis of any definite connection. Such doctrines establish a form of connection as a privileged protocol.

The rationalist conception of discourse notwithstanding, the substantive problems and connections established in any discourse are not an effect of any doctrine of causality which purports to determine what connections are or are not possible within the domain in question. What then is the pertinence of such general doctrines of causality? They are not generative of other levels of discourse or of the connections established in them. For example, certain specific Marxist analyses could be conducted under the rubric of either monism or some form of pluralism. Many Marxist discourses begin by asserting the necessary primacy of the economic and then subvert it or entirely transform the entity-category 'economic' in such a way that it is compatible with the connections they establish. Thus such doctrines in no way define the content of analyses which go beyond the repetition of the doctrine or the way in which these analyses resolve problems.

Pluralist conceptions of causality differ from monist ones not in the distribution of entities to classes, not in the postulation of connections of entities in relations of hierarchy (one dominates another), but *in the form and stability of those relations of hierarchy*. Pluralist doctrines of historical/social causation deny the validity of monism on this point. They insist on a plurality of dominant relations between entities in either a scepticist mode, where no definite general order of priority can be validated or in a dogmatic mode, where certain plural relations are general and necessary (e.g. economic changes and spiritual changes *must* go together). Pluralism specifies certain entities and a variable or combined hierarchy between them. In fact many of the definite connections between entities specified in specific analyses could coexist with either monist or pluralist general doctrines of causality.

Monist doctrines have the more difficult task of establishing the primacy of a single class of entities. Monisms can either assert the necessity of that primacy or establish it as a generalisation from some group of phenomena. A generalisation may be falsified and so such a primacy is always threatened. A monism which insists on the necessity of this primacy, and especially one which grounds it on the action of some other order of causes, cannot live with 'exceptions' in the way a generalisation can. Such 'exceptions' negate its necessity. Discourses apparently written under the aegis of monist doctrines can, however, live with discrepancy (they are bound by no necessity of consistency): the doctrine can appear in discourse now as a necessity, now as a generalisation, and 'exceptions' or plain contradictions are perfectly possible and can be accommodated. Further, specific monist doctrines as developed in discourse generally create the space for some pluralism and mobility in their hierarchy of relations between entities (e.g. the passage from Engels's letter to Bloch cited above). The space between pluralist and monist doctrines as they are developed in discourse is very slight, certainly there is no Chinese wall between them as one might 'logically' suppose.

General causal doctrines are subverted in the constraints they purport to impose on the discourse of explanation in two ways, first, by the forms of mobility and qualification of the relations of the hierarchy we have considered above, thus creating an openness which can accommodate discrepancies and contradictions, and second, by the discrepancies between the specification of the classes of entity they establish and their hierarchy, and the entities and connections between them specified in specific analyses of definite problems. What generally happens in the case of such a discrepancy is either that the openness accommodates it or that the discourse simply ignores it and maintains that the one is consistent with the other or is an effect of it. Causal doctrines can lend their sign to connections between phenomena which have no necessary relation to them (in which there is no question of a specific discrepancy but rather a non-correspondence). They can also be used as protocols to question discrepant or different connections, classically when a discourse attempts to legislate limits to another or to deny it validity. Such a denial raises questions of epistemology (mode of proof), of the legitimacy of such a legislation. It creates the ground for a debate on criteria of knowledge. Since such debates can never be settled except by *fiat* the protocols can only be imposed by *fiat*.

We have argued that general causal doctrines are not necessary for specific discursive analyses and that, therefore, the question of the precedence of one doctrine or another is not a pertinent one. Such doctrines do not produce and cannot constrain (in any valid or effective way) the entities and the connections between them that the discourses concerned with the analysis of specific problems produce. Such problems have their own, diverse, conditions of existence. What these doctrines do is to create, when they are more than a sign at the entrance to a discourse, questions of the correspondence between the connections of the general nature and the specific connections. These questions of correspondence are pertinent to the general doctrines, they concern the mode in which they insert their categories into other elements of discourse. Thus the categories may be 'slid' under those elements so that they are claimed as examples of or emanations of the general causal doctrines.

We have argued that such general doctrines and the questions they pose can be dispensed with without loss and with the benefit of dispensing with debates and problems created solely by their presence. Such doctrines do not and cannot create any specific discursive problem (for example, how credit money differs in its consequences from commodity money, or why different types of financial capitalist institutions exist and what follows from this difference—these are two crucial questions posed in our second volume) or offer the means to its solution. They do not, indeed, even create the 'theoretical context' for such a solution. Thus the notion of the general primacy of the 'economic' in no way creates the conditions for thinking of a system in which the product is circulated by means of sales and purchases in a non-commodity money medium or for dealing with the consequences of a developed capacity to create credit by financial capitalist institutions. Forms of that doctrine have in fact constituted obstacles to the analysis of such questions, stressing the primacy of production in such a way that those problems are considered unimportant (for example, insisting that commodity money must be dominant) or impossible.

This doctrine of causality—the general primacy of determination of the economic—is a weapon from a conflict long since resolved, a conflict against spiritualistic philosophies of history. The field of that conflict was necessarily one of epistemologies and doctrines of causality. To suppose that, if we let this weapon go to the museum, the full horrors of spirituality and theology will be upon us is absurd. It depends entirely on the discourse we are conducting. A spiritualistic theory of finance capital is hardly a prospect. The spiritualist alternative is a serious one only in the domain of general theories of historical causality and it is precisely this domain that we are proposing to evaluate.

To return directly to the question of 'laws of tendency', we would contend that there are three positions on the nature and status of these laws developed in *Capital*, that these positions are combined in different ways, and that together they form the complex and contradictory notion of 'law of tendency' in the discourse of *Capital*. These positions are the following.

1 These laws are conceived as falling within the class of systemic effects which are necessarily realised. Unlike the effects involved in the representation of the process to the agents, which are structural constants, tendential effects are progressively realised through the system's existence and development. They are *tendential* in that they are realised progressively and with growing effectivity. The concentration and centralisation of capitals, the socialisation of the means of production and the industrial reserve army are all

conceived in this way in certain portions of the text—notably vol. 1, ch. 32. Such conceptions of tendencies as progressively realised processes are, however, more or less exclusively confined to general or programmatic statements. Specific discursive elaborations of tendential forms, attempts to state their nature and action (in relation to other concepts and effects), generate a different form of 'law'.

2 Tendencies are also conceived as effects of the structure, which are concrete, the consequences of relations which establish pressures toward certain states of affairs, but which, through the action of those pressures themselves or by reason on the action of other similar tendencies in the system, are not realised in the form of those states of affairs. The tendency although a *real* one (a concrete effectivity) is not *realised*, or, rather, it is realised in the form of its counteraction and repetition. Such laws of tendency which generate their own or are interdicted by other counteracting forces can be either treated as analogous with constants or as spiral in effect, generating the same relations on a larger and more complex scale as the system develops. The classic example of a tendency which is counteracted by its own action and effects is that of the declining rate of profit in vol. 3. These counteracting effects are the discursive form of development of the complex possibilities of certain concepts (e.g. tendency of rising organic composition), which can specify both the law and its counteraction. Such counteracting forces are part of the general concept of the capitalist mode of production, necessary effects in all capitalisms by reason of their form of specification in the concept.

3 Tendencies of either type (1) or type (2) may be counteracted by factors or conditions which are not specified in the general concept of capitalist production but stem from states of affairs which can only be particular to definite capitalist social formations. Here, in effect, the possibility of the operation of 'mapping' is challenged. The general concept becomes a *partial* appropriation of the concrete. All the contradictions of the differing theoretical status of what is counteracted and what counteracts we noted above come into play here. In tendencies of type 2 'mapping' onto the concrete of a simple kind as in type 1 is not possible. There can be no simple *realisation* of the tendency, no progression toward a definite end state. This is because the effect of the system is its own counteraction, the tendency is realised through its counteraction and it has its effectivity through its counteraction. Hence, although

the tendency is never realised, it is real. 'Mapping' does in fact operate here, the effect necessarily does take place but in a contradictory form. Thus factors of type 3 may complicate this contradictory realisation. In this third case states of affairs postulated in certain abstract concepts of the concrete do not necessarily occur or are modified due to the action of other concrete conditions which exist outside of general concepts.

In the remaining two chapters of this part we will consider two crucial aspects of the problem of 'economic laws of motion' or 'laws of tendency' as worked out in *Capital*. In Chapter 5 the concept of the contradiction between the forces and relations of production will be considered. This concept is the way in which Marx thinks of the general framework of the 'laws of motion' as mechanisms of supersession of the capitalist system. In its most extreme form this concept states that capitalism proceeds through a self-annulling dialectic. In Chapter 6 the concept of the tendency of the rate of profit to decline will be considered. This tendency and its counteracting forces indicates the complexity of the discursive development of the concept of 'law of tendency—law of motion'. The effect of the discursive elaboration of this concept is such that it cannot be the law of any definite motion. Several oscillating and counteracting 'motions' are the form of this 'law'. These counteracting forces have a diverse theoretical status and some of them raise problems for the conception of the knowledge process postulated in other portions of the discourse.

Chapter 5

The Contradictory Combination of the Forces and Relations of Production

Forces, relations, and history in the '1859 Preface'

It is necessary to begin our discussion of these concepts in *Capital* by reference to another text. Marx's '1859 Preface' to *A Contribution* presents this relation of contradiction between productive forces and production relations in a number of condensed general theses. These theses form a necessary starting point for our discussion of the contradiction as it is presented in *Capital* because they specify its theoretical conditions of existence.

In the 'Preface' this contradiction between the forces and relations of production is presented as the general mechanism of all social development, the fundamental economic law of motion of all (except the advanced communist) societies. The distribution of social space into an economic structure and a political/legal superstructure (to which correspond definite forms of social consciousness) and the designation of the mode of producing the material means of life as primary within the economic structure make this contradiction theoretically possible. The mode of production of material life determines the forms in which the product is possessed and distributed, that is, the relations of production. It follows that a crisis within the economic structure, between its primary and its secondary elements, can produce a general crisis of the social totality. Class conflicts, social expressions of this contradiction, translate its effects from the economic level onto the level of the superstructure. Historical materialism in its classic form is necessary to the existence of this contradiction. Without the general primacy of the economic and within the economic the general primacy of the method of production this contradiction could not assume the form it does. The contradiction depends on the concept of a general privileged causality (of the economic) and on the concept of totality in which its effects are necessities inscribed within its structure. The conditions enable the couples base/superstructure, forces/relations to work as they do.

What is the nature of this general contradiction which both structures and motivates the totality? It can be presented in the form of theses drawn from the 'Preface':

1 'The totality of these relations of production constitutes the economic structure of society, the real foundation on which arises a legal and political superstructure.' Postulated here is a relation of *correspondence* determined by one of its elements; the relations of production (which represent the *form* of the economic structure) condition their political and legal expression (the notion of 'foundation' is ambiguous but it in no way subverts the general dominance of the economic level).

2 'At a certain stage of development, the material productive forces of society come into conflict with the existing relations of production or—this merely expresses the same thing in legal terms—with the property relations within the framework of which they have operated hitherto. From forms of development of the productive forces these relations turn into their fetters.' The contradiction is a relation of *non-correspondence* between the elements of the economic structure.

3 'Then begins the era of social revolution. The changes in the economic foundation lead sooner or later to the transformation of the whole immense superstructure.' (This shows how little autonomy the ambiguous notion of 'foundation' accords in the last instance to the superstructure.) Non-correspondence is located at the economic level, between the *form* in which that level is represented (the production relations) and the productive forces. This *non-correspondence* negates the *correspondence* established between the two levels of the social totality, structure and superstructure. It does so by annulling the determinacy of the economic *structure-as-form* (as the relations in which the forces are represented). The relations of production determine the correspondence between structure and superstructure (between the economic and its political/legal expressions) when they correspond to the productive forces. In providing the *form* of the structure the relations of production *represent* the determinacy of the productive

forces to the other levels of the totality. When the relations of production do not correspond to the productive forces then they cease to have this effect of representing and giving form to the economic structure as a whole (expressing through this representation the determinacy of the forces).

4 'No social order is ever destroyed before all the productive forces for which it is sufficient have developed, and new superior relations of production never replace older ones before the material conditions of their existence have matured within the framework of the old society.' The contradiction is thought of as a contradiction between a process and the form in which it is contained and through which it is represented. The envelope (the form) is torn apart at the moment when it can be replaced. The forces of production encounter the existing production relations as an obstacle when *and because* they have created the conditions of existence for new relations of production. Non-correspondence exists because the conditions of a new correspondence have become possible and necessary. The productive forces have created the conditions and the need for a new representation of themselves within the totality. The existing relations of production, which have provided the form of representation of the economic level, have in effect become identical with their political/legal expression, no longer expressing the effectivity of the forces and, therefore, being obsolete as the form of representation of the economic.

This conception of contradiction is written within a general doctrine of historical causality: first, it distributes entities to distinct classes (structure/superstructure, forces/relations); second, it gives them the order of a necessary hierarchy, one class of entities (structure/forces) is causally privileged with respect to another (superstructure/relations); and third, it raises the question of the grounding of this privilege (why is it that 'the mode of material life conditions the general process of social, political and intellectual life'?).

The contradiction between the forces and relations of production is thought of in terms of correspondence and non-correspondence. This notion is necessary to the contradiction as it is developed for the following reasons. First, it is the correspondence of one distinct entity with another, and they are linked by an external relation of causality in which one acts on another (forces→relations, structure→superstructure, forces→totality). This means that the elements in the relation of correspondence are distinct entities *apart* from the external relation, and that they can be separated one from the other. This means that the primary element can dispense with the secondary one with which it is combined. It can do so, moreover, through the external relation of causality because it is the privileged element. This form of contradiction can produce a radical supersession in which the superseded relation is entirely annulled and replaced by another (this is a possible point of difference with the classical conception of Hegelian contradiction as preservation-in-supersession). Second, this relation of the external correspondence of distinct entities actually makes possible a hierarchised organisation of this correspondence in which one element (the autonomous one) is primary and imposes the relation between them (connection/separation-annulment) on the other.

The contradiction is thought of as the relation between a process (primary—dynamic) and its form (secondary—static). The form fixed in its capacities of representation of the process becomes a 'fetter' on it; this relation being conceived on the basis of the mechanical analogy between a force and an obstacle to its action. The relations must become an obstacle because they represent (give social form to) one definite manner of producing. Material production is thus conceived as a continuously developing process and the relations of production as successive structures each of which has limits inscribed within it. Why the forces of production should so develop is never elaborated nor explained in the 'Preface', nor is it in Marx's later texts.

The transformations in the manner of producing are a trans-historical constant which makes the historical process possible. History is a succession of finite social totalities which are in turn created, shattered, and displaced by a process which must exceed and go beyond these limited forms. This process of the development of the forces of production creates the conditions of existence for the successive forms of economic structure which are its necessary (corresponding) expressions. The forms of relations of production grow out of material conditions of existence created by the manner of producing. If the primacy of the manner of producing and its inherent tendency to develop were not posited then this general conception of history would not be possible.

Relations of production are conceived as a (necessary) envelope or form which facilitates or fetters the growth of the productive forces. The effect that they have is a secondary one, that of expression or facilitation. Their positive role is limited to that of *not being an obstacle*, of expressing what they contain. In this text their existence is a curious one, they are allowed barely enough space in the discourse to play their part. In the phase of correspondence the relations express the material conditions that have made them possible; these conditions are social relations between the producers already formed by the manner of producing (which grow out of the necessities of technique). Thus, *social* relations between the producers pre-exist their expression in adequate relations of production. In the phase of non-correspondence the relations become equivalent to their own legal expression, forms without substance, without real conditions in the relationships between men in material production (these relationships require other and different forms of expression), and they continue to exist because they form the means of livelihood of the hitherto dominant class. The manner of producing the means of material life thus comes to incorporate, at the decisive moments of non-correspondence, virtually the whole of the economic structure. This incorporation of the privileged level by the forces is a function of their privilege within that level.

The 'Preface' outlines a set of concepts which provide the laws of motion for all (non-communist) economic and social systems. These motions are general and lawful because they represent the action of a basic trans-historical process, the development of the productive forces. This development is not conceived as a generalisation—'hitherto the productive capacities of economic systems have tended to increase in a cumulative manner'—rather, it is conceived as a necessary and inherent development within social life. This development is privileged because the 'mode of producing the means of subsistence' conditions human life in its totality. Historical materialism can purport to explain the primacy of the material because it is the foundation of the non-material. But it cannot purport to explain the tendency of the forces of production to develop, since this primacy of material life is a simple constant, it is equally or more pressing for hunting-and-gathering savages as it is for capitalist ones.

Only the supposition of a trans-historical *subject* can ground or provide the origin for this trans-historical process. The process conceived as the progressive development of social productive power requires the supposition that the successive associations of producers (economic systems) are in some way united, that the process has a unity (which makes it a process) and that it is the process of development *of* something. That something is *humanity*, the human species conceived as a subject. This subject has a unity (unity is theoretically necessary for there to be a concept of subject, necessary because the function of this concept is to be the support and origin of a process—it makes a process with a necessary form possible because that process is referred back to it as the principle of its origin and unity); men are united as humanity despite the differences of time and place. This subject makes history possible and is made through it. What it *is* is what it supports and makes possible. The origin supports the process and the way the process is constituted defines the origin. The '1859 Preface' lacks a positive anthropology outside the process, a fixed human nature distinct from the process of its becoming. The 'Preface' offers us no fixed human nature. It assumes humanity as a subject, the human species existing through time as a being, the history of whose endeavours can be written because it is a *single* history. But this subject has no fixed nature outside what it becomes in the process. This 'empty' anthropology is never written in the 'Preface' but an 'empty' anthropology is written elsewhere—in the *1844 Manuscripts*. In that text Man, as a species, is a being of lack. He is without a naturally given mode of livelihood or existence. As a species men must create and invent their own relation to nature. They are *material* beings, beings who must reproduce their natural conditions in order to exist, but who are without given natural conditions. History is the record of this subject's efforts to remedy this lack. But to rememdy it as *progress* is something which is not explained by this lack. Humanity in the 'Preface' must be conceived as *creative*, but the text is without the means to ground that creativity. Progress requires an origin if it is to be necessary. The subject of 1859 is doubled by what it makes possible—the process defines the origin. The subject is 'empty' and so makes this doubling as its own fulfilment possible. Yet it also subverts it. Ultimately, the pure attribute of creativity is necessary in order that the process be progressive. The subject, paradoxically, far from being empty is full of everything that it will be, it in turn doubles the process and incorporates the process as its Its becoming of Itself (a becoming beyond history, since Marx's history is one phase only of this becoming, the phase of class struggles). A process with a subject and a subject without a nature, a process which gives content to the subject and a subject whose attribute of creativity contains that content, these are the theoretical forms necessary to sustain the discourse of the 'Preface'. They are not presented in the discourse of the 'Preface'!

History is unified by this subject (the subject is what is developed) and the subject is differentiated by history (by the distinct phases of its development). The notion of a human species as a being whose nature is progressive self-creation through the constitution of its material conditions of existence makes possible the general contradiction between the forces and relations of production. It does so because it makes possible the immanent tendency of the productive forces of society to develop. These forces develop within antagonistic conditions: Marx argues that private property is a necessary condition and phase of the process of development of the productive forces and that forms of private possession impose limits on the development of humanity. The distinct modes of producing the means of material life are the stages of development of those forces and this subject, the modes represent an intersection of a level of development of productive power and forms of possession appropriate to that power. Each stage is superior to the last and may be seen 'as epochs marking progress in the economic development of society'. One epoch succeeds another because the immanent development of the productive power of humanity creates the material conditions for it: 'Mankind thus inevitably sets itself only such tasks as it is able to solve. . . .' Here the conception of humanity as subject of history is given explicit form. Only because of this subject and the process which is its existence-development can Marx ground his conception of the modes of production as succeeding one another in the order of a progress. History as the progressive development of something requires a subject as its basis of unity and its origin.

This order as progress and the subject which makes it possible may be conceived in terms of various underpinnings. The anthropology of lack is capable of various formulations: Hegelian-Feuerbachian in 1844, Darwinian-Hegelian in certain of Engels's texts, notably 'The Part Played by Labour in the Transition from Ape to Man'. But some such anthropology is required if the discourse of the 'Preface' is taken into the regions of the grounding of its privilege. Once the subject is denied its unity and its attribute of creativity the process becomes unthinkable. Why should we regard the happenings of different times and locations as capable of having the form of a unity, as the doings of a humanity whose development can be recorded? This 'obvious' unity has theoretical conditions. Racist doctrines conceive the object of a history differently, for example, and, indeed, no such discourse of history is a necessary one. Why should the productive capacity of economic systems tend to develop in an order in which superior replaces inferior? Degenerative development or stasis are equally possible conceptions.

The '1859 Preface' sets out a doctrine of causal privilege (of the forces), a privilege which makes possible an historical dynamic. Other of Marx's discourses are not hegemonised by this privilege. In portions of *Capital* (for example, vol. 1, ch. 15 and also the hitherto unpublished 'Sixth Chapter') and of the *Grundrisse* a quite different connection is essayed between the relations of production and production organisation and technique. It is a different conception of the connection and the entities connected. In 1859 one thing corresponds to or acts on another thing (defenders of the 'Preface' make much of the (secondary) reciprocal action of the relations on the forces). In these texts relations and forces are not so simply distinguished. Capitalist production, it is argued, tends to form a unity, relations-forces. Capitalist production revolutionises the instruments of production through the effects of capitalist relations of production (sale of commodities to realise profits under conditions of competition and production by means of wage labour). Capitalist production subsumes the worker to capital in the form of production techniques. The principle of unity of these techniques is different from that of handicraft production and assigns to the worker a subordinate place in the combined mechanism which is directed by capital. The activity of the worker ceases to be the connection unifying tools and raw materials, in that connection human effort and skill, individual decisions are the determining moment in the productive process, instead the connection is now established by capital in the form of combined self-acting instruments of production and by the capitalist as director of this combination. The labour process is brought into a specific kind of correspondence with capitalist relations of production, fusion. The 'forces' are conceived as the materialised form of the relations. To the extent that this position retains a causality of external connection between distinct entities (such a conception is not criticised or radically displaced) it tends to invert the one proposed in the 'Preface' (forces → relations).

A similar dominance of the relations of production also occurs when the Indian village community is considered in incidental passages in both *Capital* and the *Grundrisse*. The division of labour in these communities ensures self-sufficiency, is based on hereditary specialisation, and is therefore self-reproducing. Marx uses these communities as a crucial part of his explanation of the 'stasis' of the Asiatic mode of production (for a discussion of these passages see Hindess and Hirst, *Pre-Capitalist Modes of Production*, ch. 4).

It is true that in other portions of *Capital* it is argued that the social process of production created by capitalism (interdependent division of labour between enterprises, co-operative organisation of labour within the enterprise) comes into conflict with the relations of production based on private property. Marx conceives the relations as developing the forces beyond the point of correspondence and compatibility. This argument fails, however, as we shall see, to ascribe any effective autonomous development or causal privilege to the forces of production such that they provide the conditions for the breaking down and supersession of capitalist production relations.

The historical tendency of capitalist accumulation

Chapter 32 of *Capital*, vol. 1, 'The Historical Tendency of Capitalist Accumulation' represents one of the classic attempts to argue the contradictory non-correspondence of the forces and relations of production. It returns to the connection/contradiction of the '1859 Preface', and yet, for all its fullness and coherence at the level of exposition, sentence following sentence in measured cadences to the final expropriation of the expropriators, it falls into silence on precisely this question of the contradictory effect of the non-correspondence of the forces with the relations. The effects of this contradiction are not established theoretically, rather at crucial points the text passes into another discourse. This is most evident when Marx discusses the transition from feudalism to capitalism.

There is in this exposition no direct transition from feudalism to capitalism, 'the direct transformation of slaves and serfs into wage labourers' (*Capital*, vol. 1, Penguin edn, p. 927). Between feudalism and capitalism stands a series of forms of 'petty production' based on the possession by the independent producer of his means of production. The private property of this mode is not (in its real form) that of the capitalist mode, the latter being founded on the antithesis between capital materialised in the means of production and wage labour dispossessed of those means. 'Primitive Accumulation' resolves the one form of property into the other, it separates the mass of direct producers from their means of production and converts them into sellers of their labour-power. Marx conceives this primitive accumulation as the resolution of contradictions inherent in the petty mode of production itself. Marx stigmatises it (because he recognises in it the ideal around which the petty bourgeois of all lands unite) thus:

> This mode of production presupposes the fragmentation of holdings, and the dispersal of the other means of production. As it excludes the concentration of these means of production, so it excludes co-operation, division of labour within each separate process of production, the social control and regulation of the forces of nature and the free development of the productive forces of society. It is compatible only with a system of production and a society moving within narrow limits which are of natural origin. To perpetuate it would be, as Pecqueur rightly says, 'to decree universal mediocrity'. (*ibid.*, p. 928)

The form of the economy, relations of production based on independent direct producers, corresponds to a limited development of the forces of production. Such a system of production-relations cannot develop 'the productive forces of society' to overcome 'narrow limits which are of natural origin'.

Marx explicitly returns to the theses of the '1859 Preface', to the developing productive forces and their necessarily limited envelope. The productive forces, developing within limits, create the means by which these limits are overcome: 'At a certain stage of development . . . the petty mode . . . brings into the world the *material means* of its own destruction' (*Capital*, vol. 1, Penguin edn, p. 928—our emphasis). What are these material means? Silence. Marx enters on another discourse:

> From that moment, new forces and new passions spring up in the bosom of society, forces and passions which feel themselves to be fettered by that society. It has to be annihilated; it is annihilated. Its annihilation, the transformation of the individualised and scattered means of production into socially concentrated means of production, the transformation, therefore, of the dwarf-like property of the many into the giant property of the few, and the expropriation of the great mass of

> people from the soil . . . this terrible and arduously accomplished expropriation of the mass of the people forms the pre-history of capital. . . . The expropriation of the direct producers was accomplished by means of the most merciless barbarism, and under the stimulus of the most infamous, the most sordid, the most petty and the most odious of passions. (*ibid.*)

The discourse is moral condemnation. But it is not merely a conceptually empty, untheoretical discourse of indignation and denunciation. For the moral rhetoric is interwoven with another explanation of this transition.

At the moment when one might expect specification of the *material means* created by the petty mode which form the conditions of existence of capitalism and ensure the destruction of the petty mode's (obsolete) relations of production there is silence on this question and another discourse begins. Marx elaborates the *limits* of petty production in comparison with a system which permits co-operation and division of labour. He does not show that the petty mode creates the *material* basis for such a system. Capitalist production begins, as Marx argues, with the material basis of handicraft production, a basis which Marx argues elsewhere does not 'correspond' to capitalist relations of production. What is it in the petty mode that causes it to break down and to be superseded by capitalism? Differentiation of the petty producers? Formation of commercial and financial capital and their penetration into the commodity-producing sector? Neither of these processes can resolve the mass of the independent producers into wage labourers, they kill the few but the many survive and cling tenaciously to their means of production. It would be a very long time before the last artisan was strangled with the debts of the last peasant. What then are the means by which this transformation is accomplished, the means Marx evokes through the language of morality?

The basis for the transformation is the 'new forces and passions . . . which feel themselves to be fettered' by the petty mode. Primitive accumulation is an act of 'barbarism' motivated by 'passions'. But who is it that suffers so from these passions that they are driven to acts of barbarism? How is it that they possess the means to realise these passions in acts? Clearly, it cannot be the traders, usurers, and small manufacturers produced by any process of differentiation within the petty mode, for that would vindicate the petty-bourgeois delusions Weber is so keen to foster in *The Protestant Ethic and the Spirit of Capitalism*. How is this arduously accomplished seizure possible? It involves, as Clausewitz said of war, 'movement in a resistant medium', and, indeed, it *is* war, war against the mass of the people. This war is both arduous and necessary at all because the petty producers are *not* vanquished in production, they refuse to leave the field before the forces of competition and differentiation. They are *forced* from the land. They are forced in a process which requires the action of forces other than those which can be created by differentiation, which cannot be spoken of within the petty mode of production, the feudal landowning class and the State corresponding to the political conditions of existence of feudal rent.

The limits Marx specifies for petty production are limits relative to another system of production which does not yet exist and for which the petty mode of production does not create the economic conditions of transition. The 'passions' which arise and the force which realises them are not a part of the petty mode as such but, on the contrary, are possible only because of the relations of production of feudalism. The theses of 1859 are subverted in their very repetition. There is no way in which primitive accumulation can be accommodated to the causality in which the forces are privileged. Primitive accumulation is the creation by means of political coercion of the economic conditions of existence of capitalist relations of production. This process is effected by means of a class alliance in which the feudal landlord class is the crucial force. Marx's analysis, behind the rhetoric, reverses itself.

Perhaps Marx resolves matters differently when he comes to discuss the transition from capitalism to socialism? Marx insists that the capitalist system necessarily creates the conditions of transition, developing the forces of production to the point where relations of production based on private property become obsolete and incompatible with them. The 'expropriation' of the capitalist property-holder 'is accomplished through the action of the immanent laws of capitalist production itself, through the centralisation of capitals' (*Capital*, vol. 1, Penguin edn, p. 929). Centralisation is identified as the crucial process generating the conditions of transition. It is a necessary effect of capitalist competition that competition and crises constantly reduce the number of capitalists and place the market under the domination of fewer and fewer magnates of capital. Along with this process of centralisation through elimination proceeds the concentration of capitals. The competition of capitalists one with another and their struggles with wage labour leads to the constant revolutionisation of the means of production in the attempt to cut the costs of production, to subordinate labour and increase exploitation, and to realise a greater-than-average rate of profit. As a result the means of production commanded by enterprises grow larger and more complex, the division of labour within the enterprise and between enterprises becomes more complex. The capital required to possess the means of production steadily increases in scale. Capitalism *socialises* production. It creates a division of social labour between branches of production and generalises it on the scale of the world market. It creates interdependence between branches of production and between different specialisms in the enterprise. Production is interdependent at the level of society and co-operative at the level of the enterprise.

Marx goes on to say: 'The centralisation of the means of production and the socialisation of labour reach a point at which they become incompatible with their capitalist integument' (*ibid.*). This incompatibility between socialised production and private appropriation becomes explosive because of the appalling conditions of life it produces for the working class and because of the reduction of the capitalist class to a few functionless monopolists with a mere title to property:

> Along with the constant decrease in the number of capitalist magnates, who usurp and monopolise all the advantages of this process of transformation, the mass of misery, oppression, degradation and exploitation grows; but with this there also grows the revolt of the working class, a class constantly increasing in numbers and trained, united and organised by the very mechanisms of the capitalist process of production. The monopoly of capital becomes a fetter upon the mode of production which has flourished alongside it and under it. (*ibid.*)

The theoretical implications of this remarkable passage are numerous and need to be specified:

1 Capitalist production relations are rendered obsolete by centralisation, concentration, and socialisation, they are in effect reduced to mere titles to property distinct from the real socialised mode of production which has grown up under them.

2 Therefore, since other production relations already prevail *de facto*, the form of economy produced by the logic of concentration and centralisation is a form *appropriate to socialism*, corresponding to socialised property and incompatible with private property.

3 The effect of the division of labour and of co-operative production is to *unify* the workers as a class; further, this economic unification creates the conditions and the basis for the *political unity* of the workers (the economic organisation of the workers in capitalist production produces forms appropriate to *political* organisation).

The theoretical effects of these implications also need to be specified:

1 The compatibility → incompatibility → contradiction thesis requires that the forces and relations be considered as separate things externally connected, in this way the effectivity of the subordinate element can be dispensed with.

2 Thus the *forces of production developed within capitalism can be separated from capitalist production relations*, and in themselves already form the basis for a socialist system, the change involved in moving from one system to another is a change in economic and legal *form* and the objective conditions for this change are already created.

3 There is, therefore, strictly speaking *no process of socialist construction*, rather there is a change of the form of property and of the direction of an already existing system of production; socialism is the removal of obstacles to an already constituted set of productive forces which can now develop freely (the echoes of Stalin's *Economic Problems of Socialism in the USSR* will doubtless not escape the reader).

4 Once the property form is removed and the economic leadership changed the forms of organisation of production are appropriate to the hegemony of the working class.

These implications and effects are no more than a repetition of those of the '1859 Preface' in the context of the transition to socialism. They may be challenged with a number of questions. First, are the effects of concentration and centralisation incompatible with capitalist relations of production? Second, can such a separation be effected between production technique and organisation and the forms of possession of the means of production and of distribution of the product? Are not these techniques and this organisation specifically *capitalist* forms? Third, does the organisation of the workers in capitalist production provide the economic and political basis for the overthrow of capitalism, and the forms of economic organisation under socialism? In our reckoning the answer to all these questions must be in the negative.

Consider the analysis of centralisation and concentration. Why should these processes produce a contradiction between capitalist commodity production and the techniques and forms of organisation of that production. In the first place let us note that capitals of a certain size are necessary for certain techniques and organisational forms to be possible at all. These capitals form the conditions of existence for large-scale industry. There is thus, as *Capital* is all too well aware at other points, a definite form of *correspondence* between certain forms of the centralisation of capital and the 'forces of production' concentrated under them. In the second place it is far from being the case that the techniques and forms of organisation made possible by such capitals are incompatible with private property. The techniques and methods of large-scale industry are adapted to *commodity* production: they reflect the logic of cutting costs of production, eliminating resistance from workers, and the facilitation of selling the product in markets which correspond to the conditions created by capitalist production (primarily large industrial cities). In this thesis of non-correspondence Marx in effect denies what he demonstrates in other chapters, the subordination of the producers and the relations in which they are organised to the logic of production for profit by means of wage labour. In the third place Marx assumes that centralisation and concentration are forces which prevail for all branches in more or less the same measure.

However, there are a number of objections to this assumption. The growing social scale of big capital excludes certain commodities and branches of production from adopting the methods and scale of the dominant branches. A portion of capital retains the methods and scale which were the dominant forms in a previous era. This does not include merely handicrafts, 'putting out' and 'sweating' but also a certain scale of factory production. Thus small units of production tend to prevail in certain industries because of the conditions of the market or the product (clothing, food, furniture, etc.). There is no fixity in this, such industries may be revolutionised into a few large units. Equally, there is no reason why any given branch of production should adopt the scale employed in another. Capitals are differentiated into a range of scales by branches. Moreover, in some cases large-scale industrial production creates the conditions of existence of smaller enterprises through its specialisation of the elements entering into its product (for example, the practice of purchasing components from sub-contractors).

Again, the 'universe' of capitals to be concentrated is not given: concentration and centralisation cannot be conceived as a game of 'ten little Indians' because new branches of production (involving various scales of capitalisation and of units of production) are constantly joining the old. Marx's centripetal tendency is constructed by analysis of one set of determinants acting on the process of competition; these are the factors which are specified through the other general concepts in *Capital* (role of costs of production, tendency toward relative surplus value, etc.). It is a necessary tendency within the concept of capitalism as existence in abstraction. However, definite industrial structures, definite branches of production, definite forms of technique, and their determinants cannot be so given in the concept. It follows that either these structures can be ignored and their specific determinants dismissed as at best secondary ones or the operation of the necessary centripetal tendency specified in the concept must be modified. If the latter course is adopted then it follows that the 'effects' of competition specified in the concept cannot be unambiguously 'mapped' on to the concrete, and that no definite states of affairs are derivable from the concepts of centralisation-concentration. No necessary 'tendency' toward concentration could, therefore, be specified at the level of general concepts. No 'affects' could, therefore, be ascribed to this 'tendency'.

Marx assumes that the forms of division of labour, co-operation, and interdependence developed within capitalism can be summed up in the concept of *socialisation* and separated from the relations of production based on private property. Capitalism has created an objective 'need' for a socialist system. Interdependence is, however, *capitalist* in form, it is the connection of commodity producers and purchasers. It rests upon forms of specialisation and geographical concentration created by commodity production. Capitalist interdependence means that enterprises and their employees are dependent on chains of sales and purchases, on mechanisms of credit, etc., extending well beyond their own immediate orbit. The enterprise depends on the prevailing conditions of competition for itself, and on those commodity purchasers and suppliers on whom it is dependent—these conditions are not of its choosing. Marx is correct to argue that concentration (in so far as it takes place) increases the dependence of units on others. As the units of production and the forms of centralisation of capital become larger so the consequences of the failure of such a unit for the units associated with it and the workers they hire become more widespread and serious. The bankruptcy of British Leyland would be a major disaster for the British national economy, leading to other bankruptcies and leaving perhaps several hundreds of thousands unemployed. But it would not mean the end of capitalist relations of production. Other capitalist motor producers and other largely unrelated branches of production would survive the crash; some largely unaffected and some even benefiting from it. Capitalist interdependence is based upon commodity production and competition, its effects are limited by the existence of other producers and the relative autonomy of markets for groups of commodities.

The interdependence of units of production in capitalism cannot be thought of as *socialisation* if that term is also taken to imply forms capable of integration into a socialist system. This ambiguity in the category 'socialisation' is necessary to the argument, based on the contradiction of the forces and relations of production in ch. 32. The capitalist division of social labour into branches of production, the national and international specialisation and centralisation of production, the very forms of construction, concentration and interconnection of the plants themselves, are products of production for profit. They are by no means necessarily adapted to the needs of a socialist system. Socialist economies constructed by the people to meet their expressed needs would require work to be distributed and divided differently to how it now generally is. Marx is correct to argue that planned and co-operative production would overcome the 'anarchy' of capitalist production (our criticisms of his *theoretical* formulations involve no attempt to defend the capitalist system, rather the reverse, to provide a better foundation for its criticism and transformation). In doing so socialism must de-construct capitalist forms of economic organisation: breaking up the forms of interdependence Marx calls socialisation. In no sense do the forms of interdependence developed within capitalist economies require of necessity socialist relations of production as a form more compatible with them than capitalist relations.

On the question of the political effects of capitalist economic organisation on the working class Marx's position appears to us to be indefensible. The division of labour has not disciplined and united the working class, it certainly has not produced *political* homogeneity. There is, however, no need to refer to production organisations, industrial structures and so on to criticise Marx's position; it implies a variant of the economism and spontaneity so trenchantly criticised in Lenin's *What is to be Done?*

Marx's 'historical tendency' presents us with 'immanent laws' which resolve themselves into a contest between a few 'magnates of capital' and the masses of the exploited and oppressed. We have argued that concentration and centralisation are not linear and terminal processes resolving the universe of capitals into a few monopolists of necessity. We have argued that concentration and centralisation do not produce forms of production organisation and technique incompatible with capitalist relations of production, rather the reverse (as Marx himself argues at other places). Concentration and centralisation take place in different capitalist national economies and in different branches of production in distinct and changing rhythms. These processes, in the way they develop, are the product of many determinations and depend on the specific conditions in definite national economies. They must not be conceived of, as by Marx, as immanent tendencies in capitalism-in-general which are necessarily realised, tendencies which can be derived from the general concept of the capitalist mode of production. Such a conception is part of a form of privileged historical causality, a mechanism for the realisation of a necessary outcome of a process in certain states of affairs.

It should be noted that we have not attempted to demonstrate our argument about concentration and centralisation by reference to figures of degree of concentration in definite branches of production. This is because the point at issue is the problem in relation to which the figures are to be assessed and which form their context of interpretation. Thus for the defender of *Capital*, vol. 1, ch. 32, any tendency toward fewer and bigger units, say the number of auto-assembly firms in 1914 as against 1974 can be argued to be a sign of the immanent master tendency. Its role as sign depends on the reality of the tendency underlying it and not on itself. Equally, any 'counter-tendencies' or varying rates of concentration can be dismissed as secondary phenomena or as sectors yet to feel the main effects of the process. We are concerned with the theoretical conditions of existence of this immanent general tendency, not with the presence or absence of statistical support for it. This 'support' can always be found or denied, since the tendency in question is a phenomenon which goes beyond the particular processes which express it, and, moreover, is not set within rigorous temporal limits as to its rate of progression. For a discussion of questions of statistical interpretation and the role of statistical forms as 'evidence' see Barry Hindess, *The Use of Offical Statistics in Sociology*.

Perhaps the reader will think we have chosen easy targets. Is not the '1859 Preface' the notorious source for economic determinist and historical inevitablist accounts and critiques of Marxism? Is not 'The Historical Tendency' a classic example of Marx's 'flirtation' with Hegel, in which the 'negation of the negation' sews up the future in the necessity of a dialectical logic? Yes, this is true. But it is also true that these are the passages where Marx deals most rigorously with the theoretical foundations of the general economic laws of motion which he makes use of and exemplifies in other portions of *Capital*. In order to illustrate our arguments and perhaps convince our notional sceptical reader we will consider another, less notorious, portion of *Capital* in which Marx considers the immanent withering away of capitalist production-relations and the reduction of those relations to mere titles to property which are at best obstacles to the productive forces.

Marx on the joint-stock company and credit

The text in question is ch. 27 of vol. 3, 'The Role of Credit in Capitalist Production'. Marx refers to the capital of joint-stock companies as 'directly endowed with the form of social capital (capital as directly associated individuals) as distinct from private capital' (*Capital*, vol. 3, p. 427). Marx considers this capital to own the means of production in a pure property relation divorced from the actual organisation of production, a relation of 'antithesis as another's property to every individual actually at work in production, from manager down to the last day labourer' (*ibid.*, pp. 427–8). Marx argues that the joint-stock company results in the 'transformation of the actually functioning capitalist into a mere manager, administrator of other people's capital' (*ibid.*, p. 427).

Marx's text provides a fascinating demonstration of his equation of capitalist relations of production with the fusion of the social and technical divisions of labour in the 'capitalist' as possessor of means of production which produce commodities. Marx conceives the joint-stock company and developed-credit institutions as *transitional forms*, forms which presage the dissolution of capitalist social relations. In his treatment of stock companies and financial markets Marx reveals his failure to theorise the *enterprise*, rather than the 'capitalist', or to conceive of finance capitalist enterprises. He conceives the joint-stock company as a separation of ownership and production, ownership becoming a merely parasitic relation. Financial markets are seen solely as the sphere of operation of swindlers. The limits imposed by the fusion of function with the owning individual are superseded—'It is private production without the control of private property' (*ibid.*, p. 429).

Marx argues a variant of the divorce of ownership and control in connection with the effects of the joint-stock company. In addition to its conversion of the 'actually functioning capitalist into a mere manager', there is a corresponding conversion of the 'owner of capital into a mere owner, a mere money-capitalist' (*ibid.*, p. 427). 'Ownership' and 'control' are regarded here solely from the standpoint of their fusion in the person of the capitalist. Stock capital makes possible a transformation in the scale of enterprises, accelerating the tendency towards the socialisation of the productive forces. Ownership now appears as a purely parasitic appropriation of the product of the associated producers (including the managers)

> profit is henceforth received only in the form of interest, i.e. as a mere compensation for owning capital that is now entirely divorced from the function in the actual process of reproduction. . . . Profit thus appears . . . as a mere appropriation of the labour of others, arising from the conversion of means of production into capital. (*ibid.*, p. 427)

Ownership is reduced to a functionless title, to possession by pure property right without function in the direction of the means of production. Owners as such become mere coupon-clippers, exploiters, and parasites. Capitalist production has made its own social relations functionless and irrelevant.

Credit accelerates the concentration and centralisation of capitals:

> Success and failure both lead here to a centralisation of capital, and thus to expropriation on the most enormous scale. Expropriation extends here from the direct producers to the smaller and medium-sized capitalists themselves. It is the point of departure for the capitalist mode of production; its accomplishment is the goal of this production. In the last instance, it aims at the expropriation of the means of production from all individuals. . . . However, this appropriation appears within the capitalist system in a contradictory form, as appropriation of social property by a form; and credit lends the latter more and more the aspect of pure adventures. (*ibid*., p. 430)

The joint-stock company and the systematisation of credit accentuate the contradiction between the social character of the productive forces and the ownership of the means of production in the form of private property. The owner of capital becomes a purely parasitic *rentier* and the controller of centralised credit becomes a speculator divorced from production. The effects of credit are further to socialise the means of production and to remove whatever shreds of rationality their private ownership may have possessed: 'This is the abolition of the capitalist mode of production within the capitalist mode of production itself, and hence a self-dissolving contradiction, which *prima facie* represents a mere phase of transition to a new mode of production' (*ibid*., p. 429).

Marx's addition of the qualificatory '*prima facie*' is hardly an adequate defence; it may be left to those who wish to believe that things happened differently after Marx's death for reasons he could not 'foresee'. But it is not Marx the 'prophet' who concerns us, rather it is the economic theorist. His position was untenable the day he penned it, theoretically untenable. Marx systematically confuses capital as a social relation with particular forms of private property. property.

The unit of possession of *capital* is the joint-stock company, this form of possession exists because of the transformation of the social scale of the funds necessary to certain branches of capitalist production and it is also the condition of existence of certain types of enterprise. The shareholders do not own *capital*, rather they lend money at interest to a capital (in the form of purchasing a marketable financial asset with a dividend yield). Possession and function with regard to capital remain united in the enterprise, an economic subject quite distinct from Marx's idle and functionless money capitalist. Likewise, money funds are centralised by finance capitalist enterprises not by a few individual speculators. The forms of relation of financial to industrial capital cannot be restricted to the stock-market or to the issue of bonds. Equally, it cannot be argued that the *general* effect of finance capital has been to accentuate the crises and cycles of capitalist production through its purely speculative operations. It could be plausibly argued on the contrary that finance capitalist hegemony over industrial production, consumer credit, and the potentialities of monetary and fiscal policy of the state can in certain circumstances cushion the effects of crises and exert a stabilising effect on any downward movements in the level of production and the level of demand. Neither argument is, however, a *necessary* consequence of the development of finance capital and credit financing.

Marx fails to see that 'private ownership' in forms of 'socialised' capital does not necessarily take the form of a *rentier* class. Capital which comes into existence as capital through the sale of financial commodities (pensions, insurance), through the centralisation of the money funds of enterprises and wage earners, through the sale of share issues, and through the credit-creation policies of the state does not presuppose the existence of a *rentier* class. It supposes only enterprises, depositers/producers, and money. This capital does not correspond to personal ownership of private property, what persons *own* is titles to interest, the future payment of sums of money, etc., not capital.

The units of possession of 'socialised' capital are financial and industrial capitalist enterprises. Industrial capitalist enterprises may be subordinated through their financing to enterprises which are capitals through centralising the idle-money funds generated in the circuit of commodity-producing capital. Workers may be employed by enterprises in which their own and others' wages, savings, and pensions are the source of the capital which employs them. Capital is a social relation of production, a relation based upon possession and separation, and not upon personal titles to property. Social relations of production entailing separation can exist without the personification of exclusive possession. Capitalism is a mode of production in which profit and the requirements of forms of exclusive possession determine what is produced. The joint-stock company did not alter this fact, since it no more represents a dissolution of capitalist relations than the switch from steam to electricity as the form of motive power.

Chapter 6

The Law of the Tendency of the Rate of Profit to Decline

Discussions of this 'law' have hitherto predominantly taken the form of controversies concerning the *phenomenon* specified in it. The questions at stake in these controversies have been the following: whether or not this tendency is actually operative in capitalism, whether or not it takes the form of a progressive decline in the actual average rate of profit, whether this decline if it does take place is measureable,* and what consequences follow from this tendency or this decline, is it a terminal tendency inscribed in capitalist production?

Given the way in which the 'law' is presented and then qualified in vol. 3, pt 3 of *Capital*, a range of positions on its nature and the form of its operation is possible. This expositional complexity and the often almost delphic ambiguity of the writing cannot be simply written off as being due to the fact that it was edited into a text from notes of uneven quality by Engels. Marx enjoyed no 'author's privilege' with regard to the possibilities offered by the discourse. Even if Marx, as 'author', rather than Engels, the meticulous theoretical executor, had lived to offer us a literary resolution this

---

* The question of whether the tendency is *realised* in a declining rate of profit is distinct from that of whether it is *observable*, present in a phenomenal form in concrete profit rates. It is perfectly possible to argue that the phenomenon of decline is a *real* one but that it is not directly observable in company balance sheets. Such 'profits' are the product of a form of *presentation*, reflecting accounting methods (which may not distinguish between returns on financial assets, inflation of asset values and profits on commodity production *per se*), forms and levels of tax, and tax concessions, etc. Further, Marx argues that profits may also decline for reasons unconnected with the law.

'resolution' could only be a closure of these possibilities and would itself offer ground for debate as to its effectivity. The ambiguity with regard to the form of *realisation* of the law is integral to the form and conditions of its posing and to the space for its contradiction created by the possible consequences of other concepts in *Capital*. Equally, there can be no closure to the range of theoretical possibilities and the debate surrounding them by recourse to 'evidence' drawn from definite capitalist economies. To begin with, the simplest positivistic conceptions of the law as present or absent in company accounts can be dismissed as contradicting both the conception of method dominant in *Capital* and the argument as presented in the text. Beyond that, however, a range of positions is possible both on the nature of the phenomenon to be measured and on the methods and technical difficulties of measurement. These positions cannot be resolved because there are no definitive means for establishing the validity of criteria of validity (this argument is developed at length in Hindess and Hirst, 1977). In effect we are returned to disputes about positions taken in the text and also carried into regions of general philosophical debate. There is no answer in 'evidence' because to ask for 'evidence' is not to ask a single and unambiguous question.

We will not enter the debate on this previously dominant terrain, disputing as to the nature of the 'law' as if it were an actually existing entity. We do not argue merely that the phenomenon is not realised in the form of a progressive decline in the rate of profit and we do not simply reject the notion that it is a terminal tendency of the capitalist mode of production (both of these negative cases concerning the phenomenon can be persuasively argued on the basis of *Capital*). Both of these positions accept the existence of the entity and assign to it a definite nature. We will maintain on the contrary that there is no reason to suppose that there is a 'law' in this sense. We maintain that there can be no 'laws of tendency' at all and therefore no law of tendency of the rate of profit to decline. The 'law' is encountered in the discourse of *Capital*; that is where we confront it. The 'law' is the product of the deployment and coincidence of certain concepts in the discourse of *Capital* which make possible a thesis. This thesis is expressed as a 'law'. The difficulties with it surround the fact that the method under whose sign *Capital* is written does not provide the conceptual space for this thesis to be discounted as a mere effect of the constellation of concepts, a mere discursive possibility, and, moreover, the fact that the effect of the concepts which provide the means to formulate this thesis (and of other related concepts) is not a simple one, they also create the possibility of a number of contrary arguments or theses. The problem posed by this discursive complexity is 'overcome' in pt 3 by inscribing the contradiction between the thesis and its contraries into the reality of capitalist social relations.

It should be noted that there is no 'logical charge' in the theory of method in *Capital* which has the theoretical effect of impelling consistency. It would be possible to admit the law is a logical effect only, to deny its reality and to accept that the ensuing contradiction with the doctrine of method is something to be lived with. That this does not happen is due to no causal effects of any 'basic concepts' but is an effect of the way the discourse is written.

Our discussion of this 'law' will therefore differ considerably from its analysis in Althusser and Balibar, *Reading Capital* (pp. 283–93). Balibar's discussion of the law, the most philosophically sophisticated to date, treats the law as a real process but not as a tendency progressively realised through empirical time and culminating in some end state. Balibar conceives the law as a 'tendency' which is an effect of the structure, a form of action of the structure itself. This tendency is 'present in its effects', and those effects are phenomena which constitute both its counter-action and the conditions of existence of its future action. The tendency so conceived partakes of the form of temporality of the structure, it is the tendency of an 'eternity' (a temporality and effectivity internal to itself). Balibar identifies the action of the 'law' with 'structural causality'. This causality is a concept which appropriates a real causal process in thought. Given Balibar's epistemological position, two basic discursive options are open to him, either he can reject Marx's law, assigning it the status of an ideological residue left over from and as yet untouched by the effects of the epistemological break, or he must accept this law as part of a logical process of elaboration of concepts which appropriates the concrete in thought. Thus while Balibar rejects, on philosophical grounds, the notion of the 'law' as part of an Hegelian dialectic of supersession, or the notion of it as an empirically realised trend, nevertheless, he accepts its reality as an effect of the structure. We, on the contrary, will not attempt to accept or reject any one of the possible ontological statuses of the law in favour of another. Our discussion will be concerned with and confined to its discursive conditions of existence and effects.

Certain definite concepts are the conditions of posing the problem of the declining rate of profit. First, concepts basic to and specific to the theory of surplus value, 'constant and variable capital'. Second, the postulation of a tendency for the 'organic composition of capital' to rise, this being conceived as a basic general tendency of the capitalist mode of production. Third, the mechanism of the formation of an 'average rate of profit' such that capitals of the same size receive on average the same rate of return on capital advanced irrespective of the organic composition of these capitals.

We have seen that the epistemology advanced in *Capital* considers the deployment of concepts in discourse as a process of producing knowledge of, appropriating in thought, a concrete set of entities existing independently of discourse. For this epistemology the 'law' could never be merely a consequence of the concepts which happen to be produced and the way in which they are deployed. The discourse of *Capital* does not contradict this status which the epistemology must assign to the 'law', the law is conceived as an 'expression' of the fundamental process underlying all social reality, the tendency of the productive forces of society to develop. The 'law' is presented by Marx as a consequence of the tendency of the organic composition of capitals to rise under the conditions of the averaging of returns to capitals (creating in effect an organic composition for the total social capital, an average of the specific compositions). This tendency which produces the 'law' as its effect cannot be lightly denied this effect. This tendency toward a rising organic composition is the *capitalist form* of the universal and fundamental tendency of all social production: 'The progressive tendency of the general rate of profit to fall, is, therefore, just an expression peculiar to the capitalist mode of production of the progressive development of the social productivity of labour' (*Capital*, vol. 3, p. 209). The law 'expresses' this fundamental process, it is no chance phenomenon, and it must be distinguished from simple empirical falls in the rate of profit due to 'other reasons'.

Marx goes on to say: 'But *proceeding from the nature* of the capitalist mode of production, it is *thereby proved a logical necessity* that in its development the general average rate of surplus value must express itself in a falling rate of profit' (*ibid.*, our emphasis). The discourse gives the capitalist mode of production the status of a system whose necessity is like that of logic, in which the elements correspond as they do in the process of reasoning. Concepts and reality are intertwined in a thoroughgoing rationalism. The logical process of thought appropriates the real which has a rational (logical) order. Thought is assigned, therefore, an order from which it cannot deviate. This position has two parallel and reinforcing effects: first, discourse is subjected to rationalisation, theoretical concepts are considered as part of a necessary process, as logical effects of preceding concepts; and second, this logical necessity in discourse corresponds to a necessity in the real, the logical relations between concepts and their theoretical effects are therefore forms of representation of relations existing in the concrete. It follows that the consequences of discourse, provided it is logical, cannot be discounted. There is no evident way in which this position can dismiss a concept like the 'law' as merely the possible consequence of other preceding concepts in the discourse. This product of the interrelation of certain concepts must be a *real* tendency, an 'expression' of the 'nature' of capitalism. If this tendency is not to be *realised* in progressively declining profits then this must be because other real forces counteract it or because of the form of action of the real tendency itself.

In volume 3, chapter 14 'Counteracting Influences' and chapter 15 'Exposition of the Internal Contradictions of the Law' the text reviews a number of consequences of the concepts previously developed in it which do not lead to the conclusion of a directly expressed decline in the rate of profit. What is done here is to postulate one consequence of certain concepts (the possibility of a declining rate of profit) as the basic 'tendency' and other consequences as 'counteracting influences' or as the contradictory consequences of its action. The range of possible consequences of the discourse is ontologised into tendency and counter tendency.

The 'law' is one possible consequence of the notion of a rising social productivity of labour. It arises from the thesis of a rising organic composition of capital, but this effect is contradicted by three parallel and equally possible effects of the same thesis:

1 Increasing social productivity of labour cheapens constant capital and therefore reduces relatively the value of new means of production.

2 It also reduces relatively the cost of labour-power by reducing the value of its means of subsistence, and this, combined with and

contributing to an increase in the rate of exploitation (although this increase is set within the limits of the effects of displacement of labourers which is coupled with it), tends to increase the rate of profit.

3 Increasing social productivity and a rising organic composition create an increased tendency toward relative surplus population and therefore weakens the capacity of the working class to oppose the depression of wage levels; this reduces the pressures toward the displacement of labour and toward the introduction of more productive techniques. Similar contradictory consequences result from the fact that the 'law' operates through the forces of capitalist competition (which effect the process of 'averaging'), but these forces result in and take the form of periodic crises which write off a portion of the existing mass of capital and reduce the capital stock.

In section 2 of chapter 15 Marx argues that the processes involved in the accumulation of capital represent a contradictory unity of opposites:

> These two elements embraced by the process of accumulation, however, are not to be regarded merely as existing side by side as Ricardo does. They contain a contradiction which manifests itself in contradictory tendencies and phenomena. *These antagonistic tendencies counteract each other simultaneously.*
>
> Alongside the stimulants of an actual increase of the labouring population, which spring from the increase of the portion of the total social product serving as capital, there are agencies which create a merely relative over-population.
>
> Alongside the fall in the rate of profit [the] mass of capitals grows and hand in hand with this there occurs a depreciation of existing capitals which checks the fall and gives an accelerating motion to the accumulation of capital values.
>
> Alongside the development of productivity there develops a higher composition of capital, i.e. the relative decrease in the ratio of variable to constant capital.
>
> These different influences may at one time operate predominantly side by side in space, and at another succeed each other in time. From time to time the conflict of antagonistic agencies finds vent in crises. These crises are always but momentary and forcible solutions of the existing contradictions. They are violent erruptions which for a time restore the disturbed equilibrium. (*Capital*, vol. 3, p. 244—our emphasis)

No determinate motion such as the progressive realisation of the tendency, the tendency abstractly postulated in chapter 13, can be derived from this position. The inner motions of the capitalist mode of production are oscillating and simultaneously contradictory—they correspond to the chains of argument and counter-argument Marx's concepts make possible. All these contradictory motions (or contradictory consequences of the *same* concepts) are resolved into a unity of opposites, they are the contradictory effects of a single basic contradiction 'immanent' in capitalist production:

> The contradiction, to put it in a very general way, consists in that the capitalist mode of production involves a tendency towards absolute development of the productive forces, regardless of the value and surplus value it contains, and regardless of the social conditions under which capitalist production takes place; on the other hand, its aim is to preserve value of the existing capital and promote its self-expansion to the highest limit. . . .
>
> Capitalist production seeks continually to overcome these immanent barriers, but overcomes them only by means which again place these barriers in its way and on a more formidable scale. The *real barrier* of capitalist production is *capital itself*. (*ibid*., p. 245—emphasis in original)

This contradiction is constantly reproduced on an ever-increasing scale, but it cannot be resolved, since it consists in effects which are self-contradicting and self-reinforcing. This 'immanent' contradiction, essential to the capitalist mode of production is an 'expression . . . of the progressive development of the social productivity of labour' within capitalist relations of production. Marx grounds the tendency towards rising organic composition, and in consequence the tendency of the declining rate of profit and its contradictory nature, on this universal social tendency. But this universal tendency of social production is no longer the terminally contradictory tendency of the 'Preface' or of volume 1, chapter 32. It now peters out in contradictory effects, effects which are coupled together in a way which can never be resolved.

Volume 3, part 3 is inconclusive like the whole of *Capital* itself, that is to say the complex possibilities of the discourse are not closed off by any final *imprimatur*. What is *written* in part 3 is, indeed, complex and contradictory. Chapter 13 develops the logical potentialities and possibilities of the concept of the 'law', developing the consequences of previous concepts and extending the law as if it were the only consequence. Chapter 14 attempts to explain why these possibilities have not been *realised* in a simple progressive decline in concrete profit rates. The 'counteracting influences' are of contradictory statuses; some, like the increasing intensity of exploitation, are also consequences of the basic concepts which serve to formulate the law (rising organic composition), others refer us to definite conditions of specific capitalist national economies which cannot be given in the general concept of the capitalist mode of production, like, for instance, foreign trade. Chapter 15 conceives the very law itself as contradictory in its operation and as realised in the opposed phenomena of its operation and negation (which the formulation in chapter 13 does not).

The concept of the capitalist mode of production as existence in abstraction reveals its problematic nature at this point. The concepts involved here generate multiple and contradictory interconnections. These interconnections cannot be resolved into the forms of hierarchy necessary to create a general historical process such as that suggested in the '1859 Preface'. That process requires a privileged linear causality which results in definite and necessary states of affairs. Two possible responses can be made to this failure. First, these complex interconnections could be conceived to represent a 'map' of possible causalities, which depend for their concrete realisation (and which of them is realised) on the action of definite conditions. But then it follows that the general concept of the capitalist mode of production cannot reveal the 'laws of motion' of capital*ism*, it is rather a theory or model of the different motions possible in capital*isms*. Second, it could be argued that these complex interconnections are indeed the form of operation of the law of the declining rate of profit, but that this law is not the basic law of motion in capitalism, it is merely a way of conceiving the complex *side effects* of this basic law. Both of these positions in effect deny the centrality of the thesis of a declining rate of profit as a basic law of motion in capitalism, as part of a process impelling all such forms of existence toward a definite state of affairs.

Ultimately, neither of the portions of *Capital* we have considered, volume 1, chapter 32 and volume 3, part 3, provides a discourse which rigorously develops the causality of the '1859 Preface'. In both portions of the text this causality is accepted and yet in the way the discourse develops it is either negated or left without real theoretical support. *Capital* has no single conception of 'laws of tendency' and certainly none that could support an economic 'law of motion' which necessarily resolves capitalism into another form of totality, socialism.

Part III

Classes and the Structure of the Social Formation

Classical Marxism is far from being a unitary and coherent body of doctrines but, in spite of their considerable differences, its various forms share certain fundamental features in their conceptualisation of classes and the structure of the social formation. The social formation is conceived as a definite social totality, a unity of economic, political, and cultural (or ideological) levels and of a dominant mode of production together with other modes or elements. The correlate of the conception of social formation as a totality is the notion of an organising principle of that totality. In classical Marxism this is provided by the primacy of the economy. The precise form in which this primacy is supposed to be effected varies from one form of classical Marxism to another but in general the economic level is held to play the role of 'determination in the last instance' in that it governs the character of and relations between each of the levels.The qualification 'in the last instance' indicates that the character of the political and cultural (or ideological) superstructures cannot simply be deduced from that of the economy. The levels are 'relatively autonomous' and the political and cultural levels may exercise a reciprocal effect on the economy. 'Determination in the last instance' and 'relative autonomy' have functioned as gestural concepts in Marxist theory. They affirm both the primacy of the economy and the irreducibility of other levels to it—but they have rarely been precisely formulated and they are subject to a variety of different interpretations.

As for classes, these are conceived in classical Marxism first as categories of economic agent and second as the agents of political and ideological struggle. Once again the precise character of the supposed connection between class as category of economic agent and class as political and ideological agency varies from one form of classical Marxism to another. But however it is conceived this conception of classes is difficult to reconcile with the concepts of 'determination in the last instance' and 'relative autonomy'. If political forces are identified with classes or as representing their interests how can they also be conceived as irreducible to effects of the economy? The concept of political representation involves three elements: the content of what is represented (economic classes and their interests); the means of representation (political apparatuses and organisations); and the representation itself (the practices of those apparatuses and organisations). To say that politics is not reducible to a mere effect of economic relations is to say that there is a difference between what is represented and its representation. It is to affirm the specific and determinate effectivity of the means of representation. It follows that the means of representation cannot themselves be reducible to economic classes and their interests. But how is it possible for the means of political representation to be independent of economic classes and their interests on the one hand and yet be constrained to represent those interests on the other?

In the following chapters we shall problematise these classical conceptions. The first part of Chapter 7 outlines the classical conception of the structure of the social formation and argues that it gives rise to two distinct sets of problems. First, there are the problems arising from the character of the connections, 'determination in the last instance', 'relative autonomy', etc., posited between the distinct levels. Second, there are questions to be posed with regard to the substantive character of the social relations and practices posited in the classical conception.These problems are not entirely independent but they are nevertheless distinct and irreducible. In subsequent chapters we problematise both the character of the connections between levels posited in the classical conception and the substantive character of the levels themselves.

The second part of the chapter considers the conceptualisation of classes and argues that the classical conception of the structure of the social formation gives rise to a fundamental ambiguity in the conceptualisation of classes and class relations. On the one hand classes are conceived as categories of economic agent and on the other they are, or are represented by, definite cultural and political forces. Four main types of attempt to resolve the ambiguity are considered and all are shown to be unsatisfactory. For present purposes these types may be reduced to two basic forms. On the one hand there are positions which conceptualise classes in terms of a counterposition of subject and structure, subjective and objective conditions, social relations and structures, and so on—Lukács, Poulantzas, left-Weberian sociology. On the other hand there are positions which reject the counterposition of subject and structure and attempt, more or less rigorously, to interiorise forms of subjectivity and consciousness within the conceptualisation of the structure itself—Althusser and his associates and the very different tradition of Marxist orthodoxy represented in Stalin's *Dialectical and Historical Materialism*. In the first case the counterposition of subjective and objective (or structural) determinations entails the existence of political and cultural forms that are not reducible to class determinations—and the theory provides no means of conceptualising the effectivity of those forms. In the second case the interiorisation of forms of consciousness within the structure induces a functional and expressivist conception in which cultural, political, and economic forms and forces are reduced to effects of the structure itself. Political forces therefore have no independent effectivity: they merely perform the role assigned to them by the functional necessities, or 'structural causality', of the structure itself. In both cases there is a failure to conceptualise the conditions of the effectivity of social agents and an identification of social agent with human subject. *Either* the agent is conceived as an independent subjectivity confronting a given objective structure and its effectivity is conceptualised precisely to the extent that it acts in accordance with the 'objective' interests defined by the structure; *or* the effectivity of the agent is denied; it is conceived as a passive recipient of the forms of consciousness appropriate to its position in the structure and as acting solely in accordance with the requirements of the functioning of the structure. It will be necessary to problematise the concept of agent and to investigate its conditions of existence.

The next two chapters consider the question of the connections between distinct levels posited in Marxist theory, determination in the last instance, relative autonomy, and so on, and show that these types of connection themselves involve a particular type of rationalistic epistemological position. These arguments are based on positions developed in Hindess and Hirst, *Mode of Production and Social Formation.* Classical Marxism conceives the social formation as a definite social totality whose organising principle is represented in the forms of order of Marxist discourse. We argue that the social formation should not be conceived as a definite totality and that it is not structured by the primacy of the economy. To conceive of the social formation as a definite totality in which the economic level has primacy is to conceive the connections between economic relations on the one hand and political and ideological relations and practices on the other as governed by the organising principle of that totality, that is, in terms of determination 'in the last instance' by the economy. The thesis of the irreducibility of politics and ideology entailed in the notions of 'determination in the last instance' and 'relative autonomy' cannot be sustained. It leads either to reducibility or economism in disguise or else to a denial of the primacy of the economy. There is no middle way. We argue that connections between economic, political, and cultural relations and practices must be conceptualised not in terms of determination and causality but rather in terms of conditions of existence and the forms in which they may be satisfied. Relations of production, for example, can be shown to have definite conditions of existence in other types of social relations, law, politics, etc., but they do not themselves secure those conditions and nor do they determine the forms in which they are satisfied. If the question of the connection between relations of production and other social forms and relations is posed in these terms then the classical conception of the social formation as a definite unity of three structural levels characterised by a 'relative autonomy' and by the 'determination in the last instance' of the economy must collapse. Instead the social formation must be conceived as a definite set of relations of production together with the social forms in which their conditions of existence are satisfied.

One result of conceiving the social formation in this way is to dissolve the problem of conceptualising classes both as categories of economic agents and as political and cultural forms. If the connection between relations of production and political and cultural forces is conceived in terms of conditions of existence and the forms in which they are secured then there can be no grounds for conceiving of political and cultural forces as generated by or expressing the distribution of economic agents into classes by the relations of production. The social formation and the conflicts of social forces within it may then be conceived as providing the conditions of existence of a definite set of economic class relations. Similarly, if the question of the connection between the relations of production and the productive forces is posed in terms of conditions of existence then the notion of a definite and necessary correspondence between them must collapse. We must therefore investigate the relations between economic class-relations on the one hand and the technical division of labour in the process of production and the division of social labour in the social formation on the other.

A further reconstruction of the classical conception of classes is necessitated by an investigation of the conditions of existence of agents. It will be shown that agents cannot be reduced to individual human subjects and further, that it is both possible and necessary to conceptualise other forms of social and economic agent, for example, joint-stock companies, religious orders, people's communes, etc. A consequence of this argument is that classes may contain agents other than human individuals. It will therefore be necessary to investigate the role of management, that is, of those who perform the function of direction of the activities of these non-human economic agents.

The arguments of these chapters entail a fundamental reconstruction of the classical Marxist conceptions of the structure of the social formation, classes, and economic class relations. A short concluding chapter to this part outlines some of their consequences for the analysis of economic class-relations and their social conditions of existence, for the conceptualisation of relations of production in contemporary socialist societies, and with regard to the forms and conditions of socialist political practice.

Chapter 7

Classical Marxism

Mode of production and social formation

Classical Marxism has a definite conception of the necessary structure of society. A society is conceived as a social formation, an articulated structure of three (in some cases two) interdependent structural levels, dominated by the structure of a particular mode of production consisting of an economic, a political-legal and a cultural (or ideological) level. The levels of the mode of production are thought to be related in such a way that the first always plays a primary role, that of 'determination in the last instance'. The economy itself is structured by a definite combination of relations and forces of production. In a mode of production these relations and forces are supposed to correspond. Their failure to do so signals the end of one mode of production and the beginning of another. The transition between the two modes is effected by means of class struggle which overthrows the structure of one mode of production and installs another in its place.

The idea that this conception of the necessary structure of society is fundamental to Marxist theory has its origin in a well-known passage from Marx's Preface to *A Contribution to the Critique of Political Economy* and in a number of equally well-known and heavily quoted extracts from *Capital* and from the unfinished Introduction to *A Contribution*. In the Preface Marx summarises what he describes as 'the guiding principle of my studies':

> In the social production of their existence, men inevitably enter into definite relations, which are independent of their will, namely relations of production appropriate to a given stage in

> the development of their material forces of production. The totality of these relations of production constitutes the economic structure of society, the real foundation, on which arises a legal and political superstructure and to which correspond definite forms of social consciousness. The mode of production of material life conditions the general process of social, political and intellectual life. It is not the consciousness of men that determines their existence, but their social existence that determines their consciousness. At a certain stage of development, the material productive forces of society come into conflict with the existing relations of production or—this merely expresses the same thing in legal terms—with the property relations within the framework of which they have operated hitherto. From forms of development of the productive forces these relations turn into their fetters. Then begins an era of social revolution. The changes in the economic foundation lead sooner or later to the transformation of the whole immense superstructure. . . . (*A Contribution*, p. 21)

Here Marx presents a conception of society as structured by three loosely defined parts or levels, namely, 'the economic foundation', 'a legal and political superstructure', and 'definite forms of social consciousness'. We have seen in Part II that the Preface presents the contradiction between forces and relations of production as the general mechanism of social development. Nevertheless the relations referred to as 'on which arises', 'to which corresponds', are not rigorously defined and they are obviously open to a variety of interpretations. Or again, the assertion that 'changes in the economic foundation lead *sooner or later*' to transformations elsewhere suggests that there may in fact be real discrepancies between the foundation and the superstructure that is supposed to arise on it.

Other well-known extracts, from *Capital* and Marx's Introduction to *A Contribution*, are frequently invoked in the attempt to elucidate the precise character of the relation between the economy and other levels. Perhaps the two best-known of these extracts are a footnote in the first chapter, 'Commodities', in *Capital*, vol. 1, and a short passage from Marx's discussion of capitalist ground-rent in *Capital*, vol. 3. In the footnote Marx replies to a critic who argues that, while it may be that 'the mode of production determines the character of the social, political, and intellectual life generally' in capitalist society, other areas of life are dominant in other societies. Marx replies:

> This much, however, is clear that the middle ages could not live on Catholicism, nor the ancient world on politics. On the contrary, it is the economic conditions of the time that explain why here politics and there Catholicism play the chief part.(*Capital*, vol. 1, p. 86n)

There are two points here. First, it is trivially true that all social life depends on production, for those who do not eat do not live long enough to participate in politics or religion. But that truism tells nothing about how the economic structure of society is supposed to determine the character of the rest. Second, the second sentence tells us that politics or culture may be dominant, that is, 'play the chief part', in a certain mode of production but that it is the economy which determines what will be dominant. We seem to be presented here with a complex twofold relationship between the structural levels of a mode of production. The economy is *determinant* ('in the last instance') in the sense that it determines which structural level will be *dominant* in a given mode of production. Under capitalism the roles of dominance and determination coincide in the economy but they may be performed by different levels in other modes of production. Since the political-legal or the cultural levels may be dominant it would seem that they cannot be reduced to mere epiphenomena of the economy. Many Marxists therefore talk of the 'relative autonomy' of levels, thereby affirming both the primacy of the economy and the irreducibility of other levels to it.

The second passage occurs in ch. 47, 'The Genesis of Capitalist Ground Rent', in *Capital*, vol. 3:

> It is . . . evident that in all forms in which the direct labourer remains the possessor of the means of production and labour conditions necessary for the production of his own means of subsistence, the property relationship must simultaneously appear as a direct relation of lordship and servitude, so that the direct producer is not free. . . . Under such conditions the surplus-labour for the nominal owner of the land can only be extorted from [the direct producers] by other than economic pressure, whatever the form assumed may be. . . . Thus, conditions of personal dependence are requisite, a lack of

> personal freedom, no matter to what extent, and being tied to the soil as its accessory, bondage in the true sense of the word. . . .
>
> The specific economic form, in which unpaid surplus-labour is pumped out of the direct producers, determines the relationship of rulers and ruled, as it grows directly out of production itself and, in turn, reacts upon it as a determining element. Upon this, however, is founded the entire formation of the economic community which grows up out of the production relations themselves, thereby simultaneously its specific political form. It is always the direct relationship of the owners of the conditions of production to the direct producers—a relation always naturally corresponding to a definite stage in the development of the methods of labour and thereby its social productivity—which reveals the innermost secret, the hidden basis of the entire social structure, and with it the political form of the relation of sovereignty and dependence, in short, the corresponding specific form of state. (*Capital*, vol. 3, pp. 790—1)

Marx's argument that the feudal labourer is in no way separated from his means of production and that, consequently, relations of production must take a direct political form has been criticised at length in ch. 5 of *Pre-Capitalist Modes of Production*. (The concepts 'possession of' and 'separation from' the means of production are examined in a later chapter.) The point to notice in the present context is that Marx's position in this passage adds a further twist to the already complex saga of relations between levels. How does the form in which surplus labour is extracted 'determine the relationship of rulers and ruled'? Where the labourers are separated from their means of production the extraction of surplus labour takes an economic form. Otherwise 'other than economic pressure' is required, 'conditions of personal dependence are requisite'. It would seem that the character of the relations of production determines the form of the political-legal superstructure by determining what precise form of direct political-legal intervention in the economy is necessary for these relations of production to exist. The economy functions as 'the hidden basis of the entire social structure' by securing its own political-legal and cultural conditions of existence. Nevertheless, since Marx tells us that 'the relationship of rulers and ruled . . . reacts upon [production] as a determining element' the superstructural forms cannot be reduced simply to effects of the economy.

The classical Marxist conception of the structure of the social formation has its textual foundations in these passages and in the other famous quotations that are frequently invoked to similar effect. The basic features of the classical conception of the social formation are:

1 It represents a definite combination of structural levels (economic, political-legal, ideological) and of modes of production that produces a determinate and distinctive 'society effect', that is, it functions as a definite and relatively coherent social unity, a 'society', and it is relatively autonomous from other objects.

2 Modes of production represent sub-unities of this combination and they contribute to the 'society effect' with varying degrees of determination depending on their position of domination or subordination.

3 The 'society effect' of the social formation depends on the overall reproduction of its hierarchy of determinacy of modes of production and of the forms of the levels corresponding to that hierarchy.

4 If the hierarchy is displaced it is replaced by a new hierarchy with a new 'society effect' and a new form of social formation emerges. However, that change of form is not a change in all elements of the social formation, subordinate modes become dominant, ideological forms and state apparatuses persist with varying degrees of relative autonomy. At what point such changes of form involve a change in the nature of the social formation is open to question.

5 The levels of a mode of production are connected by relations of domination and of determination. The economic level is always determinant in the sense that it calls into being the other levels and the connections between them as the conditions of its own existence. The other levels are determined by the economy yet they are irreducible to its effects since they may 'react upon it'. The contradiction here is neatly encapsulated in the slogan of the 'relative autonomy' of the levels.

6 The economic level of a mode of production is itself structured by a definite combination of relations and forces of production. The relations and forces of a mode of production *correspond* and their failure to do so signals the end of one mode of production and the beginning of another. The transition from one mode of production to another is effected by the class struggle.

(Some forms of classical Marxism reject the notion of social formation as a hierarchical combination of modes of production in favour of the view that it consists of a dominant mode of production together with elements of other modes. A position of this kind is outlined in the Introduction to *Pre-Capitalist Modes of Production*. This difference has real theoretical effects but it does nothing to avoid the fundamental problems of the classical conception.)

The questions of class struggle and of transition may be left aside for the present. Classes are discussed in the second part of this chapter while the attempt to theorise transition clearly presupposes an adequate theorisation of modes of production themselves. For the rest it is clear that, for all its textual support in the classics, the classical conception of social formation and mode of production is not the product of any systematic demonstration in Marxist theory. The Preface to *A Contribution* states a position but does not argue for it and there is little by way of argument in the relevant sections of Marx's unfinished 'Introduction' to *A Contribution*. As for *Capital* itself, the famous quotations bearing on the question of the structure of the social formation appear as a footnote to a discussion on the nature of commodities, in a section on pre-capitalist rent that is clearly peripheral to the main theoretical arguments of the text, or as asides and points made in passing scattered throughout the text.

This absence of systematic argumentation in relation to what are frequently presented as among the fundamental concepts of Marxist theory poses a serious problem for Marxists. It is a problem that cannot be overcome by invoking the name of Marx, and possibly of Engels and Lenin too, and returning yet again to the charmed circle of famous quotations. These chapters problematise the classical conceptions of social formation and mode of production and the associated conceptions of classes. We shall see that it is necessary to displace mode of production as a primary object of theorisation in Marxist discourse and that the classical conception of social formation must be replaced by that of social formation as the form in which the social conditions of existence of economic class relations are provided.

There is, however, one influential form of defence of the classical position that should be briefly considered here. We refer to the view that since Marxism is a science the basic concepts of Marxist theory, social formation, mode of production, and so on, must be scientific. Perhaps the most recent and, within its limits, most rigorous form of this position has been advanced by Althusser and his associates, notably in *For Marx* and *Reading Capital*. Althusser advances a theory of the differential forms of theoretical discourse, the sciences and the theoretical ideologies, and of their production. In the light of this theory he proposes principles of reading which serve to identify the scientific or ideological character of a discourse and to identify its basic concepts.

It has been shown elsewhere (Hindess, *Philosophy and Methodology in the Social Sciences*) that Althusser's theory of the differential forms of theoretical discourse cannot be sustained and, further, that the Althusserian demarcation of science and theoretical ideology is dogmatic in two crucial respects. First, the identification of a discourse as scientific or as ideological is the product of a teleological mode of reading in which a conclusion known in advance, say, that Marxism is scientific and the political economy or sociology are ideological, determines the manner in which the discourse is approached. Second, with reference to the discourse of *Capital* itself Althusser effects a demarcation between concepts that are part of Marx's problematic and therefore scientific and those that are foreign to it. But that demarcation proceeds by showing that certain concepts are not consistent with concepts known already to belong to the scientific problematic. It is a demarcation, that is to say, which depends on an *a priori* identification of certain concepts as scientific.

These arguments need not be elaborated here. But it may be necessary to insist that the problems of dogmatism are in no way peculiar to Althusser's position. They are endemic to all attempts to demarcate between discourses or sets of concepts that are scientific and those that are not on the basis of general epistemological criteria. Whether those criteria are themselves derived from some version of dialectical materialism or from non-Marxist, empiricist or rationalist, philosophies makes no difference on this point. Epistemological criteria of the scientificity or validity of forms of discourse can be justified only by reference to some further set of criteria or to themselves. In the end all epistemologies depend on invoking some determinate forms of discourse as being epistemologically privileged in the sense that they cannot themselves be subject to epistemological investigation but must be accepted as given. This argument and its implications for the analysis of theoretical discourses, and of Marxist theory in particular, will be elaborated in the following chapter. For the present it is enough to note that the classical concepts of social formation and mode of production cannot be saved by invoking the name of science in their defence.

Finally, if we leave aside for the present the questions of class struggle and transition, there are two sets of questions that need to be posed with regard to the classical conceptions outlined above. First, they posit definite connections between objects that are themselves conceived as being in some sense independent. For example, a mode of production is conceived as consisting of three distinct levels which are irreducible one to another and yet one level is held to determine the character and interconnection of the others. Here relations of necessity are posited between objects that are held to be distinct and irreducible. We must therefore pose the question of the mode of connection that may be thought to hold between the distinct objects specified in Marxist discourse. Second, there are substantive questions to be posed with regard to the character of the objects posited in the classical conceptions. A mode of production consists of an *economic* level, a *political-legal* level and a *cultural* (or *ideological*) level, the economic level consists of *relations of production* and *forces of production* in a definite combination, and so on. It will be necessary to problematise the substantive character of the objects posited in classical Marxism. In particular, we shall consider first whether it is necessary or possible to conceive of political-legal forces and relations or cultural forms as organised into distinct and, in some sense, unitary structural levels, and second, the pertinence of the theorisation of modes of production as distinct and substantive unities.

While they are not entirely independent these sets of questions are nevertheless distinct and irreducible. The types of connections that may obtain between objects that are specified as distinct tells us nothing about the substantive features of the objects themselves—except, for example, in the case of objects such as mode of production or social formation which are themselves specified as consisting of the interconnection of distinct objects. The first set of questions are examined in the following chapter where it is shown that the types of connection between objects posited in the classical conceptions, domination, determination in the last instance, etc., are dependent on a definite epistemological conception of the relation between discourse and the objects of discourse. That chapter outlines the effects of a systematic rejection of epistemology for the conceptualisation of connections between objects specified in discourse and it argues that those connections must be conceived in terms of the conditions of existence of the objects specified. The second, substantive set of questions occupy the remainder of this text.

Classes

Three basic sets of questions regarding Marxist conceptualisations of classes will be considered in this text. First, there are the questions arising from the relations between the conceptualisations of classes on the one hand and of the structure of the social formation on the other. The second set of questions concerns the definition of economic class relations in relation to the means of production and, in particular, the concepts of 'possession of' and 'separation from' the means of production, the nature of the possessing agents, and the difficulties arising from the fact that Marxism has given little consideration to the possession of the means of production by agencies other than human subjects, by joint-stock companies, for example. Finally, there are the questions of the connections between economic class relations on the one hand and the technical division of labour at the level of the unit of production and the division of social labour at the level of the social formation on the other. The present discussion is concerned with the first area of questions. The second and third areas will be considered in subsequent chapters.

The classical Marxist conception of the structure of the social formation generates a basic ambiguity with regard to the conceptualisation of classes. On the one hand classes are defined primarily as a function of the opposing positions specified in determinate relations of production: bourgeoisie and proletariat, lord and serf, slave-owner and slave, etc. Where the relations of production do not specify opposing positions there are no classes and therefore, according to the classics, no state and no politics either. It follows that 'the *existence of classes* is only bound up with *particular historical phases in the development of production*' (Marx to Weydemeyer, 5 March 1852). On the other hand classes are conceived as social forces, as participants in a struggle which takes political and ideological forms. In this sense classes are, or are 'represented by', political forces and ideological forms. The difficulty here arises from the problems of reconciling a conception of classes as categories of economic agents *and* as political forces and ideological forms with a non-reductionist conception of the autonomy (or relative autonomy) of politics, law, and culture with regard to the economy.

To illustrate the difficulty consider two passages from one of Marx's best-known political analyses, *The Eighteenth Brumaire of Louis Bonaparte*. The first concerns what Marx calls 'the republican faction of the bourgeoisie':

> Under the bourgeois monarchy of Louis Philippe, it had formed the official republican *opposition* and consequently a recognised component part of the political world of the day. . . . Its character corresponded to this position under the constitutional monarchy. *It was not a faction of the bourgeoisie held together by great common interests and marked off by specific conditions of production* [this emphasis added]. It was a clique of republican-minded bourgeois, writers, lawyers, officers and officials that owed its influence to the personal antipathies of the country against Louis Philippe, to memories of the old republic, to the republican faith of a number of enthusiasts, above all, however to *French nationalism*, whose hatred of the Vienna treaties and of the alliance with England it stirred up perpetually. (Marx and Engels, *Selected Works*, p. 105)

The points to notice here are first, that a political faction is explicitly not defined by reference to economic conditions and second, that the factors introduced to account for the strength of the republican faction are manifestly non-economic in character. It seems, then, that Marx recognises the existence of political forces and a field of political conflict that is not immediately reducible to the effects of economic relations. But now consider his comments on the two Royalist factions:

> what kept the two factions apart was not any so-called principles, it was their material conditions of existence, two different kinds of property, it was the old contrast between town and country, the rivalry between capital and landed property. That at the same time old memories . . . convictions, articles of faith, and principles bound them to one or the other royal house, who is there to deny this? Upon the different forms of property, upon the social conditions of existence, arises an entire superstructure of distinct and peculiarly formed sentiments,

> illusions, modes of thought and views of life. The entire class creates and forms them out of its material foundations and out of the corresponding social relations. (*ibid.*, pp. 118–19)

The contradiction between the positions advanced in these passages is clear. If political forces are not reducible to effects of the structure of the economy then 'two different kinds of property' cannot account for what kept the two Royalist factions apart. Alternatively, if political forces are reducible to the effects of different forms of property then Marx has no business treating the republican faction as a distinct and real political force. If political forces and cultural forms are ultimately reducible to effects of class interests defined at the level of the economy then nothing remains of the irreducibility of politics and culture to economic conditions. If, on the other hand, politics and culture are irreducible then the connection between classes, conceived as categories of economic agents, and classes, or their representations, conceived as political forces or as cultural forms, must be extremely problematic.

The difficulty here is endemic to the Marxist theory of classes and of class-relations. The irreducibility of politics is widely acknowledged in practice in the classics of Marxist analysis of the conditions of concrete political practice. In *The Agrarian Programme of Social Democracy in the First Russian Revolution*, for example, Lenin insists that the balance of political forces cannot be read off from the structure of economic relations. However, the problem is not whether we should acknowledge the irreducibility of politics and culture. Rather it concerns the consequences of that acknowledgment for the conceptualisation of classes in relation to the structure of the social formation. What constitutes the unity of classes as categories of economic agent *and* as political forces and cultural forms? What are the mechanisms that articulate the political-legal and cultural (or ideological) representations of classes and class interests on to the economic classes represented? If political-legal forces and cultural forms are conceived as being mere expressions of the economy there is of course no problem: divisions at one level simply reappear elsewhere. But, if politics, law, and culture are not reducible to expressions of economic conditions, if they are autonomous, however 'relatively', then the unity of economic and politically or culturally defined classes must be problematic.

Several distinct modes of attempting to conceptualise the unity of classes in this sense may be identified in the history of Marxist theory but, for the purposes of a schematic exposition it is sufficient to identify three or four basic types. Two attempt to establish the unity of classes in terms of a confrontation between the objective determination of class position on the one hand and the subjective unity of a consciousness on the other: *either* the unity of a class as the intersubjective unity of individual human subjects having similar class positions *or* the unity of a class-subject acting as an economic, political-legal and cultural-ideological agent—i.e. either Weber and sociology or Lukács. In these positions classes are conceived in terms of the objective determination of economic position on the one hand and the will and consciousness of a subjective agency on the other. The relative autonomy of politics and culture then consists in the possibility, if not necessity, of the subject's misrecognition of its class position and its true class interests. Here the counterposition of 'subjective' will and consciousness to 'objective' class position ensures that the unity of a class must be conceived as being essentially problematic. If forms of consciousness cannot be reduced to the effects of 'objective' class position then the formation of the unity of a class cannot be necessitated in the objective structure of social relations. The third type subordinates the conceptualisation of class to the classical conception of the structure of the social formation as an essential unity of three levels organised according to the relations of domination on the one hand and of 'determination in the last instance' on the other. Here the economy plays a double role, first, as determining the structure of the whole and second, as a level represented in the structure of the whole. Classes can then be conceived as effects of the structure of the whole while the primacy of the economy in their determination follows as a consequence of its double role in that structure: classes are represented in the economy and also in the other levels as an effect of the matrix role of the economy. The most rigorous and systematic elaboration of this conception of 'structural causality' can be found in the works of Althusser and his associates. A related but in fact very different position is elaborated specifically with reference to the conceptualisation of classes in the work of Poulantzas. We shall see that Poulantzas merely adds an 'Althusserian' twist to the sociological and Lukácsian counterposition of subject and structure.

For all the considerable differences between them these modes of conceptualisation of classes can all claim substantial textual support in the writings of Marx: either in the passages usually cited in support of the classical Marxist conception of the structure of the social formation or else in *The Communist Manifesto, The Eighteenth Brumaire of Louis Bonaparte*, and other of Marx's more overtly political writings. The following brief examination of these positions is intended first, to examine their theoretical and political consequences, and second, to indicate why they are all unsuccessful.

Class as intersubjective unity

The first type of conceptualisation of class both as a category of economic agents and as a political or cultural agency belongs to left-Weberian sociology rather than to Marxism proper. Nevertheless, since it can claim some textual support in Marx's works, this type of position deserves at least a brief examination in the present discussion. The most significant passages from this point of view are those parts of *The Communist Manifesto, The Eighteenth Brumaire*, and other political writings which appear to counterpose economic class position on the one hand to class consciousness as a condition of class political action on the other.

The *Manifesto*, for example, describes the proletariat as going through various stages of development ranging from the struggle of individual labourers or the workers of a factory against their employer at one extreme to the class conscious organisation of struggle on the basis of national, or even international, political unity of the class at the other. At one extreme the class exists merely as a category of individuals organised, at best, into a multiplicity of local groups. At this stage the class does not organise for itself in pursuit of its own interests. If it unites at all 'this is not yet a consequence of their own active union, but of the union of the bourgeoisie, which class, in order to attain its own political ends, is compelled to set the whole proletariat in motion, and is moreover yet, for a time, able to do so' (Marx and Engels, *Selected Works*, p. 42). But the development of capitalist industry leads to the growth in size of the proletariat, to its concentration in particular workplaces and localities, and to improved means of communication which allow for the growth of contacts between workers in different localities. These factors together, above all, with their own experience of struggle result in the integration of the workers into a class. 'Now and then the workers are victorious, but only for a time. *The real fruit of their battles lies, not in the immediate result, but in the ever-expanding union of the workers*' (*ibid*., p. 43, emphasis added). The *Manifesto* adds that this development of the 'organisation of the proletarians into a class, and consequently into a political party, is continually being upset again by the competition between the workers themselves'.

As a second example consider the quite different position of the French peasantry described in *The Eighteenth Brumaire*:

> The small-holding peasants form a vast mass, *the members of which live in similar conditions but without entering into manifold relations with one another. Their mode of production isolates them from one another* instead of bringing them into mutual intercourse. The isolation is increased by France's bad means of communication and by the poverty of the peasants. . . . In so far as there is merely local interconnection among these small-holding peasants, and the identity of their interests begets no community, no national bond and no political organisation among them, *they do not form a class*. They are consequently incapable of enforcing their class interests in their own name, whether through parliament or through a convention. They cannot represent themselves, they must be represented. (*ibid*., p. 171)

The only point of interest in this passage lies in its contrast with the *Manifesto*'s description of the proletariat. The place of the proletariat in the capitalist organisation of production and improved means of communication facilitate the development of class political organisation. The organisation of small-holding peasant production and poor means of communication inhibit it.

It is easy to see how these, and other passages that could be quoted to similar effect, may provide the foundation for a conception of classes as *first*, a category of similarly situated individuals and *second*, under suitable conditions, as a cultural and political agency. A class *in itself* is defined by a position in the organisation of production, a position that may be occupied by a mass of distinct individuals. But that class becomes a class *for-itself* only as a function of the growth to awareness on the part of these individuals, and later of groups, of the existence of a community of interests among them. This growth to awareness is facilitated by some social conditions and by the experience of action in common and it is inhibited by other social conditions. The unity of a class both as a category of economic agents and as a political and cultural agency is therefore conceptualised first, in terms of the will and consciousness of individual human subjects and second, in terms of social conditions leading to an intersubjective unity as the basis for communal action.

The affinity of this conception with Weberian sociology will be evident. They share a common emphasis on the primacy of the will and consciousness of the individual actor as the basic explanatory principle and they both treat class situation, defined in rather different fashions, as providing a possible basis for communal action. The principle objections to any conception of the primacy of the will and consciousness of the human subject are well known and they need hardly be repeated here. Classical Marxism has always rejected any explicit conceptualisation in subjectivist terms. However, in addition to the general problems with subjectivist theory, the attempt to conceptualise the unity of classes in quasi-Weberian terms faces further severe difficulties—some of which it shares with the Lukácsian conception of classes.

First, to treat class action as a form of communal action, that is, as based on the recognition of common interests by a mass of individuals, is to admit that there may be other, non-class, forms of communal action. There is nothing about the concentration of workers in factories and large population centres as such, or in improved means of communication, to ensure that their interests as a class will be recognised and will form the basis for communal action. Shared experience of collective struggle is equally problematic in this respect since it presupposes what has to be established, namely, that it is class interests which form the basis of collective action. The problem here is that once the *recognition of common interests on the part of individuals* is thought to play a decisive role in class action then, as Weber correctly maintains, there is no reason why other 'common interests', nationality, religious belief, 'race', etc., should not play an equally decisive role in non-class forms of communal action. To conceive of class as a form of communal action, therefore, is to conceive it as one among many of the possible forms of communal action. Class action cannot then be accounted for by reference to class interests since some further explanation is required of why those interests and not others provide the basis for communal action. Short of some further explanation of the primacy of class interests over all others this conception must imply that politics and culture cannot be reduced to the expressions of interests formed at the level of the economy. To accept the conception of classes as communal agents is therefore to reject the classical Marxist conception of the social formation.

But there is another serious difficulty with this version of the Marxist theory of classes. In effect the proletariat is conceptualised in terms of an objective class situation on the one hand and a teleological process of formation into a class 'for-itself' on the other. To conceive of the proletariat in this way, as necessarily evolving into a fully conscious class 'for-itself', is to admit that politics and culture cannot be reduced to classes. This conception defines a direction in which working-class politics is supposed to evolve, namely towards a political practice based on the self-conscious attempt to realise the objective interests given by its class position. At any given time, therefore, so long as that evolution remains incomplete, working-class politics must contain elements that cannot be explained by class position. Thus politics is reducible to class interests in the case of a fully class-conscious political practice and it is irreducible to class interests in all other cases. This conception therefore affirms the existence of non-class forms of politics and yet it provides no theoretical means of conceptualising them other than in terms of their difference from what a class-conscious politics would be. Political forms must therefore be conceived, not according to their specific conditions of existence and their effectivity with regard to other elements of the social formation, but merely according to the extent of their deviation from a different and idealised state of affairs. At most, then, this conception might seem to legitimise a culturalist and propagandist mode of political practice, conceived essentially as a form of consciousness-raising, but it has nothing to offer with regard to the analysis of political forces and their effects in specific social formations.

Lukács: the concept of class-subject

In *History and Class Consciousness* Lukács elaborates a complex and sophisticated conception of classes and of history which combines a definite epistemological and ontological position with the traditional Marxist conception of the role of the class struggle in history and of the significance of class consciousness in that struggle. In common with the German neo-Kantian philosophies of history, Lukács maintains a radical distinction between the field of history and that of the natural sciences in terms of a difference in the nature of their objects and, consequently, in the form of investigation appropriate to those objects. Where the field of natural scientific investigation is governed by an external and mechanical causality the field of history is constituted by acts of consciousness. Where Lukács differs from the bulk of neo-Kantian positions is in his conception of the decisive point of reference for historical investigation. It is not the will and consciousness of the human individual that is crucial. Nor is it the role of a determinate spirit or culture in constituting a distinctive mode of life. For Lukács the decisive point of reference for historical investigation is the will and consciousness of a class.

This emphasis on class consciousness is significant for two reasons. First, it provides the point of integration of a neo-Kantian conception of history as constituted by acts of consciousness on the one hand and the conceptions of class struggle developed in Marx's and Engels's political writings on the other. Second, it appears to provide a solution to one of the most fundamental problems confronting any neo-Kantian conception of history. If history is conceived as constituted by acts of consciousness then the separation of the consciousness of the investigator from those constituting his object of investigation poses a radical problem of knowledge. For neo-Kantian philosophy the problem of historical knowledge is a problem of the interpretation of the meanings expressed by cultural objects, by artefacts and writings of various kinds and by social institutions and forms of social life. Since the cultural object is distinct from the meaning expressed in it there appears to be an insuperable problem of adequation. How is adequate knowledge of any cultural object to be established?

Lukács finds the answer to this problem in the position of the proletariat. First, since the class struggle is the motor of history it follows that the consciousness of a class offers at least the potentiality of overcoming the gulf between subject and object. Second, the position of the proletariat is uniquely privileged in that its coming to power effects the total abolition of classes. Thus the proletariat can appear as the identical subject-object of history since its own self-knowledge and its knowledge of society is not limited by the effectivity of other class-subjects:

The self-understanding of the proletariat is therefore

> simultaneously the objective understanding of the nature of society. When the proletariat furthers its own class aims it simultaneously achieves the conscious realisation of the—objective—aims of society, aims which would inevitably remain abstract possibilities and objective frontiers but for this conscious intervention. (*History and Class Consciousness*, p. 149)

History is the history of the effects of the consciousnesses of classes and it culminates in the growth to self-consciousness of the proletariat which simultaneously effects the abolition of classes and the true self-knowledge of society. For history the relation of subject to object is not an external mechanical one. It is a relation between and within consciousness and the products of consciousness—and it is for this reason that history is thought to require a method of investigation distinct from that of the natural sciences: 'For in the dialectics of society the subject is included in the reciprocal relation in which theory and practice become dialectical with reference to one another' (*ibid.*, p. 207). Lukács therefore insists that the essence of Marxism lies not in this or that substantive proposition but in the dialectical method itself. An orthodox Marxist could 'dismiss all of Marx's theses *in toto*—without having to renounce his orthodoxy for a single moment' (*ibid.*, p. 1).

This is not the place to develop a systematic critique of Lukács's position. The internal problems and incoherence of the idealist philosophies of history cannot be overcome by Luckács's attempt to marry a manifest idealism with various Marxist theses on the role of the class struggle in history. Lukács's reduction of Marxism to the dialectical method is more than a little disingenuous since his 'solution' to the problem of historical knowledge depends crucially on several specific theses of Marx concerning the role of the class struggle in history and, in particular, the role of the proletariat in the abolition of classes. In his review of *History and Class Consciousness* (Revai, 1971) Revai has shown that Lukács's solution to the neo-Kantian problem of historical knowledge cannot be sustained and Althusser has provided an effective critique of the attempted reduction of history to the actions of class (or individual) subjects. The major problems and deficiencies of his position in *History and Class Consciousness* are not overcome by the changes summarised in his Preface to the 1967 edition.

What is important for the present discussion, however, is that Lukács has provided one of the most sophisticated elaborations of the classical Marxist conception of the unity of class as both a category of economic agent and as a political and cultural agency. It is this aspect of his theory that must be considered here. Two features of his conceptualisation of classes are particularly significant. First, Lukács takes up a theme that recurs from time to time in Marx's political writings and is based on a particular formulation of the relation between base and superstructure. For example, in the discussion of the Royalist factions of the French bourgeoisie, quoted above from *The Eighteenth Brumaire*, we find:

> Upon the different forms of property, upon the social conditions of existence, rises an entire superstructure of distinct and peculiarly formed sentiments, illusions, modes of thought and views of life. *The entire class creates and forms them out of its material foundations and out of the corresponding social relations*' (Marx and Engels, *Selected Works*, pp. 118–19, emphasis added)

Here it seems that it is not the forms of property as such which create the superstructure but rather the class and its consciousness. It is this rather than the mechanistic form of the base-superstructure argument that Lukács elaborates:

> thought and existence are not identical in the sense that they 'correspond' to each other, or 'reflect' each other, that they 'run parallel' to each other or 'coincide' with each other (all expressions that conceal a rigid duality). Their identity is that they are aspects of one and the same real historical and dialectical process. (*History and Class Consciousness*, p. 204)

On the one hand the superstructural forms express the consciousness and interests of a class to the extent that that class can achieve and maintain its hegemony over society. On the other hand, the position of the class in society, its social conditions of existence, limits the forms of consciousness that are possible on the part of that class. We have seen, for example, that the proletariat is supposed to be the only class whose social conditions of existence make true self-knowledge possible. Taken together these two aspects provide Lukács with his basic principles of historical analysis and interpretation. Cultural objects are to be interpreted as more or less adequate expressions of the consciousness and interests of a class and also as expressing the necessary limitations of that consciousness. Lukács therefore treats the major social institutions of capitalist society, its forms of government and administration, its impersonal bureaucracies with their emphasis on rational calculation and technical efficiency, and so on, as expressions of a mode of consciousness characteristic of the social conditions of existence of the bourgeoisie as a class. Similarly, in 'Reification and the Consciousness of the Proletariat', he attributes the specific antinomies and contradictions of modern, that is Kantian and post-Kantian, critical philosophy to the reified mode of thought specific to the social conditions of bourgeois society.

Second, Lukács insists on: 'the distance that separates class consciousness from the empirically given, and from the psychologically describable and explicable ideas which men form about their situation in life' (*ibid.*, p. 51). Where empirically given ideas constitute 'merely the *material* of genuine historical analysis' class consciousness must be imputed as a function of class position:

> By relating consciousness to the whole of society it becomes possible to infer the thoughts and feelings which men would have in a particular situation if they were *able* to assess both it and the interests arising from it in their impact on immediate action and on the whole structure of society. That is to say, it would be possible to infer the thoughts and feelings appropriate to their objective situation. The number of such situations is not unlimited in any society . . . there will always be a number of clearly distinguished basic types whose characteristics are determined by the types of position available in the process of production. (*ibid.*)

There are several reasons for this discrepancy in Lukács's theory between imputed class consciousness and objective class interests on the one hand and the empirical consciousnesses of members of the class on the other. The class consciousness of the proletariat is not a simple or automatic reflection of its class position. While, for Lukács, the proletariat is 'the first subject in history that is (objectively) capable of an adequate social consciousness' (*ibid.*, p. 199), that consciousness can be formed only in a dialectical process of evolution. The moments of that process can represent no more than partial and inadequate expressions of imputed class consciousness:

> These gradations are, then, on the one hand, objective historical necessities, nuances in the objective possibilities of consciousness (such is the relative cohesiveness of politics and economics in comparison to cultural questions). On the other hand, where consciousness already exists as an objective possibility, they indicate degrees of distance between the psychological class consciousness and the adequate understanding of the total situation. *These* gradations, however, can no longer be referred back to socio-economic causes. *The objective theory of class consciousness is the theory of its objective possibility.* (*ibid.*, p. 79)

These last sentences give a further reason for the discrepancy between empirical and imputed consciousnesses. Following his rejection of the mechanistic conception of the relation between base and superstructure Lukács insists that the development of class consciousness cannot be necessitated by class position. The 'point of view of the proletariat' may be given by its class position but there is nothing in the class position as such to ensure that it will be adopted by members of the class. Thus, while 'only the practical class consciousness of the proletariat' possesses the ability to transform bourgeois society and thus to eliminate the reified structures of existence:

> it must be emphasised that the structure can be disrupted only if the immanent contradictions of the process are made conscious. Only when the consciousness of the proletariat is able to point out the road along which the dialectics of history is objectively impelled, *but which it cannot travel unaided*, will the consciousness of the proletariat awaken to a consciousness of the process, and only then will the proletariat become the identical subject-object of history whose praxis will change reality. *If the proletariat fails to take this step the contradictions will remain unresolved and will be reproduced by the dialectical mechanics of history at a higher level in an altered form and with increased intensity.* It is in this that the objective necessity of history consists. (*ibid.*, pp. 197–8, emphasis added)

Lukács reproduces at the level of the class subject all the problems of the subjectivist conception of history as a function of the will and consciousness of actors. If consciousness is not reducible to its social conditions of existence, if imputed class consciousness is not necessarily realised, then Lukács's allusion to 'historical necessity' is no more than a rhetorical flourish expressing at best an assertion of blind faith with no possible basis in his argument. If, on the other hand, we were to take seriously the assertion of 'historical necessity' then we would have to conclude that class consciousness is ultimately necessitated by objective conditions—and in that case Lukács's theory would be nothing but a complex and attenuated economic reductionism.

In either case Lukács's argument entails the conclusion that politics and culture are not reducible to class determination. *Either* consciousness is ultimately reducible to class position at the end of a long process of development (it must then be irreducible to class position at all other points), *or* consciousness is irreducible to class position: class consciousness may develop but there is no necessity for it to do so. Forms of politics and culture that do not express class interests and that are irreducible to class determinations are therefore a real possibility.

Lukács's theory therefore requires that there be non-class forms of politics and of culture, but he provides no means whatever for conceptualising these forms except in terms of their discrepancy from imputed class consciousness. In effect, Lukács's conception reproduces the theoretical and political effects of the conceptualisation of class as an intersubjective unity. Political and cultural forms must be conceived not in terms of their specific conditions of existence and effectivity with regard to other elements of the social formation, but rather in terms of the extent of their failure to reflect imputed class consciousness. While this conception may also serve to justify the culturalist and propagandist politics of consciousness-raising it has nothing to offer with regard to the analysis of political forms and their effects in specific social formations.

Classes as effects of the structure

The positions discussed so far have attempted to conceive of the unity of a class by means of a counterposition of the objective determinants of a structure on the one hand to the subjective unity of consciousness on the other. The unity of the class as an economic, political, and cultural agency is a function of subjective or intersubjective unity of consciousness while the determination of that unity as a class is the effect of its position in the structure. The counterposition of subject and structure ensures that the unity of a class must be conceived as essentially problematic. If forms of consciousness cannot be reduced to simple effects of the structure then the unity of a class cannot be necessitated by the structure. These positions therefore entail the irreducibility of politics and culture to class determinations but they provide no means of conceptualising political and cultural forms other than in terms of their relative success or failure in expressing those class determinations. At best, then, these positions may generate a teleological mode of analysis in which political and cultural forms are to be evaluated in terms of their deviation from ideal and imputed forms which really do express the real objective interests of the class in question. Political forms are analysed as more or less adequate *expressions* of class positions and not in terms of their effectivity with regard to other social relations and practices.

In contrast a third basic mode of conceptualising classes in Marxist theory rejects the counterposition of subject and structure and attempts, more or less rigorously, to interiorise forms of consciousness within its conceptualisation of the structure itself. Classes and class struggle are effects of the structure. They are called into being as a function of specific relations of production while the specific forms of struggle are effects of the particular structure of the social formation in question. The classical Marxist conception of the structure of the social formation involves a dominant mode of production in combination with subordinated modes or elements. The dominant mode of production is itself structured by its differentiation into three 'relatively autonomous' levels governed by the 'matrix' role of the economy which determines the character of and relations between these levels. Here the economy plays a double role, first, as determining the structure, and second, as a level represented in the structure. It follows that classes can be conceived as effects of the structure while the primacy of the economy in their determination is a function of its double role. Classes are represented in the economy and they are represented in the other levels as an effect of the 'matrix' role of the economy. Althusser, for example, maintains that

> To conceive of the nature of a social class it is essential to bring together the determinations of the economic base, of the juridico-political superstructure, and of the ideological superstructure. It is equally essential to be aware of the interplay

> within this combined determination so as to account for the way in which dominance may shift between the different determinations. . . . (quoted in Terray, *Marxism and 'Primitive' Societies*, p. 144)

The unity of these multiple determinations is itself the result of the 'structural causality' which, in Althusser's view, governs the structure of the social totality. Structural causality means that the structure must be conceived:

> as a cause immanent in its effects in the Spinozist sense of the term, that *the whole existence of the structure consists in its effects*, in short that the structure, which is merely a specific combination of its peculiar elements, is nothing outside its effects. (*Reading Capital*, p. 189)

Here the unity of a class reflects the unity of the structure of which it is an effect. Class may be conceived both as a unity and as represented at each of the economic, political, and ideological levels precisely because, for all their 'relative autonomy', these levels are themselves just so many effects of the structure of the whole.

We will return to the consequences of this mode of conceptualising classes in relation to the structure of the social formation in a moment. But first it is necessary to notice that the conception of classes and class struggle as called into being as effects of the structure is in no way restricted to the exponents of the theory that the structure of the social formation is governed by a 'structural causality'. The most rigorous elaborations of that concept are to be found in the works of Althusser and his associates. A related position but with very different effects as regards the conceptualisation of classes has been developed by Poulantzas. His position will be considered separately below. However, the idea that classes and class struggle are effects of the structure may also be found in the famous quotations which provide the foundations of the classical Marxist conception of the structure of the social formation. We have already cited Marx's claim 'that the *existence of classes* is only bound up with *particular historical phases in the development of production*' (Marx to Weydemeyer, 5 March 1852). Or again, consider the extract from Marx's Preface to *A Contribution to the Critique of Political Economy* quoted in the first part of this chapter. It is clear that the primacy accorded by that passage to the relation between the relations of production and the productive forces may readily be interpreted as lending support to the view that the precise interplay of relations and forces determines the level of class conflict in any society. A well-known tradition in Marxist thought presents a theory of history in which the level of class conflict is conceived as an effect of the extent to which the relations of production lag behind the productive forces. A concise pedagogic expression of this conception is given in Stalin's *Dialectical and Historical Materialism* which maintains that the development of the productive forces is the motor of history:

> First the productive forces of society change and develop, and then, *depending* on these changes and *in conformity with them*, men's relations of production, their economic relations change . . . however much the relations of production may lag behind the development of the productive forces they must, sooner or later, come into correspondence with—and actually do come into correspondence with—the level of development of the productive forces, the character of the productive forces. (*Dialectical and Historical Materialism*, p. 31)

Here the non-correspondence of relations and forces of production is enough to bring about its own rectification through the transformation of the relations of production. Advance the productive forces sufficiently and, sooner or later, the relations of production will advance themselves. It is clear that the class struggle must be relegated to a secondary level of effectivity in this conception. It develops as an effect of the discrepancy between relations and forces of production, and its role is to clear away that discrepancy. Thus:

> having developed productive forces to a tremendous extent, capitalism has become enmeshed in contradictions which it is unable to solve. . . . This means that capitalism is pregnant with revolution, whose mission is to replace the existing capitalist ownership of the means of production by socialist ownership. This means that the main feature of the capitalist system is a most acute class struggle between the exploiters and the exploited. (*ibid*., pp. 37–8)

Here the existence of classes and the character of the relations between them are ultimately reducible to effects of the structure of the economy, while the effectivity of the class struggle is confined to its performance of the historical role assigned by that structure.

The teleological character of that position is evident. But its effects on the conceptualisation of classes in relation to the structure reappear in the very different position of Althusser and his associates. If the social formation is conceived as governed by a structural causality then every level and element must be conceived as an effect of the structure. Classes and the conflict between them are effects of the structure and its structural causality. Consider just two examples. The first concerns the question of the transition from one mode of production to another. Althusser explicitly rejects all teleological conceptions of history—including that of the forward march of the productive forces. For Althusser and his associates there is nothing in the structure of any mode of production which necessitates its supersession. On the contrary, each mode of production must be conceived as an 'eternity in Spinoza's sense' (*Reading Capital*, p. 107). The mode of production secures its own conditions of existence and is therefore capable of eternal reproduction. In *Reading Capital* the transition from one mode of production to another is not conceived as the necessary effect of the ever-forward march of the productive forces but each period of transition is conceived as involving a definite non-correspondence between the relations and the forces of production. There are two types of structure of production: in a mode of production the relations and the forces correspond and in a structure of transition they fail to correspond. In the first case there is a reciprocal limitation between the relations and the forces such that each serves to reproduce the other. However:

> In the form of non-correspondence, which is that of the phases of transition such as manufacture, the relationship between the two connexions [the relations and the forces of production] no longer takes the form of a reciprocal limitation, but becomes *the transformation of the one by the effect of the other* . . . in which the capitalist nature of the relations of production determines and governs the transition of the productive forces to their specifically capitalist form. (*ibid.*, p. 304, emphasis in original).

The essentialist and fundamentally teleological character of *Reading Capital*'s doctrine of structural causality has been shown in ch. 6 and the Conclusion of *Pre-Capitalist Modes of Production*. In effect, *Reading Capital* replaces the overt, transformative teleologies of the ever-forward march of the productive forces and of the Hegelian theories of history by a covert and inconsistent teleology in which the conception of mode of production as eternal, as stationary and repetitive, is combined with a transformative conception of the stricture of transition as essentially finite.

However, what must be noted in the present context is the effect of the doctrine of structural causality on the conceptualisation of classes and class struggle. If the period of transition is brought to an end through the transformation of the productive forces by the relations of production, then the class struggle as such, or the conflict of political forces, can have no independent effectivity. At most the class struggle merely performs the role assigned to it by the structure of production.

As a second example of the consequences of Althusser's position consider the treatment of the reproduction of the relations of production in his paper, 'Ideology and Ideological State Apparatuses' (in *Lenin and Philosophy*). The term 'structural causality' does not appear in this paper, but Althusser explicitly refers the reader to the arguments of *Reading Capital* in the course of a brief recapitulation of the Marxist conception of the structure of the social formation. In a postscript to this paper Althusser insists on the importance of adopting 'the point of view of the class struggle':

> For in a class society the relations of production are relations of exploitation, and therefore relations between antagonistic classes. The reproduction of the relations of production, the ultimate aim of the ruling class, cannot therefore be a merely technical operation training and distributing individuals for the different posts in the 'technical division' of labour. . . . The reproduction of the relations of production can therefore only be a class undertaking. It is realized through a class struggle which counterposes the ruling class and the exploited class. . . . In fact, the State and its Apparatuses only have meaning from the point of view of the class struggle, as an apparatus of class struggle ensuring class oppression and guaranteeing the conditions of exploitation and its reproduction. (*Lenin and Philosophy*, p. 171)

That seems clear enough: we must never forget the class struggle. But if we consider the problem of reproduction posed in this paper and Althusser's solution to it it is clear that the postscript's insistence on 'the point of view of the class struggle' is no more than a rhetorical flourish. Althusser poses a functional problem, namely, 'how is the reproduction of the relations of production secured?' A functional problem requires a general functional mechanism for its solution: 'for the most part, it is secured by the exercise of State power in the State Apparatuses, on the one hand the (Repressive) State Apparatus, on the other the Ideological State Apparatuses' (*ibid*., p. 141).

Furthermore, in keeping with the doctrine of 'determination in the last instance' by the economy, it seems that the specific character of this functional mechanism is itself given by the relations of production in question. In the case of the feudal mode of production 'it is absolutely clear that *there was one dominant Ideological State Apparatus, the Church*' (*ibid*., pp. 143–4). On the other hand:

> the ideological State apparatus which has been installed in the *dominant* position in mature capitalist social formations as a result of violent political and ideological class struggle against the old dominant ideological State apparatus, is the *educational ideological apparatus*. (*ibid*., pp. 144–5)

The class struggle which Althusser invokes in this passage belongs to the long period of transition between the dominance of feudalism and that of capitalism.

The ideological State apparatus secures its functional objectives by distributing human agents to the places required by the social division of labour and by ensuring that those agents are suitably equipped to play the roles required of those places. Thus each category of agent:

> is practically provided with the ideology which suits the role it has to fulfil in class society: the role of the exploited . . . the role of the agent of exploitation . . . of the agent of repression, or of the professional ideologist. (*ibid*., p. 147)

Paul Hirst has shown that Althusser's solution involves two related errors: the identification of the relations of production with the functions assigned to economic agents in the social division of labour and the identification of economic agents with human subjects. The important point in the present context, however, concerns the functional character of Althusser's problem and the functional mechanisms he invokes for its solution. The ideological

State apparatuses appear as the means to the fulfilment of a given functional end. The means has no determinate effect on the form for which it is functional (the relations of production) other than the function of reproduction itself. It is merely the agency or support of the function assigned to it by the relations of production whose reproduction is to be secured.

This functionalism returns us to the doctrines of 'structural causality' and the 'determination in the last instance' of the economy. The economy determines the other levels of the social formation by securing its own conditions of existence, the ideological State apparatuses, the repressive State apparatus, and so on, and these in turn have a reciprocal action on the economic base by providing the conditions necessary to its functioning. Structural causality collapses into the closed and empty circle of functional determination. Each component part of the structure exists as an effect of the structure and it exists because of the functions it performs for the structure. Althusser maintains that 'the whole existence of the structure consists in its effects' (*Reading Capital*, p. 189) which is to say that it consists in the performance of the functions necessary to its existence.

We have considered two examples from the work of Althusser and his associates, the treatment of the problem of transition in *Reading Capital* and the treatment of reproduction in 'Ideology and Ideological State Apparatuses'. In both cases the conclusion is the same, namely, that the doctrine of structural causality requires that there be no independent effectivity of the class struggle. At most the class struggle, the conflict of social and political forces, performs the role assigned to it by the structure of production. In a period of transition the transition is effected because that is the nature of the structure of transition. In all other cases reproduction is secured because the 'determination in the last instance' of the economy secures the conditions of its reproduction. In both cases class struggle may exist but it is merely one functional effect of the structure amongst others. It is all very well for Althusser to maintain in the postscript to his ideology paper: 'To adopt the point of view of reproduction is therefore, in the last instance, to adopt the point of view of the class struggle' (*ibid.*, p. 171). Of course it is. Althusser might equally well invoke the 'point of view' of the forces of production or the family. If each and every aspect of the social formation is an effect of the structure of the whole then they are all equivalent to one another. In the functionalist world of structural causality all points of view are the same.

Poulantzas: the counterposition of class and structure

As a final example consider Poulantzas's conceptualisation of classes in relation to the structure of the social formation. In *Political Power and Social Classes* and to a lesser extent in subsequent works Poulantzas appears to base his position on the work of Althusser in *For Marx* and *Reading Capital*. In fact he merely provides an Althusserian gloss on the basic counterposition of subject and structure characteristic of the sociological and Lukácsian positions considered earlier. Where Althusser rejects the counterposition of subject and structure and attempts to interiorise forms of consciousness within his conceptualisation of the structure of the social formation Poulantzas resolutely refuses to do so. Instead he proposes a fundamental distinction between the structure of the social formation on the one hand and the field of social relations on the other. Classes are 'the result of an ensemble of structures and of their relations' (*Political Power and Social Classes*, p. 63) and consequently they cannot be conceived as existing at a particular level in the structure of the social formation. Classes: 'do not manifest themselves inside the structure, but entirely as the *global effect of the structures in the field of social relations*, which, in class societies, themselves involve the distribution of agents/supports to social classes' (*ibid*., p. 64). While Poulantzas's position is by no means equivalent to that of Lukács we shall see that his insistence on the distinction between structures and social relations generates similar theoretical effects.

Consider first Poulantzas's demarcation between the field of social relations and the structures of the social formation. Poulantzas argues that a clear demarcation is essential on this point as a precondition of any serious critique of anthropologism of the subject 'whether in its historicist or humanist forms' (*ibid*., p. 65) but he does not directly establish the necessity of that demarcation. Nevertheless its theoretical basis appears very clearly in his distinction between relations of production on the one hand and *social* relations of production on the other. The relations of production denote specific combinations of agents and the material-technical conditions of labour. On the other hand:

social relations of production are relations among agents of

> production distributed in social classes, i.e. class relations. In other words, the *'social' relations of production*, class relations, manifest themselves, at the economic level, as an effect of this specific combination: agents of production/material-technical conditions of labour constituted by the *relations of production*. (*ibid.*, p. 65)

Social relations are relations between human agents. Social relations of production are effects of the economic structure, of the relations of production:

> but we can also speak in all strictness of political 'social' relations and of ideological 'social' relations. These social relations, as class relations isolated here with respect to the instances of the political and the ideological, manifest themselves as the effect of the political and ideological structures on social relations. (*ibid.*, pp. 65–6)

In effect Poulantzas posits a field of intersubjective relations that is structured by the intervention of the economic, political, and ideological structures of the social formation. This interpretation is confirmed by a footnote later in the text:

> Structure/Institution: These two concepts must be clearly distinguished. By institution will be meant *a system of norms or rules which is socially sanctioned*. . . . On the other hand, the concept of structure covers the organizing matrix of institutions. (*ibid.*, p. 115, emphasis added)

The reference to 'norms or rules' clearly belongs to a sociological problematic of intersubjective relations. The two fields, of structures and of intersubjective relations, are mutually irreducible since the one involves people and things in specific combinations while the other involves people only. Poulantzas therefore rejects both 'economism', which reduces social relations to structures, and 'anthropologism of the subject', which reduces structures to effects of social relations. Classes and class practices belong to the field of social relations. They are therefore subject to the effects of the structures but are not reducible to those effects:

> The determination of the practices by the structure and the intervention of the practices in the structure, consist in the production by the structure of limits of variation of class

> struggle: it is these limits which are effects of the structure. (*ibid.*, p. 95)

Class practices are limited by the effects of the structure but they are not determined by them.

Poulantzas counterposes the 'objective' determinations of the structures to the realm of human subjects and their intersubjective relations and he insists that they are mutually irreducible. He presents class determination as an effect of the structures, i.e. of political and ideological determinations as well as economic ones, and it is this that defines the objective interests of a class. But class *interests* in this sense, determined by the structure, are not necessarily identical to the *positions* taken by the class in the concrete conditions of struggle. That follows directly from the irreducibility of social relations to structures. Thus the structure of the social formation gives class determinations which define class interests and the political and ideological positions which correspond to those interests. But in any particular conditions of struggle the position taken by a class may differ from its objective interests. In the conclusion to *Classes in Contemporary Capitalism* Poulantzas insists that there is no necessity for class position to correspond to class determination:

> We must rid ourselves once and for all of the illusions that have often affected the revolutionary movement, throughout its history, to the effect that an objective proletarian polarization of class determinations must necessarily lead in time to a polarization of class positions. (*Classes in Contemporary Capitalism*, p. 334)

In effect we are presented with a principle of reduction of politics and ideology to class determinations as effects of the structure together with an insistence that political and ideological positions are irreducible to those determinations.

The parallel with Lukács is evident. In both cases the structure provides an objective determination of class interests and in both cases those interests must be clearly distinguished from representations in the consciousnesses of agents. The structure determines class interests but it cannot ensure that they will be recognised. The theories of Poulantzas and of Lukács therefore entail the existence of political and cultural/ideological practices that are strictly irreducible to class determinations. Nevertheless the two positions are not entirely equivalent, for where Lukács interprets superstructural forms as more or less adequate expressions of the consciousness and interests of a class Poulantzas sees them as expressing class relations. For example, in discussing political apparatuses Poulantzas tells us that they are 'never anything other than the materialization and condensation of class relations' (*Classes in Contemporary Capitalism*, p. 25). Thus: 'The State is not an "entity" with an intrinsic instrumental essence, but it is itself a relation, more precisely the condensation of a relation' (*ibid.*, p. 26). Poulantzas's equivocation over the discrepancy between structures and social relations is apparent in these formulations. On the one hand political apparatuses are reducible to class relations: they are *never anything other than*. . . . On the one hand they are not reducible to class relations: they materialise or condense them and may therefore differ according to the forms of 'materialisation' and 'condensation'.

But in spite of these differences the fundamental consequences of the counterposition of subject and structure appear in Poulantzas's work as they do in Lukács's. His theory requires that there be non-class forms of politics and of ideology, but he provides no means of conceptualising these forms except in terms of what is required by objective conditions. Once again political and ideological forms must be conceived not in terms of their specific effectivity with regard to other social practices and relations but rather in terms of their failure to reflect the objective interests of a class. For all that Poulantzas castigates sociological and Lukácsian conceptualisations of class in relation to the structure of the social formation his own theory must lead to similar theoretical and political consequences.

Chapter 8

Determination in the Last Instance

Classical Marxism posits a connection between the economic base and other structural levels such that those levels are determined 'in the last instance' by the economy on the one hand while on the other they retain a real, though 'relative', autonomy and an independent effectivity of their own. Here the political and the ideological-cultural levels are conceived as distinct and irreducible objects whose essential character is nevertheless determined by another object, the economy. The economy itself is thought to be structured by relations of production and forces of production in a definite and necessary correspondence. This correspondence is necessary in the sense that any non-correspondence is essentially self-correcting: it induces the social changes necessary to restore correspondence. Sometimes primacy is accorded to the productive forces (as in *Dialectical and Historical Materialism*) and sometimes it is accorded to the relations of production (as in *Reading Capital*) but in both cases the structure of causality is the same: failure of one object to correspond to another creates the conditions which restore correspondence. In these conceptions relations of necessity are posited between objects that are held to be in some sense distinct. The concept of one object has necessary consequences for the conceptualisation of other, distinct objects. For example, if the political and ideological-cultural superstructures must correspond 'in the last instance' to the economic base then the essential features of those superstructures can be deduced directly from the concept of the economy.

In order to establish what is involved in these conceptions of determination and dominance consider the conceptualisation of relations of production. Relations of production concern the social distribution of the means and conditions of production, that is, the distribution of possession of and separation from the means of production among different categories of economic agents. The concepts of 'possession of' and 'separation from' are examined in a later chapter and it is enough for present purposes to say that possession of certain means of production involves the capacity to control the functioning of those means in the production process and to exclude others from their use. Possession of certain means of production by one category of agent therefore entails the separation of other categories of agent from those means. Those who are separated from the means of production have access to their use only on the terms of a definite economic relation governing the distribution of the product of that process. For example, in capitalist relations of production means of production are possessed in the form of commodities purchased by the capitalist. The capitalist purchases labour-power in exchange for wages and the production process takes the form of the production of commodities by means of other commodities, namely, means of production and labour-power. The labourers are separated from the means of production and have access to them only on condition of the conversion of their labour-power into a commodity. The distribution of the product between labourers and capitalists therefore takes place through the intermediary of the market in which labour-power is exchanged for money and money is exchanged for commodities.

Now, if relations of production are specified in this way it is clear that they must presuppose other social relations and conditions. Capitalist relations of production require that means of production and labour-power take the form of commodities. They therefore require a legal system which defines and sanctions definite forms of property, especially property in the form of commodities, and definite forms of contract, especially contracts to buy and sell. In addition since means of production, labour-power, and products all take the form of commodities capitalist relations of production entail the organisation of production on the basis of monetary accounting by the capitalist or his agents. They therefore require the existence of definite forms of calculation and of training in the application of those forms. Similarly, since relations of production necessarily involve means and processes of production, capitalist relations of production must presuppose 'forces of production' amenable to capitalist calculation and control.

This list of what is presupposed by determinate relations of production could easily be continued. The point to notice here, however, is that determinate relations of production cannot be specified without an explicit or implicit reference to the effects of other social relations and practices. Those relations and practices are not given in the concept of the relations of production in question. To say that capitalist relations of production presuppose a legal system with definite forms of property and contract is merely to specify some abstract and general conditions which a legal system must meet if it is to be compatible with capitalist production. Similar points may be made with regard to forms of calculation and 'forces of production'. The relations of production presuppose that other social relations and practices satisfy certain abstract and general conditions, that certain effects are secured by those relations and practices. But the concept of determinate relations of production does not tell us in what precise form those effects will be secured nor does it tell us the precise character of the relations which secure them.

Let us call those effects that are presupposed in the specification of determinate relations of production the *conditions of existence* of those relations. To specify the social relations and practices which secure those effects is to specify the form in which those conditions of existence are secured. Relations of production can only be conceived as articulated on to other social relations and practices otherwise their conditions of existence would not be secured. But the concept of determinate relations of production cannot tell us the form in which those conditions will be secured nor what social relations and practices will secure them. The concept of capitalist relations of production allows us to infer that some form of commercial law is presupposed. But what is presupposed here is at such a level of generality that it takes no account of the differences between, say, British and Japanese commercial law or of the effects of those differences on the structure of and relations between enterprises in the respective economies.

Now the theses of the determination in the last instance by the economy and of the correspondence between relations and forces of production go much further. Rather than the limited position that specific social relations presuppose definite conditions of existence these theses maintain that certain types of social relations are capable of securing their own conditions of existence. The legal and cultural conditions of existence of capitalist production are secured by the action of the capitalist economy. Similarly, for the correspondence thesis: in one version the forces of production themselves generate the social conditions required to bring about the corresponding relations of production, and in the other version the relations of production bring the productive forces into line. In all cases the conditions of existence presupposed by an object, the economy, the forces or relations of production, are secured through its own effectivity.

A relation between concepts, between, say, the concept of determinate relations of production and the concept of conditions of existence that may be derived from it, is transposed by the thesis of determination in the last instance into a relation of determination between the objects specified in those concepts. The thesis of the *relative* autonomy and independent effectivity of those conditions of existence follows directly from this conception. Since the derivation of conditions of existence cannot itself give the precise form in which those conditions will be secured it would seem that the determination of its own political-legal and ideological-cultural conditions of existence by, say, a capitalist economy must be essentially incomplete. Certain abstract and general features of the superstructure are determined 'in the last instance' by the economy while the remaining features are left to the play of other determinations. It is only this space for the intervention of other determinations that allows what is determined 'in the last instance' by the economy to react upon it. This conception appears to underlie Marx's comment that:

> The specific economic form, in which unpaid surplus labour is pumped out of the direct producers, determines the relationship of rulers and ruled, as it grows directly out of production itself *and, in turn, reacts upon it as a determining element.* (*Capital*, vol. 3, p. 791, emphasis added)

Whatever acts on the economy as a determining element cannot at the same time be determined by the economy in all its particulars.

Epistemological conceptions of the relation between discourse and its objects

We can now approach the central problem of the thesis of

determination in the last instance by the economy and the related theses of classical Marxism. Determination in the last instance transposes a certain type of relation between concepts on to a relation of determination between the objects specified by those concepts. That transposition involves a rationalist epistemological conception of the relation between concepts and objects: that is, it posits a realm of discourse, a distinct realm of objects specifiable in discourse and a definite correlation between the two such that certain relations in the realm of discourse reappear as relations of determination in the realm of objects. To question the thesis of determination in the last instance is to question the epistemology it involves, either from the standpoint of another epistemology or from that of a systematic rejection of the epistemological enterprise as such. This chapter establishes the epistemological features of the thesis of determination in the last instance and argues that the critique of this thesis from the standpoint of a different epistemology merely exchanges one indefensible dogmatism for another. In rejecting epistemological conceptions of the relation between discourse and its objects it argues for a conceptualisation of relations of production and other objects in terms of their conditions of existence and the specific forms in which those conditions are satisfied.

An epistemology is a form of theoretical discourse which posits both a distinction and a correlation between a realm of discourse on the one hand and a realm of objects specifiable in discourse on the other. To say that the realms are distinct is to say that the existence of the realm of objects is not dependent on the existence of discourse. To say that there is a correlation between them is to say that certain elements or forms of discourse correspond to, or designate, members of the realm of objects and their properties. Different epistemologies conceive of the supposed correspondence in different ways but in all cases certain elements or forms of discourse are thought to give direct knowledge of the realm of objects. In rationalist epistemologies the world is conceived as a rational order in the sense that its parts and the relations between them conform to the order of concepts and the relations between them, the concept giving the essence of the real. The thesis of determination in the last instance involves an epistemology of this kind. It is precisely because certain concepts do give the essence of the real that a relation between concepts, between the concept of the economy and the concept of its conditions of existence which can be derived from it, can be transposed into a relation of determination between objects.

Now, the widespread and influential critique of 'determination in the last instance', which proposes to subject that thesis to empirical investigation, merely counterposes one epistemology to another. To say that the relation between objects is to be established at the level of observation is to claim that the discourse of observation, that is of human experience, has privileged access to knowledge of the real. In effect, it is to posit an empiricist epistemology in which the correlation between the realm of discourse and the realm of objects is supposed to be effected through the agency of the experience and judgment of human subjects. In this case all claims to knowledge are thought to be susceptible of evaluation in terms of basic observation statements which purport to represent what is *given* in the experience of human subjects. Empiricist epistemologies may well recognise the necessity of theoretically abstract forms of discourse which do not themselves directly designate the given, but these forms are always conceived as being directly or indirectly reducible to the privileged level at which discourse really does designate what is given in the experience of human subjects.

But, for all their differences, both the Marxist thesis of determination in the last instance and its empiricist critiques are posed upon a common ground of epistemological problems. Each presupposes a realm of discourse, a distinct and independently existing realm of objects and an epistemologically privileged form of discourse which directly effects a correspondence between the two realms. To posit such a correspondence is to claim that the particular forms of discourse in which it is effected do give direct access to knowledge of objects and relations between them. Those forms of discourse are therefore epistemologically privileged in the sense that their direct access to the realm of objects is a logically necessary consequence of the initial epistemological postulates. *That* they have such direct access is beyond dispute: they therefore provide a final and irrefutable foundation against which all other forms of discourse may be measured, but they are not themselves open to further investigation. Empiricist epistemologies posit the discourse of experience as the ultimate point of reference of all claims to knowledge of the world. Rationalist epistemologies, on the other hand, whether or not they allot any role to human experience in the formation of knowledge effectively posit a uniquely privileged level of concepts by reference to which all claims to meaningful discourse may be evaluated.

Consider, for example, the theory of the differential forms of theoretical discourse, the sciences, and the theoretical ideologies, advanced in *Reading Capital*. Although Althusser makes a serious attempt to break with the classical epistemological problem of knowledge the result of his arguments is to remain within a classical philosophical framework and to develop a distinctive type of rationalist epistemology. (That argument is elaborated in Hindess, *Philosophy and Methodology*, and Hindess and Hirst, *Mode of Production and Social Formation*.) In the rationalism of *Reading Capital* the discourses of the sciences are each governed by a scientific problematic, a definite and distinctive system of concepts. The result of scientific discourse is the construction of scientific thought-objects which are said to constitute the 'appropriation of the concrete in thought'. The scientific appropriation effect is secured by the functioning of the concepts of the scientific problematic. Those concepts therefore provide the ultimate point of reference against which all claims to knowledge in the appropriate domain may be measured. Thus, for example, Althusser claims to establish the unscientific character of the conception of social relations of production as intersubjective relations by showing that that conception is incompatible with what he regards as the basic concepts of *Capital*. In addition, Althusser explicitly denies the possibility of forms of theoretical discourse in which the scientific or unscientific character of problematics may be established. The sciences provide their own internal criteria of validity. It follows that the 'scientific' character of a scientific problematic must be accepted as absolutely given: it cannot be open to further investigation.

Finally, it should be noted that the different epistemological conceptions of the relation between discourse and its objects entail different conceptions of the relations between objects themselves. Empiricism conceives of objects of discourse as given in the experience of human subjects. They are represented in discourse as a function of that experience mediated by the exercise of the human faculty of judgment. Relations between objects, then, can only be conceived as given in experience itself. The classical empiricist conception of relations between objects is therefore in terms of a mechanical, external causality representing nothing more than the existence of regular and recurrent correlations between observed phenomena. These relations must be established in, or tested against, the judgment of experience. For empiricism theoretically derived relations must, with the possible exception of logic and pure mathematics, be subjected to the tests of experience. Thus the thesis of determination in the last instance, regarded by classical Marxism as beyond any merely empirical refutation, must be regarded by empiricism as an empirical generalisation at best. In rationalist epistemology, on the other hand, where the world is conceived as a rational order, concepts give the essence of the real and relations between concepts therefore represent the essential form of the relations between objects. The classical rationalist conception of relations between objects is therefore in terms of an expressive causality, an internal relation between an essence and the phenomenal forms of its appearance. These relations between objects may be established through purely theoretical argument. In the case of those epistemologies such as Kant's which are neither purely rationalistic nor purely empiricist relations between objects can only be conceived in terms of the distinct and competing claims of reason on the one hand and experience on the other.

Now the central problems of epistemologies, and therefore of all epistemologically derived conceptions of causality, determination, and the like, concern the inescapable dogmatism that is entailed in the epistemological project itself. An epistemology posits a distinction between two realms and it affirms that a correlation between them is effected in certain specific forms of discourse, the discourse of experience, of a scientific problematic, or whatever. But once a particular form or forms of discourse are singled out as epistemologically privileged then a series of interrelated consequences must follow. First, it follows that there are uniquely privileged forms of discourse which provide the means of designating existing objects. These privileged forms provide a touchstone against which all claims to knowledge may be judged. Any discourse not itself of the privileged form must be reducible to, or at least compatible with, approved discursive forms if its claims to knowledge are to be seriously entertained. Empiricist epistemologies conceive of meaningful discourse as reducible to the discourse of experience. Rationalist positions, on the other hand, posit some privileged levels of conceptualisation that are not established through the experience of human subjects and they affirm that all claims to knowledge must be compatible with those privileged levels. The inescapable dogmatism of these positions should be evident. To affirm that all claims to knowledge must be measured against discourse of a particular form is in the same movement to render that form immune to further questioning. There can be no demonstration that such-and-such forms of discourse are indeed privileged except by means of forms of discourse that are themselves held to be privileged. If the discourse of experience provides the touchstone against which all claims to knowledge must be measured then how is the validity of the discourse of experience to be established except by a circular reference to experience itself? Or again, if certain concepts are thought to give the essence of the real how is it possible to establish that they really do so except by means of concepts which do give the essence of the real?

Second, to affirm a uniquely privileged form of discourse is to affirm that objects independent of discourse exist in the form of actual or potential objects of discourse. Their properties must therefore be such that they can indeed be designated in and described by discourse of the privileged form. Each epistemology therefore entails a corresponding ontology which affirms, at the very least, that the totality of what exists includes all those objects designated in and described by the privileged forms of discourse. Similarly, we have seen that each epistemology entails its own particular conception of the relations between objects and its own particular forms of causality and determination. Finally, the existence of uniquely privileged forms of discourse provide each epistemology with the foundations of a series of epistemological critiques of other discourses.

The full implications of these consequences have been discussed elsewhere (*Mode of Production and Social Formation*) and they need not be considered here. What must be noted is that any epistemology involves a whole series of interrelated positions all of which rest on a single and fundamental epistemological postulate, namely, *that there is a realm of discourse, an independently existing realm of objects (in the mode of objects appropriable in specific forms of discourse), and that such-and-such a form of discourse effects a correlation between the two realms*. There can be no hope of demonstration for such a postulate. The epistemological enterprise therefore opens up a field of mutually incompatible positions between which there can be no rational debate, but at best merely a series of more or less tortuous affirmations of the same fundamentally opposed positions. But the dogmatism of epistemology is not merely a feature of each epistemology considered separately, it is constitutive of the epistemological enterprise as such. Whatever their differences at the level of precisely how the correlation between discourse and its objects is to be effected all epistemologies share the presumption that the mode of existence of objects is such that they may be appropriated in suitable forms of discourse. We have seen that there can be no demonstration that precisely such-and-such a form of discourse is the one that does the trick. To that extent each epistemology is dogmatic. But how do we know that the trick can be done at all? The fundamental epistemological postulate tells us that the mode of existence of objects allows them to be appropriated in discourse. But there can be no demonstration of that postulate without recourse to forms of discourse which do claim to designate the objects that we held to be appropriable. The epistemological enterprise is dogmatic through and through and it is the dogmatism of the enterprise itself which ensures the dogmatism of each of its attempted resolutions.

Concepts, objects of discourse and their conditions of existence

The preceding discussion has shown that the epistemological enterprise is essentially arbitrary and dogmatic. There is no necessity to conceptualise the relations between discourse and the objects it refers to in terms of both a distinction and a correlation between a realm of discourse and an independently existing realm of objects. Nothing, beyond an entirely arbitrary epistemological fiat, compels us to conceive of a world which, at one and the same time, is independent of discourse and exists in the form of objects that are both extra-discursive and specifiable in discourse. But, in the absence of the epistemological conception, it is no longer possible to refer to objects existing outside of discourse, or the forms of discourse that are held to designate them, as the measure of the validity of discourse. On the contrary, far from providing an external measure for discourse, the entities referred to in discourse are constituted solely in and through the forms of discourse in which they are specified. Objects of discourse cannot be specified extra-discursively, they can be conceived only through the forms of discourse in which they are specified or in other related, complementary or critical, discourses. There is no question here of whether *objects of discourse* exist independently of the discourses which specify them. Objects of discourse do not exist at all in that sense: they are constituted in and through the discourses which refer to them. The distinction/correlation structure of epistemology depends on the conception of objects existing independently of knowledge yet in forms appropriate to knowledge itself. To deny that conception is to reject epistemology and the field of problems defined within it.

What are the consequences of this rejection of epistemology for the conceptualisation of objects and the relations between them and for Marxist theory in particular? First, it is necessary to insist that the rejection of epistemology does not involve the replacement of one dogmatism by another. The dogmatism criticised above is a necessary consequence of the basic postulates of epistemology. To posit a correlation between a realm of discourse and what is thought to be an independent realm of objects of discourse is to suppose that certain forms of discourse (the discourse of experience, of the sciences, etc.), directly effect that correlation. Those forms of discourse therefore provide a touchstone against which all other discourses may be evaluated but they cannot themselves be subject to that evaluation. Epistemologies are dogmatisms in that they necessarily posit certain forms of discourse as being immune to further evaluation. To deny epistemology is to remove the foundation of that dogmatism.

Second, it follows that there can be no privileged form of discourse of the kind posited in epistemology. Those privileged forms provide epistemology with definite points of closure of discourse by purporting to represent the order of the real itself. The thesis that there is a uniquely privileged empirical level of discourse in terms of which all theses, hypotheses, and the like may be evaluated is the product of empiricist epistemology. Similarly the thesis that certain concepts, say, the basic concepts of Althusser's scientific problematics, provide an ultimate point of reference to which all other concepts must conform is the product of a rationalist epistemology. These theses must be rejected along with the epistemologies on which they are based. There can be no privileged basic concepts of Marxism or other fields of theoretical discourse. Balibar's project, in pt 2 of *Reading Capital*, of identifying *the* basic concepts of historical materialism and Althusser's dismissal of theoretical humanism on the basis of its difference from what he regards as the fundamental concepts of Marxist theory are the products of a rationalist epistemology and must be rejected with it. But if there are no basic concepts then neither Marxism nor any other theoretical discourse can be subject to the arbitrary forms of theoretical closure promised by the epistemologies. The concepts of different modes of production specify distinct objects of discourse. They function as the means of formation of other concepts, as means and instruments of analysis and argumentation, but they cannot function as the epistemologically privileged basic concepts of rationalist conceptualisations. These concepts have no necessary primacy in Marxist discourse and they cannot serve as absolute criteria governing the criticism or formation of other concepts. They represent a means of conceptualisation in discourse, not a privileged source of deduction. Theoretical discourses are not simple deductions from or extensions of basic concepts. On the contrary, the difficulties and problems generated in and by a body of concepts may well provide the grounds for transformation, revision, and re-organisation of the concepts themselves. For example, the problems and inconsistencies of the classical Marxist concepts of mode of production, social formation, and classes identified in the preceding chapter, clearly call for fundamental reappraisal of those concepts. To treat them as basic or fundamental concepts in the manner of Althusserian rationalism is to foreclose on the possibility of such fundamental reappraisal. The following chapters argue for the displacement of the concept of mode of production and for a reconceptualisation of relations of production and of their relationship to other social relations and practices.

But first it is necessary to outline the implications of a rejection of epistemology for the conceptualisation of objects and of the relations that obtain between them. Consider the case of the relations of production outlined in the first part of this chapter. We have seen that the specification of determinate relations of production involves explicit or implicit reference to the consequences of other social relations and practices. Determinate relations of production presuppose that certain conditions are met by legal and cultural forms, they presuppose definite means and conditions of production, agents capable of occupying the positions of 'possession of' and 'separation from' those means of production, and so on. We have called these conditions which are presupposed by determinate relations of production the *conditions of existence* of those relations. What must be noted here is that the concepts of those conditions of existence do no more than specify certain abstract and general conditions which are presupposed by the relations of production in question. Capitalist relations of production presuppose a legal system which allows the formation of particular kinds of contractual relations and exchanges. The concept of the legal conditions of existence of capitalist relations of production therefore imposes definite constraints on the type of legal system compatible with the conditions of capitalist production. But it cannot tell us precisely how the necessary forms of contract will be provided for nor what other properties the legal system might possess. Similarly for all the other conditions of existence of the relations of production. To derive those conditions from the concept of determinate relation of production is not to specify the social relations and practices responsible for providing those conditions. We must therefore distinguish between conditions of existence and the social relation and practices which provide them. The first *can* be inferred from the concept of determinate relations of production but the second cannot. Relations of production must be conceived as articulated on to other social relations and practices but we cannot deduce what those relations and practices will be from the relations of production themselves.

The consequences of this position for the conceptualisation of the connections between relations of production and other elements of determinate social formations will be considered in the following chapter. But, if mode of production and social formation are not conceptualised in epistemological terms as definite objects of discourse existing independently of discourse itself then the form in which the conditions of existence of determinate relations of production are provided cannot be conceived either, in the manner of rationalism, as derivable in principle from the relations of production whose conditions of existence they secure or, in the manner of empiricism, as empirically given to theory. Rationalist and empiricist conceptualisations of the connection between relations of production and other social relations and practices both ensure that the effects of those other social relations cannot be conceptualised. In the one case they are treated as derivable in essence from the concept of the relations of production. Those relations are treated as securing their own conditions of existence and the effects of other social relations are therefore conceived as given in the relations of production themselves. In the other case the conditions of existence are conceived as given outside of theory and therefore as dependent on the circumstances of the case, as lying essentially beyond the range of theoretical determination.

The thesis of determination in the last instance by the economy provides an excellent example of the theoretical effects of rationalist positions in which certain concepts and forms of discourse are thought to give the essential features of objects capable of independent existence, determinate unities, of being. Certain concepts give the essence of the real and what is presupposed by those concepts must therefore be represented in the real. We have seen, further, that what can be derived in the way of conditions of existence does not fully specify the precise forms in which those conditions of existence are provided. The thesis of determination in the last instance by the economy defines a theoretical space for other determinations to intervene at the superstructural levels. These other determinations are real and they have their effects on the economic base, the superstructure 'reacts upon it as a determining element' (*Capital*, vol. 3, p. 791), but they are inessential. Determination in the last instance therefore allows classical Marxism to bring together rationalist and empiricist conceptualisations so that while empirically given variations may be recognised, and accorded some significance, the essential features of the social formation are nevertheless thought to be determined by the dominant relations of production. Features not determined by the economy are recognised and deemed inessential, and therefore ultimately ineffective, in one and the same movement.

The argument that disposes of determination in the last instance disposes also of the 'correspondence' that is alleged to hold between the relations and the forces of production. It is clear that relations of production and forces of production may each provide certain of the conditions of existence of the other. Relations of production presuppose that production takes place, and it can do so only under some definite forms of organisation, with definite means of production and under definite conditions. Similarly all 'productive forces' presuppose that production takes place under definite social conditions and according to some definite social form of possession of the means and conditions of production. They may be possessed privately or collectively but if they are not possessed at all then no social agency has the capacity to control their functioning. We have seen that the concept of conditions of existence cannot give the form in which those conditions are secured. Conceptualisation in terms of conditions of existence and the forms in which those conditions are secured therefore cuts the ground from under the classical Marxist conception of the economy as essentially structured by a definite correspondence between relation and forces of production.

Finally, and more generally, the critique of epistemology and the argument for analysis of objects in terms of their conditions of existence and the forms in which they are secured destroys the foundations of all epistemologically conceived relations whether these are thought to be relations of knowledge between a subject of one kind or another and objects which confront it or relations of causality and determination. The significance of these points for Marxist theory is not restricted to conceptualisation of the structure of the social formation and the relations between its parts. The preceding chapter has shown that attempts to conceptualise classes in relation to the structure of the social formation have failed to conceptualise the conditions of existence of agents. Rather they have conceived the relations of agent to the structure in terms of some combination or other of a relation of knowledge on the one hand and a relation of determination on the other. In this sense conceptions of epistemology and theories of class consciousness and its significance tend to go hand in hand. The critique of epistemology requires that the conditions of existence of agents be reconsidered. That will be the task of a later chapter.

Chapter 9

Mode of Production, Social Formation, Classes

This chapter considers the implications of the critique of 'determination in the last instance' and related positions for the conceptualisation of the structure of the social formation and of classes. We shall see that it is necessary to reject both the pertinence of the concept of mode of production and the conception of the social formation as a totality organised into two or three distinct but articulated structural levels. The correlate of the conception of totality is the notion of an organising principle. The social formation is not a totality governed by an organising principle, determination in the last instance, structural causality, or whatever. It should be conceived as consisting of a definite set of relations of production together with the economic, political, and cultural forms in which their conditions of existence are secured. But there is no necessity for those conditions of existence to be secured and no necessary structure of the social formation in which those relations and forms must be combined. As for classes, it will be argued that if they are conceived as economic classes, as categories of economic agents occupying definite positions of possession of or separation from the means and conditions of production, then they cannot also be conceived as, or as represented by, political forces and ideological forms. It follows that the concept of class struggle cannot be retained in its classical forms and that there can be no justification for a 'reading' of politics and ideology for the class interests they are alleged to represent.

Concepts of mode of production and social formation

We have seen that the classical Marxist conception of the social formation posits a definite combination of modes of production organised into three structural levels (economic, political, and cultural-ideological). The social formation functions as a relatively coherent social whole, a 'society', and it is relatively autonomous from other objects. In this structure one mode of production is dominant and the others are subordinated to it. The modes of production are themselves organised into three structural levels, or two in the case of the communist modes of production, and they are governed by the 'determination in the last instance' of the economy. Finally, the economy itself is structured by a definite combination of relations and forces of production in which, according to the version of classical Marxism in question, either the relations or the forces are dominant.

Now, the argument of the preceding chapter undermines the concept of mode of production in two distinct respects. First, the thesis of determination in the last instance has the effect of transposing a relation between concepts, between the concept of an economy on the one hand and those of its conditions of existence on the other, into a relation of determination between objects—so that the economy secures its own conditions of existence in the form of suitable political and cultural-ideological levels. That transposition cannot be justified except in terms of a rationalistic epistemological position which has the effect of dogmatically rendering a certain body of concepts immune to criticism and argumentation. To reject that dogmatism is to reject the transposition of relations between concepts into relations between objects. It follows that the relationship between the economy and its conditions of existence cannot be conceptualised in the manner of 'determination in the last instance'. Starting from the concept of the economy it is possible to specify its social conditions of existence in the form of definite political, legal, and cultural presuppositions. The concept of the economy entails definite abstract and general conditions which must be satisfied by political, legal, and cultural forms if they are to be compatible with the economy in question. The concept of the economy gives us the concepts of its conditions of existence but it does not tell us the form in which those conditions will be provided. Thus the economy has definite conditions of existence but it cannot ensure that those conditions will be satisfied and, if they are satisfied, it cannot determine the forms in which they are met.

Pre-Capitalist Modes of Production directed a related argument against the concept of structural causality advanced by Althusser and Balibar in *Reading Capital.* Structural causality refers to a definite relationship between a structure and its parts and that the parts constitute the totality of the conditions of existence of the structure while the structure itself provides the conditions of existence of its parts. The continued existence of the structure is logically entailed by its existence. It is for this reason that Althusser refers to the structure as 'eternity in Spinoza's sense' (*Reading Capital*, p. 107). Since the structure constitutes its own conditions of existence, it cannot be dependent on any external conditions. Here too a relation between concepts is transposed on to a relation between objects, for the existence of the parts is held to be secured by the action of the structure to which they belong. Althusser presents structural causality as a *philosophical* category whose field of application is therefore more general than that of determination in the last instance. Far from being restricted to Marxism, structural causality is pertinent to a variety of theoretical discourses: 'psycho-analysis, linguistics, other disciplines such as biology, and perhaps even physics' (*ibid.*, p. 187). Nevertheless, in its application to Marxist theory the effects of structural causality are equivalent to those of determination in the last instance. The economy plays a double role. It is present as a level in the structure and it determines the relationships between the levels of the structure. It is determinant on the one hand and it may be affected by the other levels on the other.

The critiques of structural causality and of determination in the last instance lead to the conclusion that the economy cannot be conceived as securing its own conditions of existence. In effect it lands to a reduced concept of mode of production consisting of an economy, a definite combination of relations and forces of production, having definite political, legal, and cultural conditions of existence which cannot be secured through the action of the economy itself. That conclusion is argued in the closing chapters of *Pre-Capitalist Modes of Production.* Mode of production in the reduced sense is not equivalent to the economic level of the classical conception since it does not play the role of determination in the last instance or the matrix role assigned to it by Althusser's structural causality. But this reduced concept still retains the notion of a necessary correspondence between relations and forces of production. This brings us to the second respect in which the concept of mode of production is undermined by the argument of the preceding chapter.

Starting from the concept of relations of production it is possible to show that each specific set of relations of production must have some conditions of existence that can be secured only by definite means and processes of production. If there is no production then the concepts of 'possession of' and 'separation from' the means and conditions of production are vacuous. Similarly, each specific set of forces of production has conditions of existence that can be satisfied by definite relations of production. Forms of organisation of labour presuppose the capacity of some agent or agents to control the functioning of the means of production. It is easy to show, in other words, that relations and forces of production each presuppose the other. Relations of production have some of their conditions of existence secured by forces of production, and forces of production depend upon relations of production for some of their conditions of existence. So far, so good. If the thesis of the correspondence of relations and forces of production went no further than this it would be unexceptionable. Unfortunately the correspondence thesis goes far beyond the rather trivial assertions that possession of means of production presupposes production and that production presupposes the capacity of some agent or agents to control it.

In fact we have seen that the thesis of correspondence goes hand in hand with either the thesis of the primacy of the forces of production (as in the Marxism of the 2nd International and of Stalin's *Dialectical and Historical Materialism*) or the thesis of the primacy of the relations of production (the Chinese position, also advanced in *Reading Capital* and, with significant differences, in *Pre-Capitalist Modes of Production*). Once the necessity of correspondence is affirmed then some means of effecting and restoring correspondence must be posited. Both theses maintain that non-correspondence may occur and, if it does, then correspondence will be restored through the transformation of either the relations or the forces of production. For the thesis of the primacy of the forces any non-correspondence is corrected through the transformation of the relations of production. Conversely, for the thesis of the primacy of the relations of production, correspondence is effected through the transformation of the productive forces. There is a necessary correspondence between relations and forces in the sense that, in the event of non-correspondence occurring, the one acts so as to bring the other into line. Either the relations or the forces act so as to secure their own economic conditions of existence. Once again a relation between concepts is transposed on to a relation of effectivity between objects: what is presupposed in the *concepts* of the forces (relations) is brought into being through the effectivity of the forces (relations) themselves.

The thesis of the necessary correspondence of relations and forces of production therefore falls victim to the same general argument that disposed of the thesis of determination in the last instance and of structural causality. But if correspondence is not necessitated then the connection between the relations and the forces of production can be conceptualised only in terms of conditions of existence and the forms in which they are secured. *Either* the articulation of relations and forces of production is conceived in terms of some kind of necessity so that the character of one thing, the relations or the forces, is deducible from the concept of the other, *or* it must be conceived in terms of the connection between social relations and the forms in which their conditions of existence are secured. We have seen the problems of the first alternative. The second means that there is no reason to posit modes of production as distinctive objects of analysis in Marxist theory. Once the *necessity* of correspondence between the relations and forces of production is denied, once each is conceived as merely subject to certain abstract and general conditions if it is to be compatible with the conditions of existence of the other, then there are no grounds for maintaining that to each distinctive set of relations (forces) of production there must correspond an equally distinctive set of forces (relations) of production. The attempted theorisation of modes of production, where one set of relations necessarily correspond to one set of forces, as distinctive and primary objects of analysis involves a correlative neglect of the problems of conceptualising the conditions of existence of more complex forms of economic class-relations constituted by the combinations of distinct relations of production. The significance of this point will become clearer in a later chapter which examines the concepts of class and of the possession of and separation from the means and conditions of production.

We can now move on to the classical Marxist conception of the structure of the social formation. If, as we have argued, it is necessary to reject the pertinence of the concept of mode of production for Marxist theory then it is impossible to maintain the classical conception of the social formation as a combination of modes of production. Similarly, the attempt of *Pre-Capitalist*

Modes of Production to break away from the conception of a combination of modes by conceptualising the economic level of a social formation as consisting of a dominant mode of production together with *elements* of other modes cannot be sustained.

But there is also a more general problem which concerns the conceptualisation of the social formation as a definite internally differentiated social totality, a 'society' with differential levels of effectivity and forms of ontological primacy. In the classical conception social formation is conceived as a combination of modes of production and of structural levels such that one mode is dominant and one level is primary. The economic level of the dominant mode of production has an ontological primacy in the sense that it determines 'in the last instance' the overall articulation of modes of production and structural levels in the social formation as a whole. The subordinate modes and the structural levels are assigned a definite effectivity as a function of the character of the economic level of the dominant mode of production. Quite apart from the problems of the concept of mode of production this conception of social formation raises in a different form the difficulties we have already encountered with the thesis of determination in the last instance and of the necessary correspondence of relations and forces of production. The conception of the social formation as having a definite and necessary structure governed by definite and necessary relations of effectivity between its parts rests on the epistemological conception of the social formation existing independently of the discourses in which it is specified. To see this it is sufficient to return to the question of the position of the relations of production *vis-à-vis* the rest of the social formation. The concept of definite relations of production gives us the conditions of existence of those relations in the form of certain abstract and general conditions which must be satisfied by political, legal, and cultural forms if they are to be compatible with the presence of those relations of production. For example, capitalist relations of production presuppose some form of commercial law which recognises certain forms of property and contract, in particular, contracts to buy and sell commodities and to exchange labour-time against money wages. But, if relations of production presupposes conditions of existence provided by other social relations they cannot generate those conditions of existence or determine the social relations which provide them. Neither the concept of the relations of production nor the concept of any other part of the social formation can sustain the thesis of the necessary effectivity or ontological primacy of that part.

If the relations of necessity and ontological primacy are not given in the concepts of the parts and social relations that are held to constitute the social formation then they must be established in some other fashion. It is precisely because the social formation is conceived as a definite social unity existing independently of the discourses which specify it that relations of necessity may be conceived as given in the social formation itself, as given independently of discourse and therefore as necessary to discourse if it is to be able to specify the social formation. We have seen that to conceive of a realm of objects existing independently of discourse and yet specifiable within it is also to posit a definite level or form of discourse as giving direct and privileged access to members of the realm of objects. The classical Marxist conception of the structure of the social formation involves a rationalist epistemological position in the sense that it posits a uniquely privileged body of concepts, the basic concepts of historical materialism, as directly representing the essential structure of the real itself. The essential structure of the real is therefore conceived both as represented in discourse and as external to it. The internal differentiation of the social formation, the definite and necessary relations of effectivity between its levels, and the primacy of the economic level of the dominant mode of production are conceived as existing independently of discourse and as being represented in it through the basic concepts of Marxist theory. In this sense the classical Marxist conception of the structure of the social formation involves both the concepts of particular social relations and practices, relations of production, law, politics and the State, ideology, etc., *and* a definite rationalist epistemological conceptualisation of the relation between discourse and its objects.

Now, we have argued that the epistemological project is not a necessary one and that the relations between discourse and its objects does not need to be conceived in terms of both a distinction and a correlation between a realm of discourse and an independently existing realm of objects. But in the absence of such an epistemological conception it is no longer possible to conceive of objects existing *outside* of discourse (and represented in its basic concepts) as the measure of validity of discourse. On the contrary, in the absence of such specifiable yet extra-discursive objects the elements specified in discourse must be conceived solely in and through the forms of discourse in which they are constituted. What is specified in theoretical discourse cannot be specified extra-discursively: it can be conceived only through that discourse or a related, critical, or complementary one.

What are the consequences of a rejection of epistemological conceptualisation for the classical Marxist conception of the social formation and its structure? We have seen above that the concepts of determination in the last instance, correspondence of relations and forces of production and mode of production can no longer be sustained. The more general point to notice is that the conception of the social formation as having a definite and necessary structure with definite and necessary relations of effectivity between its parts cannot be sustained either. In effect all those concepts formed through the positing of necessary correspondence and necessary forms of effectivity, dominance, and determination, must be rejected since they are, at least in part, a function of epistemological conceptualisation. We are left then with the concepts of definite social relations and practices, relations and forces of production, law, and so on, but there is no necessary form in which these concepts must be articulated into the concept of the essential structure of a social formation.

What, then, of the discursive primacy accorded to the economy in Marxist theory? In the classical conception the discursive primacy accorded to the economy and to production in particular involves a definite conception of the ontological structure of a realm of modes of production and social formations existing independently of Marxist discourse: the analysis of social formations begins with production and the economy because they determine the essential character of all other social relations and practices. In the absence of epistemological conceptualisations there can be no ontological primacy accorded to production, the economy or any other feature of the social formation. The discursive primacy of the economy cannot be justified by reference to the essential structure of any independently existing realm of objects. If, as we have argued, social relations are to be examined in terms of their conditions of existence and the forms in which those conditions are provided then there can be nothing in the social relations themselves or their interrelationships to justify the according of discursive primacy in any particular relations or set of relations. On the contrary, discursive primacy can only be a function of the posing of definite problems for theorisation. If relations of production and their conditions of existence are presented as a problem for theorisation then those relations must be accorded primacy in the discursive resolution of that problem.

For example, the concepts of social formations developed in Marxist theory are a function of definite political and theoretical problems. These concepts and those of modes of production have been developed on the basis of a variety of problems deriving from the most diverse sources and elaborated in terms of diverse means of conceptualisation: political ideologies (socialism and communism); historical and anthropological debates and the historian's practice; problems arising in the process of theoretical exposition (e.g. the elaboration of the concept of simple commodity production in *Capital*); political and theoretical debates with Narodnism and legal Marxism in the case of *The Development of Capitalism in Russia*, etc. Problems created by politics, or generated within Marxist theory or by other forms of theorisation constitute the objects of theorisation and problematisation in Marxist discourse. The manner in which problems are posed and theorised does not depend on the development of Marxist theory alone. It is also a function of Marxist politics and of the extent to which political problems are allowed to generate problems for theorisation.

The political objectives of a socialist transformation of economic class relations pose the problem of relations of production and their political and cultural conditions of existence as primary objects of theorisation for Marxism. The concepts of social formations provide a theorisation of the forms and conditions in which production and distribution, political and ideological practices are effective. They are a means of conceptualising effectivity, of the calculation of effects, of the movements of production and distribution, the possibilities and results of political action, and so on. Concepts of social formations specify economies and economic class-relations, their political and legal conditions of existence, and the possibilities of their transformation. The conceptualisation of social formations therefore involves conceptualisation of:

1 relations of production and economic class-relations;

2 the specific means and processes of production and forms of distribution of the products and their relationship to the specific forms of possession of and separation from the means

of conditions of production and of economic class-relations;

3 forms of State and of politics;

4 cultural and ideological forms, for example, the forms of calculation employed in the organisation of production and of trade, forms of political calculation, etc.;

5 relations with other social formations;

6 conditions and possibilities of the transformation of some of these forms and relations—for example, of the transition from capitalism to socialism.

Social formation in this sense does not designate a 'society', a social totality existing independently of the discourses in which it is specified, and governed by the organising principle of 'determination in the last instance' or 'structural causality'. Nor does it represent particular states of such an entity or stages of its dissolution into some other form of social totality. Neither the necessary supersession nor the persistence of a social formation or its elements can be deduced from the concept of the social formation itself. The political, legal, and cultural elements of a social formation cannot be reduced to the classical Marxist formula of economic base and its attendant superstructures. Political, legal, and cultural conditions provide the forms in which the conditions of existence of relations of production are secured, but these conditions are not reducible to their effects at the level of the economy, and they cannot be conceived as organised into definite structural levels which merely reflect the structure of an underlying economic base.

Economic classes, politics, and culture

Classical Marxism conceives of classes first, as categories of economic agents defined by position in respect of possession of and separation from the means and conditions of production and second, as entities that constitute, or are represented by, definite political forces and cultural forms. We have seen that any conception of the irreducibility of politics and culture to the economy must render that conception of classes extremely problematic. If classes are conceived as categories of economic agent then they cannot also be conceived as political and cultural agencies. It follows that political institutions and practices, ideologies and other cultural forms cannot be conceived as classes or the direct representation of their interests.

In order to establish that conclusion it is necessary to show that in the absence of determination in the last instance or structural causality the conception of political and cultural forms as representing economic classes and their interests cannot be sustained. The social formation must now be conceived as including a specific set of economic class-relations together with the economic, political, and cultural forms in which the conditions of existence are secured. Political and cultural forms are not determined, in the last instance or otherwise, by the system of economic relations. Given that conception of the social formation, is it possible to conceive of political and cultural practices as representing economic classes and their interests?

The concept of representation implies a distinction between what is represented, economic classes and their interests, and the representation itself, the political and cultural practices of specific organisations and institutions. Classes do not immediately and directly represent themselves. When we examine political and ideological struggles we find State apparatuses, political parties and organisations, demonstrations and riotous mobs, bodies of armed men, newspapers and magazines, etc., but we do not find *classes* lined up against each other. Nor do we find that the issues in political struggle take the form of direct conflicts between classes for political hegemony or over the specific character of the relations of production, feudalism versus capitalism, capitalism versus socialism, or whatever. The classics of Marxist political analysis have always insisted on the specificity of the forces and issues at stake in political conflict, on the fact that political struggles are not directly and immediately reducible to classes and their interests. For example, in 'The Discussion of Self-Determination Summed Up' Lenin attacks the ultra-left economist reduction of politics to such a conflict of classes in the following terms:

> To imagine that social revolution is *conceivable* without revolts by small nations in the colonies and in Europe, without revolutionary outbursts by a section of the petty-bourgeoisie *with all its prejudices*, without a movement of the politically non-conscious proletarian or semi-proletarian masses against oppression by landowners, the church and the monarchy, against national oppression, etc.—to imagine all this is to

> *repudiate social revolution*. So one army lines up in one place and says 'We are for socialism', and another, somewhere else, and says 'We are for capitalism' and that will be a social revolution . . . whoever expects a 'pure' social revolution will *never* live to see it. (*Collected Works*, vol. 22, pp. 355–6)

What is at stake is the recognition of the main political issues and the forces engaged in them. In practice the classics of Marxist politics have come to terms with the specificity of political forces and issues. But in theory Marxism insists that political and ideological struggles should be conceptualised in class terms. This discrepancy is contained in the concept of representation, in the difference between what is represented, classes, their interests and struggles, and its representation in specific political and ideological forces, issues, and struggles. To talk of representation in this context is to treat specific political struggles as representing or expressing something that is not immediately present in them. The content of representation is not immediately present: it must be read off from the specific forms in which it is represented. Lenin frequently insists that the balance of political forces cannot be derived from economic class-relations. In *The Agrarian Programme of Social Democracy in the First Russian Revolution* he assesses the balance of class forces by means of an analysis of political organisations, their programmes, and ideologies. The specificity of political struggles is recognised and it is read as representing the struggle of economic classes. The idea of representation appears to provide Marxism with a genuine alternative to the economistic reduction of political and ideological struggle to economic class-relations. Political forces are not reducible to classes, they *represent* them.

Can this concept of representation be sustained? It involves three aspects: what is represented—class interests and the conflicts between them; the means of representation—political organisations, institutions, etc.; and the representation itself—the practices of these organisations, institutions, etc. If the representation is not directly reducible to what it represents that can only be because of the specific effectivity of the means of representation. The difference between what is represented and its representation presupposes a specific and determinate effectivity of the means of representation. It follows that the means of representation, political organisations and institutions, modes of political organisation and struggle, cannot themselves be reducible to classes and their interests. Thus to conceive of politics and culture in terms of the representation of class interests is to admit political and cultural forms that are in principle irreducible to classes and their interests. The representation itself is always a function of two independent elements, the content and the means of representation. If these elements are not independent then the representation is directly reducible to what it represents.

A similar conclusion results from Gramsci's attempts to develop an anti-economistic Marxism. Political and cultural struggle is to be conceived as a war of position conducted between forces representing distinct and antithetical principles of social organisation and the classes which function as the principle social bearers of these principles. To talk of a war of position is to talk of a terrain upon which the war is fought and of specific and determinate features of that terrain, of the points at which particular battles may be won and lost. The notion of a war of position between classes and the forces which represent them therefore entails at least an implicit conception of a terrain that is in principle irreducible to classes and their interests.

But, if the means of representation are irreducible in principle to classes and their interests then two problems must arise for the problematic of representation. First, how are the means of representation constrained to function so that they do produce a representation of class interests? Second, how are the interests represented to be read off from their political and cultural representations? The first problem merely poses another version of the problem of 'relative autonomy': how is it possible to be autonomous on the one hand and not autonomous on the other? How is it possible for the political and cultural means of representation to be independent of economic classes and their interests on the one hand and yet be constrained to represent those interests on the other? The problem is insoluble. If political institutions, organisations, etc., are not determined, in the last instance or otherwise, by the system of economic class-relations then they cannot also be constrained to function as the means of representation of those relations.

For example, in the Lukácsian and the left-Weberian interpretations of Marxism discussed in Chapter 7, class interests are supposed to be determined at the level of the economy and the representation of those interests in politics, ideology, etc., is conceived as being a function of the will and consciousness of a multiplicity of actors. The means of representation, in this case the will and consciousness of human subjects, are independent of the interests whose representation they are supposed to provide. We have seen that these positions necessarily entail the conclusion that politics and culture are irreducible in principle to economic classes and their interests. If the representation of economically determined interests depend on acts of recognition and of will on the part of a plurality of independent human subjects then there can be no necessity for those interests to be represented at all. We have seen the theoretical and political effects of these positions. Political institutions, organisations, and practices are to be seen as the more or less adequate expressions of the interests of economic classes. In effect, political forms are recognised as being irreducible to economic classes and their interests but no attempt is made to conceptualise their effectivity with regard to economic class-relations or other elements of the social formation.

But the example of subjectivist conceptions of class illustrates a general feature of the problematic of representation. *Either* the political and cultural means of representation are determined by the economy and representations are immediately and directly reducible to the classes and interests represented, *or* the means of representation are not determined by the economy and there is no necessity of the political and cultural representation of classes and their interests at all. The problematic of representation is as unstable and ultimately incoherent as that of relative autonomy and for essentially the same reasons. Far from providing a coherent alternative to the economistic reduction of political and ideological struggle to the effects of economic class-relations the notion of representation merely involves a complicated economism. For economism political and ideological forces are ultimately reducible to the effects of economic class-relations and the interests constituted by them. In political analysis economism leads to the reduction of political forces and issues to interests determined elsewhere (basically in the economy). They are analysed not in terms of their specific conditions of existence and their effectivity with regard to other social relations and practices but rather for the interests they are thought to represent. In the absence of determination in the last instance or some equivalent economism cannot be sustained. We have seen that the qualification 'in the last instance' has a gestural character: it asserts the primacy of the economy while affirming that politics and ideology cannot simply be reduced to its effects. But if the social formation is not governed, 'in the last instance' or otherwise, by the primacy of the economy then political and ideological forces cannot be reduced to the effects of economic class-relations. Either political and ideological forces are reducible to classes or fractions of classes or they are not. To deny economism is to reject the classical conception of the economic-political-ideological unity of classes. It is to maintain that political and ideological struggles cannot be conceived as the struggles of economic classes. There is no middle way.

The resolution of the second problem, namely, how are the interests represented to be read off from their political and cultural representations, follows from that of the first. Either representation is no more than a complicated economism or it shatters the classical conception of classes. For economism there is no real problem of reading the interests represented in the specific political and ideological struggles of the day. Economism merely draws the consequences of the thesis of determination in the last instance. It involves a reductionist conception of the social formation in which the essential features of law and politics are determined by the economy. Determination in the last instance admits of features that react back on the economy and are not determined by it. These exist but are inessential. Similarly for economism: political and ideological struggles are essentially reducible to the interests of classes and the irreconcilable conflict between them. The specific manifest political and ideological struggles of the day may well have other functions which disguise their real character. Such features exist and they have real effects—for example, they confuse the uninitiated and dissimulate the essential class character of these struggles. They have real effects but they are inessential. For economism there is no problem of separating the essence, economic classes and their interests, from the manifest forms of its appearance, the specific political and ideological struggles of the day. There is no problem here simply because the essential interests are known independently of the concrete forms of their representation: they are given in the concept of the economy itself.

If we reject economism and if we take that rejection seriously then the question of representation cannot arise. Political and cultural practices, issues, and struggles do not represent interests determined elsewhere, at the level of the economy. It follows that specific political forces, issues, and struggles can no longer be interpreted as *essentially* representing something else. There can be no question of the analysis of politics through the separation of the essential class struggle from the inessential dross with which it is clothed. Some political parties and organisations claim to represent the interests of a class (many others do not). But those 'interests' cannot be understood as 'objectively' given, as determined by economic class-relations and then recognised by the party or organisation in question. They are constituted in terms of definite political ideologies by means of specific political and cultural practices. Class 'interests' are not given to politics and ideology by the economy. They arise within political practice and they are determined as an effect of definite modes of political practice. Political practice does not recognise class interests and then represent them: it constitutes the interests which it represents.

The economistic reduction of politics and culture to class 'interests' generates a definite mode of political calculation in which organisations and programmes are evaluated in terms of their pertinence to those 'interests'. This mode of political calculation is employed in one form or another by Marxist parties and groupings and more generally throughout much of the non-Marxist left. It is a possible mode of political calculation but it is not a necessary one and, as we have seen, it has no coherent theoretical basis. Great Marxist political leaders like Lenin and Mao Tse-tung have gone beyond economism in practice: they have confronted the specificity of political struggles and forces and have come to terms with it. But they have not gone beyond economism in theory: they have not criticised the problematic of representation and the basic economistic principles it enshrines and they have provided no theoretical alternative to it. In *The Agrarian Programme of Social Democracy in the First Russian Revolution*, for example, Lenin recognises the specificity of political struggles and he assesses the balance of political forces by means of an analysis of political organisations, their programmes and ideologies. But he interprets this balance as a balance of *class* forces.

If the problematic of representation provides no coherent theoretical alternative to economism then it is necessary to reject the analysis of politics in terms of the actions of classes and their representations. The evaluation of political issues and forces is a function of definite political objectives and definite ideologies, socialism, liberalism, feminism, or whatever. For Marxism this means abandoning the evaluation of political issues and forces in terms of the essential interests of classes. It means evaluating them in terms of a definite conception of socialist organisation and ideology and an estimation of the dominant political issues of the day. Marxists will have to clarify their standards of evaluation of political forces, their conceptions of what a socialist movement is and what its objectives are, and their conception of what the crucial struggles of contemporary politics are. Only the analysis of these struggles and of the specific groups, parties and organisations engaged in them can tell us who our political allies may be.

Summary and conclusion

This chapter has developed the implications of the critique of 'determination in the last instance', 'structural causality', and related positions for the classical Marxist conceptions of mode of productivity, social formation, and of classes. We have argued that the pertinence of the concept of mode of production must be rejected and that the social formation cannot be conceived as organised into two or three distinct but articulated levels governed by the determination in the last instance of the economy. The classical conception of the social formation involves concepts of particular social relations and practices, relations of production, forces of production, law, politics and the State, ideology, and so on, on the one hand, and a definite rationalist epistemological conceptualisation of the relations between discourse and its objects on the other. In the absence of that epistemological conceptualisation the necessary correspondences and necessary relations of effectivity, dominance, and determination posited in Marxist theory can no longer be sustained. It follows that the conception of the social formation as having a definite and necessary structure with definite and necessary relations of effectivity between its parts cannot be sustained either. The discursive primacy accorded the economy in classical Marxism cannot then be justified by reference to the essential structure of the social formation. We have argued that the according of discursive primacy to any particular relations or set of relations can only be a function of the posing of definite problems for theorisation. The concepts of social formations developed in Marxist theory are a function of definite political and theoretical problems. The political objectives of a socialist transformation of economic class-relations pose the problem of relations of production and their political and cultural conditions of existence as primary objects of theorisation for Marxism. We have therefore argued for a conceptualisation of social formations in terms of a definite set of relations of production, the economic, political, and cultural forms in which these conditions of existence are secured, and the possibilities of transformation of these forms and relations.

The second part of the chapter examined the conceptualisation of the connections between economic class-relations, politics, and culture in terms of the political and cultural 'representation' of classes and their interests in the practices of definite groups, institutions, and organisations. We have argued that the problematic of representation is essentially unstable and that it provides no coherent theoretical alternative to the economistic reduction of everything to a more or less direct manifestation of the state of the economy. The choice for Marxism is between a systematic economism and a rejection of the classical conception of politics and culture in terms of the necessary representations of economic classes and their interests. The first alternative returns us to the thesis of determination in the last instance and its effects, while the second means that political and ideological struggles cannot be conceived as, or as representing, the struggles of economic classes. The evaluation of political issues and forces can no longer be conceived as a matter of the essential interests of classes. It is a matter of definite political objectives and ideologies. For Marxism both the conceptualisation of the social formation and the analysis of political and ideological forces and struggles within it must be a function of the posing of definite political problems for theorisation.

Politics, law, and culture cannot be conceptualised in terms of the representation of economic classes. It follows from the discussion of the structure of the social formation that the articulation of economic class-relations on to other features of the social formation must be analysed in terms of the conditions of existence of economic class-relations and the forms in which those conditions are secured. Economic class-relations involve definite forms of possession of and separation from the means of production on the part of economic agents. They presuppose some legal or customary recognition of entities capable of assuming the capacities of agents and therefore some definition of what may or may not be a legal or customary subject, human individuals, organisations, communities, or whatever. Agents and their social conditions of existence are discussed in Chapter 11. In addition economic class-relations presuppose agents capable of organising production and operating the means of production under conditions of definite forms of possession. This involves legal or customary definitions and sanction of rights and obligations (law of contract, property, etc.), and the existence of forms of calculation consistent with the performance of the relevant capacities. For example, capitalist forms of possession involve an organisation of production in which the elements of the production process including labour-power take the form of commodities. They therefore presuppose both some form of commercial law which recognises and sanctions the conditions of commodity production and exchange and the employment of definite forms of monetary calculation and accounting in capitalist's organisation of the production process. Capitalists are not born with the skills of double-entry book-keeping let alone the more sophisticated accounting practices employed in modern capitalist enterprises. Without appropriate forms of monetary calculation and the social means of training people in their use capitalist relations of production cannot survive.

But neither the distribution of agents endowed by law, custom, and by training with the capacities appropriate to performing the functions of possession or non-possession, nor the technological conditions of production are sufficient to determine the precise conditions of production or of the distribution of the product between economic agents. For example, under capitalist conditions the capacities of capitalists and labourers and the socially available technological forms do not suffice to determine either the conditions of labour or the division between wages and profit. To say that production takes place under capitalist forms of possession is to say that it presupposes, *inter alia*, legal recognition of the forms of wage-labour contract. And that implies the possibility of a whole variety of legal interventions in the conditions of contract—minimum wage legislation, regulations of working hours and working conditions, redundancy and pension rights, and so on. These and other legal interventions are *possible* but not necessary given the capitalist organisation of production.

But the wage-labour contract must always be *determinate*, that is, it must specify definite conditions and obligations on the parties to that contract. There must always be some legal specifications of the forms of contract that are possible and of those that are legally precluded and, within those limits, each wage-labour contract presupposes some further determination of the particular conditions specified in the contracts. These conditions of contract are not determined by capitalist relations of production as such—since they presuppose only that these be determinate wage-labour contracts. They are determined by the outcome of the struggle of definite social forces acting, say, on the legislative and juridical apparatuses of the State, on conditions voluntarily agreed between employers and workers' organisations, etc. Capitalist relations of production presuppose legal relations of contract as one of their conditions of existence but they do not determine the form that regulation takes. Similarly, wage-labour presupposes a definite system of wage levels. At any given time wages are fixed at such-and-such a level, neither more nor less. Those levels are not determined by the relations of production and the technological conditions alone but also by the intervention of definite political, legal, and cultural determinations. Wages may be fixed by the State, determined by individual bargaining subject only to legal constraints and the expectations of participants, or they may be fixed by means of the struggle of organised bodies of labourers and capitalists. But they will always be fixed at some level. Wage-labour presupposes some definite legal recognition and legal regulation of the conditions of contract and some definite level or levels of wages. It therefore presupposes the struggle of definite social forces the outcome of which has the effect of determining those conditions and levels. Where there are capitalist relations of production there must be conflicting political and ideological forces.

This example of the conditions of existence of capitalist wage-labour illustrates the more general point that determinate relations of production always presuppose definite political, legal, and cultural conditions but they do not determine the form in which those conditions are provided. Those conditions have definite effects, e.g. on the level of wages and other conditions of employment, and they may be modified by political and ideological struggles. In certain cases the very existence of the relations of production in question *may* be subject to the effects of these struggles. Economic class-relations presuppose the existence of political struggles whose outcome has differential effects on the precise relations of the classes or particular categories of agents within them (e.g. workers in a particular union or factory). But those forces cannot be reduced to effects or reflections of economic class-relations. Where there are economic class-relations there must be political and ideological forces having differential effects on those classes. But there are no grounds for supposing that those forces are the products of the classes representing themselves and their interests in political and ideological forms. There is no necessity for political and ideological forces to be polarised around the memberships of the different classes.

Similarly, the action of such forces has no necessary implications regarding the maintenance or non-maintenance of the relations of production in question and their conditions of existence. The political and ideological struggles which intervene in the determination of the level of wages and working conditions under capitalism may or may not call into question the conditions of existence of capitalist production-relations. There is nothing in capitalist relations of production as such to ensure any of the forces engaged in those struggles will be or will tend to become socialist. Since politics do not simply reflect or represent economic class-relations it follows that the working class is not automatically or essentially socialist, that working-class politics are not automatically progressive. The USA is an excellent example of a situation where the conditions of wage-labour and the levels of wages are determined, *inter alia*, by the conflict of workers' and employers' representatives but without the intervention of any significant socialist forces. Forces will have to be won for socialism. There is nothing in capitalist production-relations as such which necessarily generates such forces let alone ensures that they will be successful.

Chapter 10

Possession of and Separation from the Means of Production

The concepts of possession of and separation from the means of production are central to the analysis of economic classes. Marxist theory has defined economic classes in terms of the relations of agents to the means of production and those relations are defined by specific relations of production. In his discussion of ground-rent in *Capital*, vol. 3, Marx suggests that a major distinction between capitalist and pre-capitalist forms of rent is that in the latter the direct producers are not separated from the means of production. Consequently, exploitation under these conditions must take the form of a coercive relationship between non-labourers having no function in the process of production and the direct producers themselves. This argument involves two positions: first, that class-relations must be conceived as relations between labourers and non-labourers; second, that economic class-relations are possible on the basis of a non-separation of labourers from their means of production. The second position has been criticised in *Pre-Capitalist Modes of Production*, while the first is rendered problematic by our analysis of slave and feudal relations of production—and, indeed, by Marx's analysis of the role of the capitalist in the organisation of capitalist production. This chapter examines the concepts of possession of and separation from the means of production and the concepts of labourer and non-labourer. It argues that economic class-relations always involve the effective possession of the means of production by economic agents of one category and the consequent separation of other agents from those means. Marx's treatment of pre-capitalist relations of production as essentially non-economic in form involves a crucial conflation of forms of possession of and separation from the means of production on the one hand and their legal and political conditions of existence on the other.

The definition of economic class-relations in terms of effective possession of and separation from the means of production leaves open the questions of the nature of the possessing agent, that is, of who or what may occupy the position of possession, and of the connections between economic class-relations, the organisation of production and the division of social labour. These questions will be considered in the two following chapters. The first argues that Marxism has given little consideration to the possession of the means of production by agencies other than individual human subjects, by joint-stock companies, religious orders, communities, and so on. That chapter attempts a general analysis of agents and their conditions of existence and it shows that there is no foundation for the identification of agents and individual human subjects. The next chapter considers the organisation of production and the division of social labour. It is particularly concerned with attempts by Marxists to equate class position with technical function in the social organisation of production—for example, the attempts by Poulantzas and others to differentiate between proletariat and petty bourgeoisie in terms of a distinction between productive and unproductive labour. Finally it considers the role of management and the position of managers in the light of the possibility of possessing agents other than human subjects.

Relations of production

In his analysis of capitalist production Marx presents the position of the labourer with regard to the means of production in terms of a relation of separation. The labourer is separated from his means of production in the double sense that, first, they are the legal property of another (the capitalist) and second, that the capitalist rather than the labourer has the capacity to set the means of production to work. It is because he retains the effective capacity to set the means of production to work that the capitalist (or his agent) plays a vital role in the organisation and co-ordination of the capitalist labour process. It is for this reason that the labourer can work only on condition that he sells his labour-power to a capitalist and agrees to work under his supervision. The worker receives his wages and the capitalist receives the product of the labour process. The capitalist has effective possession of the means of production while the labourer is effectively separated from them and it is the distinctive character of capitalist forms of possession and separation that governs both the mode of distribution of the product between capitalists and labourers and the forms of organisation of the labour process that are possible (complex co-operation, division of labour in the workplace, etc.).

By contrast, in 'The Genesis of Capitalist Ground-Rent' in *Capital*, vol. 3, Marx treats the direct producer in pre-capitalist agricultural production as the possessor of his means of production. He therefore argues that exploitation under those conditions is not a function of *possession* by members of the exploiting class but rather of more or less direct coercion exercised by that class over the producers:

> It is . . . evident that in all forms in which the direct labourer remains the 'possessor' of the means of production and labour conditions necessary for the production of his own means of subsistence, the property relationship must simultaneously appear as a direct relation of lordship and servitude, so that the direct producer is not free. . . . Under such conditions the surplus-labour for the nominal owner of the land can only be extorted from (the direct producers) by other than economic pressure, whatever the form assumed may be. . . . Thus conditions of personal dependence are requisite, a lack of personal freedom, no matter to what extent, and being tied to the soil as its accessory, bondage in the true sense of the word. . . . (*Capital*, vol. 3, p. 790)

It is clear that in this and other similar passages Marx is not attempting a systematic conceptualisation of pre-capitalist production but is rather concerned to make use of pre-capitalist forms in order to highlight certain distinctive features of capitalist production. However, the contrast Marx draws, which has been taken over by a majority of Marxist historians in dealing with pre-capitalist societies, is seriously inadequate. It has been criticised at length in chapter 5 of *Pre-Capitalist Modes of Production* and it will be enough for present purposes simply to outline the major problems generated by the attempt to conceptualise pre-capitalist economic class-relations in terms of the non-separation of producers from the means and conditions of production.

Notice first that the pertinence of 'other than economic pressure' is by no means restricted to the conditions Marx specifies.

Capitalist forms of possession are equally dependent on definite legal and political conditions of existence. In particular they presuppose legal definition and sanction of private property in the means of production. Otherwise there would be nothing to prevent the labourers from ignoring the capitalists and simply setting their own means of production to work as and when they chose. Marx himself makes a similar point by means of the example of Mr Peel:

> Mr. Peel took with him from England to Swan River, West Australia, means of subsistence and of production to the amount of £50,000. Mr. Peel had the foresight to bring with him besides, 3,000 persons of the working class, men women and children. Once arrived at his destination, 'Mr. Peel was left without a servant to make his bed or fetch him water from the river.' Unhappy Mr. Peel who provided for everything except the export of English modes of production to Swan River. (*Capital*, vol. 1, p. 766)

If productive property is available for the taking then the supply of labourers cannot be taken for granted. Economic class-relations always presuppose definite non-economic conditions of existence. What is distinctive in Marx's account of the case where the labourer possesses his own means of production is not so much that 'other than economic pressure' is a condition of existence of economic class-relations but rather that class-relations appear to consist of nothing but these non-economic forms of extortion.

In effect Marx's argument posits relations of production that are essentially non-economic. Where the labourers possess their means of production exploitative class-relations take the form of coercive relationships having no function in the organisation of production. Relations of production have no bearing on production itself. In this conception it seems that feudal lords must appear as parasites pure and simple: they cream off a portion of what is produced on their estates and they play no further part in the organisation of production. Since feudal lords take no part in the organisation of production it makes no difference to that organisation whether feudal relations are present or absent or are replaced by some other mode of creaming off a portion of the product, taxation, fraud, banditry, 'protection', and so on. The concept of *feudal* relations of production must then lose all specificity: *either* all modes of appropriation of the product from possessing agents must be assimilated into a single category *or* they must be differentiated according to the specific legal, political, and cultural means employed. In the second case the principle of differentiation of pre-capitalist relations of production must be essentially arbitrary in the sense that it cannot be derived from and has no bearing on the organisation of production itself.

This arbitrariness is particularly clear in Anderson's discussion of feudalism in the Conclusion of *Lineages of the Absolutist State*. Anderson follows Marx's argument that exploitation in pre-capitalist societies operates through extra-economic coercion. In consequence he maintains: 'pre-capitalist modes of production cannot be defined *except* via their political, legal and ideological superstructures, since these are what determines the type of extra-economic coercion that specifies them' (*Lineages of The Absolutist State*, p. 404).

The distinct forms of political, legal, and ideological superstructure define distinct modes of production. Anderson's position therefore leads to a series of essentially arbitrary typological distinctions since there is no theoretical basis for determining the pertinence of any superstructural distinctions. Thus, after defining feudalism in the manner of traditional Marxist historiography Anderson argues that there were important differences between European and Japanese feudalism:

> within the intra-feudal relationship between lord and overlord, above the village level, vassalage tended to predominate over benifice: the 'personal' bond of homage was traditionally stronger than the 'internal' bonds of investiture. . . . The expressive 'order' of the lord-vassal relationship was provided by the languages of kinship, rather than the elements of law: the authority of the lord over his follower was more patriarchal and unquestionable than in Europe. (*ibid.*, p. 414)

These differences pose a real problem for Anderson's argument. Given his earlier insistence on the necessity of distinguishing between different legal and political configurations Anderson can hardly maintain that, in spite of superstructural differences, European and Japanese feudalism are instances of the same mode of production. The problem of course is that once political, legal, and cultural differences are thought to distinguish distinct relations of production there can be no theoretical grounds for maintaining that differences in the forms of law and politics represent *either* distinct relations of production *or* merely different instances of the same essential relations. The demarcation between pre-capitalist relations of production must therefore be reduced to a matter of theoretically arbitrary *fiat*.

But, to return to Marx's argument, there is a significant contradiction in his account of the relations between the labourer and the 'nominal owner of the land'. On the one hand the labourers possess their own means of production and on the other hand they are unfree, 'being tied to the soil as its accessory.' On the one hand the 'nominal owner of the land' plays no part in the organisation of production and on the other hand he controls his land and his bondsmen's access to it. The contradiction here is clear: since land is an indispensable means of agricultural production Marx's 'direct labourer' cannot possess the totality of his means and condition of production if he does not also possess his land. If the labourer is unfree and 'tied to the soil as its accessory' then what Marx describes as 'the nominal owner of the land' is in fact the possessor of an indispensable means of production. But to say that is to say that economic class-relations between, say, feudal lords and serfs are a function of possession of the land by the lords and the correlative separation from it of the serfs. *Pre-Capitalist Modes of Production* has argued that the feudal landowner does play a crucial role in the organisation of production not only with regard to the divisions of the land between different uses and its allocation to peasant households but also with regard to the provision of certain means of production operating at a scale beyond that of the individual peasant (for example, large-scale drainage works, flour-mills, etc.).

Now, if feudal landowners possess the land then the specificity of feudal relations of production must be defined in terms of a definite mode of possession of an indispensable means of production. Feudal relations of production are economic relations, they are relations of possession and separation. We must therefore distinguish between feudal, or other non-capitalistic relations of production, their legal, political, and cultural conditions of existence and the forms in which those conditions of existence are satisfied. In failing to make these distinctions Marx's argument effectively dissolves pre-capitalist economic relations into legal, political, and cultural forms and therefore leads to a disjunction between the sphere of production and possession on the one hand and that of economic class-relations on the other.

Possession and separation

We have argued, against Marx's position in his analysis of ground-rent, that economic class-relations must be conceived in terms of the effective possession of the means of production by one category of economic agents and the consequent effective separation of another category of agents. *Possession in Separation* is therefore the crucial concept for the analysis of classes: the modes of possession and of separation and the forms of what is effectively possessed distinguish the different types of class-relation. In all cases, however, effective possession involves a capacity to control the functioning of means of production in the process of production and to exclude others from their use. We shall argue that the possessing agent has a definite and necessary role to play in the functioning of the means of production in his possession. In this sense the analysis of possession must always involve analysis of the unit of production. Effective possession is not to be identified with the legal concept of ownership or with the performance of certain functions of direction. The joint-stock company, for example, is an economic agent distinct from its shareholders and its managerial employees. It is the company, rather than its shareholders, that exercises effective possession of its means of production and it employs managerial wage-labour to perform the tasks of direction and supervision. (The question of management is discussed more fully in Chapter 12.) Correlatively effective separation from certain means of production implies that the use of those means can take place only under some form of control by their possessor, and it means that the possessor can therefore exert some control over the distribution of the product or the use of those means. Thus, for each mode of possession in separation we have a class of possessors and a class of separated non-possessors. For example, in the case of capitalist relations of production, the capitalist possesses various instruments and raw material in the form of commodities, and workers may engage in production only on condition that they sell their own commodity, labour-power, to the capitalist. Here the capitalist controls and organises the production process in which he brings together certain commodities at the beginning of the process so as to obtain other commodities at the end. The capitalist sells, or tries to sell, his products to other capitalists or to workers. Thus capitalist possession of the means of production involves a definite form of organisation of the production process in which labour-power is purchased, under definite contractual conditions, from the worker by the capitalist and enters production as his property, as one commodity amongst others. And it involves a definite form of distribution of the product, through commodity exchange and the division between wages and profits.

Two further examples are worth considering since they concern cases where the possessor of some means of production is separated from the possession of others. Class-relations do not merely concern the separation of *labourers* from the means of production, for petty commodity producers and capitalists may themselves confront classes who possess certain of their necessary means of production. Thus landowners may confront capitalists as a definite class by reason of their exclusive possession of a finite and necessary condition of production (for farmers and industrialists alike). The landowner, in effect, manages an estate by regulating the uses to which different portions of his land are put by the tenants and by virtue of his control over the provision of means and conditions of production, such as drainage or irrigation, which may extend beyond the land of any one tenant. By virtue of this effective possession the landowner obtains a definite economic return in the form of rent payments, charges for the right to introduce changes in tenanted property (erection of new buildings, changes in field boundaries, etc.), and in the value of the property that reverts to the owner at the close of the period of tenancy. The landowner's possession is effective through the competition of capitalists for the rental of land and is dependent on legal recognition and defence of landed property. His economic return is a function of the conditions which determine the level of rent, and other charges, that can be extracted from capitalist tenants. These conditions may include political interventions by the State such as, for example, the Corn Laws which affected the level of agricultural prices, and therefore of rent. In this case we have two modes of effective possession and consequently two forms of control over production (the landowner manages his estate while the capitalist directs the immediate production process) and two forms of distribution of the product (between landowners and capitalists and between capitalists and workers). The existence of a landowning class is not a necessary consequence of capitalist forms of possession but it may arise from the social relations of particular social formations as a result of definite political, legal, and economic conditions. Similarly, petty commodity producers may confront forms of merchant's capital which provide the conditions necessary for these producers' insertion into a social division of labour by means of, say, long-distance trade. This position gives merchant's capital control over the conditions of realisation of commodities produced. Again, this form of dominance of merchant's capital is not a necessary consequence of all forms of petty commodity production. It depends on a specific division of labour between definite social formations under particular conditions of exchange.

These examples are enough to show that, under definite social conditions, the possession in separation of *certain* of the 'means of production' can provide the foundation for economic class-relations. They also demonstrate the importance of a clear specification of what is entailed in the general concept 'means of production'. The 'means of production' are sometimes conceived, as in some of Marx's analyses, as instruments of production, that is, as elements of the production process distinct from both the objects of labour and the labourer. But the examples of landownership and of slavery (in which the slave is separated from all 'means of production' including his own labour-power) indicate that the object of labour (land) and the labourer may be the objects of an exclusive possession and that such possession may serve as the basis of class-relations. Similarly, the example of merchant's capital shows that conditions outside the immediate production process (the conditions of realisation of the commodities purchased) may be the objects of an exclusive possession. If the concept 'means of production' is restricted to the instruments of production then it cannot form the sole foundation for relations of possession and separation.

Thus, for the analysis of economic class-relations it is necessary to generalise the concept 'means of production' to include whatever conditions of production may be the object of an exclusive possession. 'Means of production' must then be defined as: *all the conditions necessary to the operation of a particular labour process which are combined in the units of production in which that process takes place.* If any of these conditions is the object of an effective possession by a definite category of agents and if the agents who operate or direct the labour process are separated from them then that possession provides the basis for class-relations. We shall see that class-relations may be distinguished on the basis of the relations to the labour process established by different forms of exclusive possession.

This general definition of 'means of production' requires that relations between the 'unit of production' or 'enterprise' and the systems of circulation or distribution of the conditions of production must be analysed if class-relations are to be rigorously determined. That analysis must be conducted for the social relations of specific social formation, and those relations cannot be deduced from any investigation of the ownership of units of production alone. Analysis of class-relations necessarily involves the theorisation of units of production and of their modes of articulation with the social relations of distribution of the means of production and of the product of these means.

The forms of distribution of the conditions of production to the units of production may themselves, under certain conditions, be the locus of class-relations. A division of social labour, that is, the division of the production of society into distinct branches producing different specialised categories of product, which operates through commodity circulation, will in general have the consequence that units of production may obtain the means of production through simple sales and purchases; exchanges are the distribution of forms of *possession* different in content. Where, however, a definite category of agents monopolises the means of circulation for a category of units of production, as in our example of merchant's capital and long-distance trade, then it may have a control amounting to effective possession of certain of the means of production. This may be so if the conditions of production depend upon the realisation of the product circulated. If so, then merchant's capital can impose its prices for reasons additional to the discrepancy between its purchases and sales; it controls through its monopoly interdiction of circulation and reproduction of the means of production (successive sales and purchases being the production-realisation-reproduction cycle for the petty producer). Here a limited social division of labour and the commodity-relations corresponding to it provide the foundation for class-relations. Successive cycles of sales and purchases reproduce the control merchant's capital exercises over the condition of production, the petty commodity producer obtains them under conditions which subordinate him to the terms of exchange imposed by merchant's capital. Hence struggles for 'free', i.e.

non-monopoly, trade have often been directly pertinent to economic class-relations. Merchant's capitalist monopolies allied with absolutist or capitalist States have used State power and their own armed forces to suppress independent capitalist traders and the development of competitive market-relations. Class-relations stem from the mode and terms of combination with the means of production imposed upon the separated non-possessor.

In the analysis of what the means-conditions of production *are* and the forms of their possession and distribution, it is essential to avoid the economistic reduction of these forms to technique and the concentration of analysis on the immediate forms of the labour process. It is necessary to abandon the forms of economism which make the process of production essentially prior to and determinant of circulation and distribution. However, not all relations of circulation and distribution are the locus of class-relations. To constitute class-relations the interdiction of circulation/distribution must control necessary conditions of production and the effect of the cycle of production/distribution must be to reproduce this capacity of control in the hands of a definite category of agents.

It follows that a crucial part of the analysis of the class relations in a social formation is a theoretical analysis of the division of social labour, the mode of articulation of production with the distribution of the conditions of production, and an analysis of the characteristic forms of unit of production. The social division of labour, and therefore class-relations, cannot be fully determined without theorisation of these forms. The social relations of production cannot in general be conceived solely as the relations between the 'direct producers' and their 'exploiters' (the agents who appropriate the surplus product from the direct producer). This is a major defect of the mode of analysis followed in *Pre-Capitalist Modes of Production* since in that text all other class-relations are considered as auxiliary or secondary. Hence its failure to consider or theorise petty commodity production, merchant's capital, etc., and to analyse forms of reproduction process. These points confirm the argument of the preceding chapters concerning the necessity of displacing mode of production as a primary object of analysis and of replacing it by social formation conceived as a determinate form of economic class-relations, their conditions of existence, and the forms in which those conditions are provided.

Labourer and non-labourer

> The essential difference between the various economic forms of society, between, for instance, a society based on slave labour and one based on wage-labour, lies only in the mode in which this surplus-labour is in each case extracted from the actual producer, the labourer. (*Capital*, vol. 1, p. 217)

Here and in other passages Marx represents relations of production as so many types of relation between labourers (direct producers) on the one hand and the non-labourers who exploit by appropriating their surplus labour on the other. In this respect the classics of Marxism have conceived the distinctive feature of classless societies, primitive communism, socialism, and communism as being that the means of production are the collective property of the labourers themselves. This has generally meant that the relations of production distribute the means of production to units composed of labourers without the intervention of possessing non-labourers and, consequently, that the distribution of the product of those means of production takes a non-exploitative form.

But what are 'labourers' and 'non-labourers'? If the category of 'non-labourer' is to include all economic agents who are not, in some sense, direct producers then the status of more and more functions must become problematic as the division of social labour becomes more complex. The category of 'non-labourer' has suffered from a lack of clear definition in Marxist theory. It is used, but not defined rigorously or consistently, in *Pre-Capitalist Modes of Production*. The analysis of the slave and feudal modes of production in that text render the concept of non-labourer confused and problematical since both the slave-owner and the feudal landowner play a crucial role in the organisation of production. This lack of definition is related to two features of classical Marxism. First, the dominance of 'exploitation' as the form of the analysis of relations of production results in a tendency to identify the appropriator of the surplus product and the non-labourer. This is particularly true, for example, of the classical conception of feudalism in which the feudal landlord class is thought to play no part in the organisation of production but rather to be totally parasitic and to appropriate the surplus product by coercive means. Second, Marxism is plagued by a 'philosophy of labour' in which the (manual) labourer is conceived as the agency of transformation of raw material and as the sole creator of value. This involves a tendency to concentrate analysis of production on the labourer and, in effect, to consider other agents as secondary or ancillary to the 'direct producer'.

In fact the categories of 'labourer' and 'non-labourer' are totally inadequate to the analysis of class-relations and they entail a serious misrepresentation of the respective functions of possessing and non-possessing agents in the organisation of production. Both categories must be displaced if they are not to obscure the relationship between the division of functions technically necessary to an economy (the technical division of labour) and the forms of possession of and separation from the means of production (the social division of labour). It is necessary to replace the distinction between labourer and non-labourer by a more complex conception of the relations between technical functions and possession.

Consider what is involved in the concept of effective possession of the means of production. We have seen that each particular mode of possession of means of production involves a capacity to control the functioning of those means in the process of production. The existence of that capacity must require the performance of certain technical functions, by or on behalf of, the possessing agent. For example, under capitalist conditions elements of production including labour-power enter the production process in the form of commodities purchased by the capitalist. His capacity to control the functioning of those commodities in the production process therefore involves him in the direction and supervision of the labour process and, since he is working with *commodities*, in the calculation of monetary costs and returns. If those functions are not performed by the capitalist or on his behalf then he ceases to have effective possession of the means of production: either those means enter into another possession or they do not enter into production. Similarly for members of the landowning class discussed above: while they may play no part in the direction and supervision of the immediate labour process their effective possession of land let out to capitalist tenants depends on the performance of definite technical functions in the determination of what types of production may take place in different parts of the estate, in the determination of the level of rent and other charges, and so on.

These examples will suffice to illustrate a general point, namely that each form of effective possession presupposes a corresponding differentiation of technical functions in production such that certain functions are performed by or on the part of the possessing agent. Conversely, it is clear that the modes of possession impose definite limits on the technical functions that are possible: the functions of direction and supervision and the physical operation of many types of machine and of production processes presuppose modes of possession in which a plurality of labourers may be brought together in a single unit of production; the function of estate management presupposes the existence of landed estates; and so on. The connections between the social and the technical divisions of labour is therefore that each imposes definite limits on what is possible for the other. In particular:

1 The differentiation of certain technical functions (direction, supervision, co-ordination, manual labour) is a condition of existence of certain forms of effective possession of the means of production. However, this point should be interpreted with great care. To say that a particular differentiation of functional tasks is a condition of existence of a particular mode of effective possession is not necessarily to say that those tasks are executed by members of different classes. The differentiation of functional tasks is also an effect of the division between mental and manual labour and of the existence of particular forms of managerial organisation—and these are not reducible to any simple effect of class-relations. Thus, capitalists may employ specialist managerial agents who are no less separated from the means of production than the manual labourers whom they direct. The crucial point here is that certain functional tasks must be performed *by or on the part of the possessing agent.* The significance of the qualification 'on the part of' will be considered in the next chapter. For the present it is enough to notice that there may be a distinction between the 'responsibility' for the performance of certain tasks and their execution such that one devolves to the possessing agent and the other to his employee.

2 Effective possession presupposes that the means and conditions of production are distributed to units of production in a manner which provides the foundation for the monopolisation by a definite category of agent of certain of these means and conditions and thereby for the control they exercise over production.

The connection of possession and function, that certain functions are occupied as a consequence of possession and others as a consequence of the separation associated with it, makes possible a rigorous specification of the social division of labour. It does not follow that agents who possess in separation certain of the means of production have no place in the technical division of labour, rather the occupancy of places in it, is as a function of the social division. *Forms of possession which involve a corresponding separation may result (depending on the means of production possessed) in the distinction of the function of the* direction of the *means of production from other functions and the determination by the possessor of the occupancy of that function*. Thus, for example, co-ordination, a technically necessary function in any process of production combining various activities to a single end, is a function that devolves onto the capitalist or his agent in the capitalist modes of production.

The technical division of labour is dependent on the social relations of production, in the sense that it is the relations between the agents which create the conditions of existence for certain forms of technical division of labour (an example is the forms of organisation of the labour process which are an effect of slavery, see *Pre-Capitalist Modes of Production*, ch. 3). However, the places created in this socially conditioned technical division are necessary places, functions necessary to the relation of production and circulation, or to the process of production as a complex of phases and techniques. It follows that agents like capitalists and slave-masters may perform technically necessary functions within the forms conditioned by the relations of production, they are not pure 'exploiters' without economic function. Their control of the product is a function of their control or direction of the process of its production.

The effects of a philosophy of labour in creating the category of 'labour' (= transformative activity) makes the capitalist a 'non-labourer'. The problems of whether capitalists 'work' or not is irrelevant to the analysis of the connection between relations of possession and economic functions. The 'non-labourer', like the categories of 'productive' and 'unproductive' labour, derives from a conception in which the *source* of the surplus product is the dominant problem. This source is the labour of transformation, non-labourers appropriate the products of the direct labourer. The problem with this analysis is that it supposes a discrepancy between production and the relations of production, as if the activities of the direct producers can be considered as a distinct process with a labour product (attributable to the labour of transformation) upon which are superimposed the relations of production which appropriate this product. Where this discrepancy is evident, as in the classical concept of feudal rent, then the linkage of production and appropriation is based upon coercion (direct or ideological). Capitalism does not involve such coercion as its basis of appropriation of the surplus product because an unequal exchange is inscribed in forms of equal exchange. Marx clearly argues that the capitalist performs the technically necessary function of co-ordination, he calls it 'a productive job, which must be performed in every combined mode of production' (*Capital*, vol. 3, p. 376). In terms of the analysis in vol. 1, however, the capitalist is a 'non-labourer'—his activities are necessary but as a preliminary to the process of transformation of the product by labourers which is a process of the expansion of value. Labour conceived as the agency of transformation and as the source of value must reduce the capitalist to a 'non-labourer'. The 'exploiter' cannot be a producer of what he appropriates.

The difficulty with this form of connection of production and the relation of production is that it cancels out the effectivity of the relations themselves. The 'non-labourer's' activities (a function of the articulation of the technical and the social divisions of labour) materially affect the forms and level of production and do not merely appropriate a portion of a given labour product as the 'surplus product'. Thus, for example, a feudal landlord (e.g. a monastic order, cf. Kosminsky) maximises the proportion of the estate devoted to demesne land, organises production on it more rationally than the tenants do their own plots, and closely supervises the labour services performed by the tenants—by these actions the product on the demesne land is increased. Similarly, the capitalist and functionaries have a direct effectivity on the level and forms of production. This is clearly recognised in *Capital* (vol. 1 on 'relative surplus value') but only in terms of the problems of value analysis. The origin of the product and value in transformative labour prefigures the activities of the capitalist—the effects of capitalist calculation, organisation, and supervision are represented in terms of the intensification of labour and the increasing rate of exploitation. The product and the surplus value inscribed in it have their origin in the labour performed; a process the capitalist makes possible but in which he plays no direct part. Once the function of transformation is recognised as an effect of the process and not simply of certain of its agents, then the whole 'labourer'/'non-labourer' problem disappears. The displacement of the question of the source of profit, and the essentialisation of labour associated with it, makes possible the recognition of the effects of investment decisions, innovations in technique and methods of production organisation as changes in the productivity of the process initiated by capital. The labour contributions of the agents are not calculable in the product and are irrelevant since it is only in and through the process that they are effective. There is no need to fall into the perverse inversion of Marx's position and contend that Henry Ford and Frederick Taylor were more 'productive' as 'labourers' than the workers whose activities they revolutionised.

The notion of the 'non-labourer' obscures what is central in the articulation of the social division of labour with the technical. Functions annexed to certain categories of agents as a consequence of possession have a real effectivity on the process of production. The category 'non-labourer' hides what the possessor does, he directs the means of production he possesses in the service of an exclusive possession. Where possession confers the capacity to direct the labour process the 'non-labourer' and his agents occupy the pivotal positions in the technical division of labour and separated agents secondary ones. Appropriation of the product depends upon the possession-connection and not on the labour contributions of the agents; where the possessor directs the labour process he nevertheless occupies a technically necessary function which enables him to direct that process in the service of that possession. All appropriation as the consequence of an exclusive possession requires at least a minimum level of direction of the means of production possessed.

All class-relations depend upon forms of possession which are also forms of separation, and as a consequence combination with the means of production involves either the payment of a portion of the product for the capacity to use them, or the performance of subordinate functions in a process of production directed by the possessor. These forms of possession are sanctioned, provided with their political conditions of existence, by the State, but they are not themselves political or legal relations. The analysis here generally confirms the position argued in *Pre-Capitalist Modes of Production*, ch. 5, that class-relations are *economic* relations, that is, they are relations which are represented in the political and not forms of domination deriving from it. Far from differentiating between class-relations based upon domination and those based upon economic forms, a quite different differentiation of types of class-relations will be proposed here. This will be based on the relation between possession and function. The two types of class-relations are the following:

1 Where possession of certain of the means of production confers upon the possessing agent the capacity to direct the labour process and where the separated agent is combined with those means in a capacity subordinate to this direction.

2 Where possession of certain of the means of production confers upon the possessing agent the capacity to determine certain of the conditions of direction of the labour process, but in which its direction is a function of the possessor of other of the means of production; examples would be merchant's and usurer's capital, and certain forms of landlordship.

These two categories are not exclusive. For example, a capitalist farmer may employ wage labourers and operate under conditions of rental, maintenance, and performance imposed by a landlord. They differ in the role the possessing agent plays in relation to the labour process. The second type rests on the economic subordination of *directors of the labour process*, that is, it presupposes relations of distribution of the means of production such that forms of exclusive possession interpose themselves between these relations of distribution and the labour process. In addition to this classification, modes of possession may be distinguished according to whether they are communal or non-communal (private) in form. The implications of communal possession for the analysis of class-relations and for the mode of differentiation of technical functions will be considered in the concluding chapter.

As Marx makes clear in his *Critique of the Gotha Programme* the mode of distribution of the product is a consequence of the distribution of the means of production. It is not an effect of the technical contribution of the agents to the process of production. The distribution of the means of production enables the 'possessor' to effect a definite form of appropriation of the product and this requires of the 'possessor' a definite level of direction of the means of production sufficient to retain effective possession. The function of direction therefore fuses elements of the social and technical divisions of labour. We have seen, for example, that Marx argues that the capitalist (or his agent) performs the technically necessary function of co-ordination. The use of the category 'non-labóurer' to refer to the possessing agent is an absurdity: it recalls the petty-bourgeois philosophies of labour which Marxism attempted to displace, gospels of work and ultra-egalitarian notions of an equal distribution of the fruits of labour. The 'non-labourer' performs definite functions which are technically necessary to production. Neither the possible combinations of relations of production nor the forms in which their conditions of existence are provided can be reduced to an effect of relations between 'labourer' and 'non-labourer'. It follows that to concentrate on *that* dichotomy must be to obscure crucial theoretical problems facing Marxist analysis.

We have argued that the social and technical divisions of labour are interdependent in that each provides conditions of existence of and limitations on the other. But there is no simple correspondence between the divisions of economic agents into classes according to the modes of possession and separation on the one hand, and the technical division of labour within the unit of production or the division of the social labour force into industries as sectors on the other. This obvious point is worth stressing since it implies that there may be a whole series of differences within the total social labour force that are in no way reducible to *class* differences. A clear example would be the differences in wages and conditions of labour for different occupations in capitalist social formations. Capitalist modes of possession entail a definite form of distribution of the product (through wage payments and commodity circulation) and a corresponding form of direction and supervision of the labour process by the capitalist as his agent. Within the limits of these forms differences in the level of wages or in the conditions of labour will be the effects of differences in the markets for different types of labour, the hierarchical organisation of enterprises, the outcome of struggle between organisations of possessing and non-possessing agents, legal regulation of the wage-labour contract, and so on. Those differences are not deducible from, or effects of, the effective possession by capitalists of the means of production. In particular the manual/non-manual distinction, while it is necessary for capitalist modes of possession, is not itself a class distinction. Non-manual workers *may* be paid differently from manual workers and they may have different conditions of work but they are equally separated from the means of production. Effective possession by the capitalist presupposes a differentiation of functional tasks in which the functions of organisation of production (direction, supervision, calculation) devolve on to the capitalist or his agents. Capitalist possession therefore presupposes the division between mental and manual labour but *that* division is not itself a class division. It exists in socialist societies and, while it may be an obstacle to the complete socialisation of production, it does not vanish with the overthrow of capitalism and is by no means easy to eliminate. The division between mental and manual labour may well be pertinent to political debates and struggles but it is not a class division and it gives no basis for the location of managers as a class distinct from that of other wage labourers.

Chapter 11

Agents and Social Relations

The definition of classes in terms of different positions with regard to possession of and separation from the means of production poses the question of who or what is capable of occupying these positions. Marxism has traditionally conceived of classes as consisting of human individuals so that Lenin, for example, can define classes as:

> large groups of people, differing from each other by the place they occupy in a historically determined system of social production, by their relation, (in most places fixed and formulated in law) to the means of production, by their role in the social organisation of labour, and, consequently, by the dimensions of the social wealth of which they dispose and the mode of organising it. Classes are groups of people, one of which can appropriate the labour of another owing to the different places they occupy in a definite system of social economy. ('A Great Beginning', *Collected Works*, vol. 29, p. 421)

We have seen that classes and human individuals themselves have been conceptualised in terms of more or less sophisticated versions of two basic types of position. Either they are conceived in terms of the counterposition of subject and structure, subjective and objective conditions, social (i.e. intersubjective) relations and structures, and so on—as in Lukács, left-Weberian sociology, Poulantzas. Or forms of subjectivity and consciousness are interiorised within the conceptualisation of the structure itself—as in Althusser and his associates and in the orthodox Marxism of the second and third Internationals. Both types of position fail to conceptualise the conditions of the differential effectivity of social agents and they tend to identify the concepts of agent and human subject. In the first the agent is conceived as an independent subjectivity confronting given objective conditions and its effectivity is conceptualised only to the extent that it chooses to act in accordance with its structurally determined 'objective' interests. These versions of Marxism posit an essential autonomy on the part of the will and consciousness of subjective agencies and they therefore entail the theoretical indeterminacy and ultimate incoherence of the subjectivist sociologies and theories of history. In the second type of position the agent is reduced to a passive recipient of the forms of consciousness appropriate to its position in the structure and it is denied any independent effectivity. Marx outlines a position of this kind in his Preface to the First German Edition of *Capital*:

> But here individuals are dealt with only in so far as they are the personification of economic categories, embodiments of particular class-relations and class-interests. My standpoint, from which the evolution of the economic formation of society is viewed as a process of natural history, can less than any other make the individual responsible for relations whose creature he socially remains, however much he may subjectively raise himself above them. (pp. 20–1)

Where classical and neo-classical economic theory conceives the economic agent in terms of a definite human nature (a function of definite needs and attributes in the one case and a definite calculating psychology in the other) Marx conceives the capitalist as a personification of capital. He is the incarnation of a social force; an empty subject endowed with forms of consciousness appropriate to his social position. In *Capital*, for example in his discussions of capitalist calculation and the chapter 'Illusions Created by Competition' in vol. 3, Marx analyses the subjectivity of the capitalist as a function of appearances generated by the action of the structure itself.

The capitalist is a mere 'aliquot part' of the total social capital and the mode of experience of the appearances of its structure is universal in form. It is the same for all aliquot parts of the social capital. Thus, while he avoids a naive anthropology or psychologism through the use of this incarnation structure, Marx nevertheless presupposes a definite human nature in the form of an essential faculty of experience on the part of the human individual.

Without the intermediary of a faculty of experience the appearances of the structure would be unable to form the consciousness of the capitalists. The reduction of the capitalist to the personification of an aliquot part of social capital provides no means of conceptualising the differential effects of capitalists' calculations and organisation of enterprises on the conditions of production and of capitalist competition. If calculation by capitalists does have an effectivity, then the capitalist cannot be reduced to the personification of capital.

A distinct but related reduction of the agent to its social position can be found in Althusser, especially in 'Ideology and Ideological State Apparatuses' (*Lenin and Philosophy*) where he poses the problem of the reproduction of the relations of production. Althusser's problem and his proposed solution has been criticised by Paul Hirst in another publication ('Althusser and the Theory of Ideology'). What is of interest for the present discussion is that Althusser effectively reduces the reproduction of relations of production to the distribution of human subjects to places in the social division of labour and the endowment of those subjects with an ideological formation appropriate to the social position they are destined to occupy. The relations of production are conceived as relations between human subjects who are themselves 'personifications' of their social positions. Paul Hirst has shown that Althusser makes two related errors: first, the identification of the relations of production with the functions assigned to economic agents in the social division of labour and second, the identification of economic agents and human subjects. It is the second identification and its effects which most concern us here. Since economic agents are human subjects, it follows that the mechanisms Althusser invokes to mould agents to forms appropriate to their economic place must function by means of the structure of human subjectivity. Where Marx invokes appearances generated by the economy and a faculty of experience on the part of the individual to provide agents with suitable consciousness Althusser invokes ideological State apparatuses which function by ideology. Althusser conceives of ideology as involving a distinct level of the social formation. The ideological level is the site of ideological practice, a practice which works on men's consciousnesses by constituting representations of the imaginary relationship of individuals to their real conditions of existence. Ideology constitutes men's consciousnesses and men live in ideology in the sense that all acts of consciousness are necessarily ideological. Althusser therefore advances the double thesis: '1. there is no practice except by and in ideology; 2. there is no ideology except by the subjects and for subjects' (*Lenin and Philosophy*, p. 159).

The human subject is a creature of ideology and ideology is therefore a condition of existence of all forms of social practice. There is a duality between Althusser's conception of agents as human subjects and his conception of ideology as an integral part of all social practices. Because ideology is constitutive of the consciousness of subjects it follows that where there are subjects there must be ideology. On the other hand, since ideology is integral to any social practice and since it operates on the consciousness of subjects it follows that the agents of a social practice can be agents only if they are also subjects:

> No human, i.e. social individual, can be the agent of a practice if he does not have the *form of a subject*. The 'subject-form' is actually the form of historical existence of every individual of every agent of social practices. (*Essays in Self-Criticism*, p. 95)

Althusser's conceptions of ideology and of the agent as subject are interdependent and mutually supportive: each ensures the necessity of the other. The essential character of the human subject ensures the eternity of ideology as an ingredient of all social practices and the role of ideology as an essential ingredient of all social practices ensures that agents must have the form of subjects. Thus if we posit ideology we must also posit the agent as subject and if we posit subjects we must also posit ideology. If we accept Althusser's conception of one then we must accept his conception of the other. But why should we not reject both? Althusser provides no argument on this point. In effect his conception of the agent as subject and the correlative conception of ideology are introduced by *fiat*.

This chapter presents a tentative and provisional analysis of the concepts of agents and their social conditions of existence. It argues that there is nothing in the concept of agent to ensure that all agents must be conceived as human subjects and shows how concepts of social agents other than human individuals may be constituted. While much of the argument will be conducted primarily with reference to economic agents it should be clear that it has more general implications. The problem of the conceptualisation of agents and their conditions of existence is by no means restricted to the category of economic agent and it is equally pertinent to the conceptualisation of law and politics and of other forms of social practice.

The concept of agent as subject

An agent is an entity capable of occupying the position of a locus of decision in a social relation while a social relation is a relation between agents, possibly involving other objects, for example, means of production. A set of relations of production involves at least two categories of agent together with the means of production which they possess or are separated from. The interdependence of the concepts of agent and social relation ensures that no conceptualisation of one is possible without at least some implicit conceptualisation of the other. Thus, to posit universal attributes of agents by maintaining, say, that they must all be subjects, is to posit a correlative universality at the level of social relations—they must all be relations between subjects. Conversely, to deny universality at the level of agents is also to deny it at the level of social relations: it is to maintain that specific types of agents (social relations) can be defined only with regard to specific types of social relation (agent). To treat, for example, States as agents capable of entering into social relations is to posit types of social relations in which human individuals cannot occupy positions as agents. In the following section we argue that no universality can be posited either at the level of agents or at that of social relations and that agents or social relations must always be conceptualised by reference to specific types of social relations or agents.

But first it is necessary to consider what is entailed in the contrary position, namely, that all agents are subjects and all social relations are relations between subjects. The effect of identifying all agents as subjects is to posit a set of universal subjective attributes of will and consciousness as characteristic of all social agents. These universal attributes may allow of the differentiation of agents through the development of specialised and distinctive capacities but such capacities cannot be conceived as essential attributes of the agents concerned. In Althusser's Ideology paper, for example, the differentiation of the social labour force through the development of specialised capacities in agents—technical skills and also 'the "rules" of good behaviour, i.e. the attitude that should be observed by every agent in the division of labour, according to the job he is "destined" for' (*Lenin and Philosophy*, p. 127)—is an effect of the ideological State apparatuses and, in the case of capitalism, of the educational ideological State apparatus in particular. Ideological apparatuses work through ideology, that is, they have as their objectives the transformation of men's consciousness. In sociology the differentation of agents is conceived as a function of the free choice of ultimate values, of primary and adult socialisation operating through a variety of discrete institutions, and so on. But in all cases the development of specialised capacities on the part of agents is conceived as operating through and by means of the universal attributes of will and consciousness possessed by all subjects *qua* subject. Similarly, if agents are conceived in terms of universal subjective attributes then social relations must have a necessary and universal form: they are relations between subjects and they exist in and through the will and consciousness of subjects. Specialised social relations therefore depend on specialisation of the wills and consciousnesses of the agents participating in these relationships. Thus Althusser treats the reproduction of the relations of production as if it were equivalent to the distribution of subjects endowed with suitably specialised subjectivities to the separate positions defined by the social division of labour.

The conceptualisation of all agents in terms of universal subjective attributes poses real problems with regard to the conceptualisation of the effectivity of and differences between agents. The agent as subject may be conceived as free or as more or less unfree. Positions of the first type are advanced by Weber and the bulk of subjectivist sociology. In this case agents are constitutive of social relations not only in the limited sense that social relations can exist only through the universal attributes of agents but also in the sense that all social relations are reducible to decisions on the part of one or more agents. If agents are free then their actions and decisions cannot be conditional on social conditions outside the agents themselves. Social relations can therefore have no determinate effectivity of their own and such effectivity as they may possess is always reducible to that of the agents constituting those relations.

For Weber social relations and social collectivities:

> must be treated as solely the resultants and modes of organisation of the particular acts of individual persons, since these alone can be treated as agents in a course of subjectively understandable action. (*Theory*, p. 101)

The insistence on subjective understanding follows from the conception of agents as free subjects: if subjects are constitutive of social relations then the analysis of those relations must reduce to the analysis of the subjectivity of the agents which constitute them.

Now, to claim that agents are subjects and that they are free is to claim that certain crucial features of agents are subject to no external conditions of existence whatever. The agent's decisions and choices are the effect of its freely functioning consciousness. The contents of consciousness must therefore include not only perceptions and conceptualisations of conditions external to the subjectivity of the agent in question but also features that are in no way dependent on those conditions. In Weber's sociology these features are called 'ultimate values'. They are independent of all social and material conditions and they are freely chosen by individual human subjects. Once chosen, the agent's ultimate values govern its decisions and actions unless and until they are supplemented by the choice of other ultimate values. It has been shown elsewhere (Hindess, 'Humanism and Teleology in Sociological Theory', 1977b) that this type of position is a humanist version of a more general rationalist conception of action. This conception posits a realm of nature, an independent realm of ideas (ultimate values, meanings or whatever) and a mechanism of realisation of ideas in the realm of nature. The mechanism may be individual human subjects, as in humanist versions, or supra-individual social systems and institutions, as in anti-humanist versions. In its humanist or anti-humanist forms the rationalist conception of action presents more or less secularised variants of the traditional religious counterposition of the material and the spiritual realms with men as the pig in the middle. These conceptions are unable to reconcile the conflicting effectivity of the material and the spiritual realms: if the spirit is willing but the flesh is weak what is it that ensures the dominance of one or the other in any given situation? However, even if that problem is set aside, the rationalist conception of notion has no means of conceptualising the articulation of conflicting ideal elements, say, two opposing ultimate values. *Either* it must maintain that the ideal realm contains no inconsistent elements—in which case its accounts of social action can be shown to be vacuous. *Or* in any situation of action where two ultimate values conflict the victory of one or the other has no determinate conditions of existence. The situation is therefore indeterminate. These arguments have been developed at length in another work and they need no further elaboration here.

All forms of the rationalist conception of action are incoherent and indeterminate but the humanist versions pose additional problems of their own. The most significant in the present context concerns the conditions of existence of the actions of agents. In these conceptions it is only certain features of the agent as subject that have no determinate conditions of existence. All Weberian subjects are dependent on the satisfaction of the biological conditions of existence of human animals, and since they are free *subjects* as well as animals, they presuppose definite ideal conditions in the form of a freely floating realm of ultimate values. But the particular choice of ultimate values made by an individual subject has no determinate conditions of existence. A realm of ultimate values is a condition of existence of the *possibility* of choice but the choice itself is essentially indeterminate. In the end, therefore, to conceptualise agents as free subjects is to preclude conceptualisation of the conditions of existence of their actions.

The polar opposite to the conception of the agent as subject freely constituting actions and social relations is the view of the subject as literally the subject of (i.e. subjected to) the system of social relations in which it is implicated. The subject is the creature of its relations. Thus, for Althusser:

> the individual is interpolated as a (free) subject in order that he shall submit freely to the commandments of the Subject, i.e. in order that he shall (freely) accept his subjection, i.e., in order that he shall make the gestures and actions of his subjection 'all by himself'. There are no subjects except by and for their subjection. That is why they 'work all by themselves'. (*Lenin and Philosophy*, p. 169).

Each subject is conscious of itself as a fully acting agent. It is free in the imaginary world of its conscious representations but in reality it is the subject of its distinctive place in the structure of the social formation. In effect the subject is the passive recipient of the form of subjectivity appropriate to its position in the system of social relations but, since it is a subject, it *experiences* its subjection in the mode of freedom. Strictly speaking Althusser's subjects do not enter into relations 'which are independent of their will'. On the contrary, their wills are the product of the relations they are made to enter.

For Althusser the constitutive subject which generates social relations as an effect of its freely chosen praxis has a necessary place but it is solely in the Imaginary, in the ideological realm of forms of subjectivity and consciousness. In reality the social formation requires subjects as supports of the positions defined by its structures and social relations and its ideological State apparatuses and to ensure that subjects are indeed endowed with the subjectivities appropriate to the positions which they occupy. Subjects are not constitutive of the social formation, but they are necessary to it. Since ideological State apparatuses act on and through the consciousness of men, the provision of suitable agents as supports depends on the agents being already constituted as subjects. The specialised capacities of agents are an effect of the structure of the social formation, but their universal subjective attributes, which are necessary if the specialised capacities are to be formed at all, are not. They are presupposed by the structure, not constituted within it. As subjects agents are endowed with a faculty of experience which allows them to receive and to interiorise the forms of subjectivity appropriate to the position they will occupy in the structure. The functioning of the structure therefore presupposes subjects with the universal attributes of the knowing subject. Althusser does attempt to theorise mechanism of formation of subjects, but, as Paul Hirst has shown, his attempt is ineffective since the mechanism he postulates presupposes precisely what has to be explained, namely the subjective faculty of experience. Thus, far from being a systematic anti-humanism in the sense of conceptualising a subjectless structure, Althusser's conception of the social formation requires the concept of subject, a concept which is not itself theorised but is simply incorporated as a necessity.

Now consider the problem of conceptualising the actions of agents in Althusser's theory. Subjects are free agents only in the realm of the Imaginary. In reality they are always the subjects of their place in the structure of the social formation and such effectivity as they may appear to possess is merely the effectivity of their place in the structure. The difficulty with this conception is that it provides no means of conceptualising the differential effectivities of the actions of different agents. The action of any one agent is a function of its subjectivity, of the perceptions and calculations provided for it by the structure as precisely the subjectivity necessary to the performance of the functions defined by its position in the structure. The action of the agent, that is to say, is strictly reducible to the function it performs in the structure of the whole. And the same holds true of every other agent. Differences between agents therefore reflect differences in the functions necessary to the existence of the structure. Now recall that Althusser regards all social relations as relations between subjects, that is, as existing solely in and through the consciousness of the agents participating in those relations—so that the reproduction of the relations is strictly equivalent to the reproduction of suitably endowed agents in appropriate positions. Since the social formation consists in the totality of its social relations, and the reproduction of those relations is an effect of the structure itself, we must conclude that the structure reproduces itself as a necessary effect of its own existence. Thus, Althusser's conceptualisation of agents as the subjects of the structure returns us to the form of structural causality in which, as we have seen, the structure is to be conceived as 'eternity in Spinoza's sense' (*Reading Capital*, p. 107). How then are we to conceive the differences between agents and the consequences of those differences? The conditions of existence of each agent and of each action of that agent are given in the structure. But if they are all equally the effects of the structure then how are we to account for their specificity? If there are differences between one effect of the structure and another it cannot be the action of the structure alone which differentiates them. By reducing the distinctive and specialised capacities of all agents to effects of the structure Althusser effectively denegates their specificity. He therefore reproduces the structure of what he castigates as an expressive totality in which all phenomena are effects of a single inner essence—they are all effects of the structure.

Finally, of course, there are a variety of positions which fall between the polar types discussed above. These involve either a non-individualistic version of the rationalist conception of action which purports to subordinate the actions of human individuals to the functioning of supra-individual social mechanisms (social and cultural systems for example) or a counterposition of subject and structure. The first type has been discussed in another publication

(Hindess, 'Humanism and Teleology') which shows that while they escape the more absurd consequences of an individualistic theoretical humanism they cannot avoid the more general problems of the rationalist conception of action. They are incoherent and theoretically indeterminate. The second type has been examined in the discussion of classes in Chapter 7. We have seen that while they affirm the irreducibility of subject to structure they can conceptualise the effectivity of subjects only to the extent that their actions accord with the 'objective' interests defined by the structure—that is, to the extent that they act as if they were reducible to the structure. Whether they are conceived as free or as the more or less unfree creatures of their social relations the conceptualisation of agents in terms of universal subjective attributes can provide no means of conceptualising the effectivity and conditions of existence of particular agents and the particular actions they undertake.

Agents and the conditions of existence of agents

An agent is a locus of decision within one or more social relations and the locus of action as a function of the decisions it takes. Agents differ from other objects which enter into social relations not only in the sense that they may effect movement and changes but also in the sense that their actions are dependent on decisions. A piston-rod may act on a crankshaft but it does so because of a definite mechanical connection between them. It does not *decide* whether to act on the crankshaft or not. An industrial capitalist deploys labourers and means of production within the confines of a definite enterprise or enterprises but he does so solely as a function of his decisions on the one hand and of the social relations which allow them to be effective on the other.

How are agents and the decisions they take to be conceptualised? In the preceding section we have considered one type of answer, namely that agents must be conceived in terms of universal subjective attributes. To be an agent is to be a subject: it is to act in terms of the functioning of a will and a consciousness endowed with a faculty of experience. A subject may be conceived as free or as more or less unfree. We have seen that if it is free then its particular decisions can have no determinate conditions of existence. On the other hand if it is free only in the imaginary realms of consciousness, if in reality it is the creature of its social relations, then its 'freely made' decisions in fact dissolve into effects of the structure of the social formation. The social formation is then reduced to an expressive totality in which each of its agents merely express what is given in their perceptions of the whole. The structure is then a self-generating spiritual essence—an 'eternity in Spinoza's sense'—whose existence suffices to secure the totality of its conditions of existence. These polar positions effectively preclude the possibility of conceptualising the conditions of existence and effectivity of particular agents and their actions either by denying the possibility of determinate conditions of existence altogether for certain crucial features of agents or by dissolving the specificity of agents and their actions in the universality of the structure. Intermediate positions counterpose the freedom of subjectivity to the determinism of the structure, thereby taking on some of the fundamental problems of both polar types.

These positions share a common essentialism and a common problem. Their essentialism consists in the presumption that to be a locus of decision is to partake of a decision-making essence and of the universal attributes necessary to the functioning of that essence—to be a locus of decision is to be a subject, it is to partake of the essence of subjectivity. Their common problem is generated by their essentialism: how can differences between agents be conceptualised as a function of a common essence? Either the differences are real and inexplicable (they have no determinate conditions of existence) or they are unreal and determinate (they are just so many expressions of the same essential structure of the social formation)—or else they are somewhere in between.

If we are to avoid essentialism and its problems then the question of the conditions of existence of agents must be carefully posed. To pose the question of the agent as a universal question independent of any determinate conditions is to require that the answer be unconditional and therefore essentialist. Instead the question must be posed in relation to the determinate conditions in which the agent as locus of decision must operate. Since agents function as loci of decisions in determinate positions in determinate social relations it follows that an important part (but by no means all) of these conditions must depend on the social relations in which the agents participate. To say that the question of the conditions of existence of agents must be posed, *inter alia*, with reference to the social relations in which they participate is to say that they are not constituted by the possession of universal attributes.

To illustrate what is involved here let us consider the case of relations of production and the agents implicated in them. Relations of production have been conceived in terms of determinate forms of possession of and separation from the means of production. Effective possession involves a capacity to control the functioning of means of production in the process of production and to exclude others from their use. Effective separation therefore implies that the use of these means can take place only under some form of control by the possessing agent and it means that the possessor can exact some control over the distribution of the product of the use of those means. In the case of capitalism the elements of the production process take the form of commodities: means of production are possessed as commodities and the distribution of products takes the form of commodity exchange.

Capitalists purchase means of production and they purchase labour-power in exchange for wages. What does this tell us about the agents implicated in capitalist production? Consider first the capitalist, the agent of possession. If an agent is to function as a capitalist it must be capable of possessing commodities and of entering into contracts to buy and sell commodities. That is, it must be legally recognised as an agent for the purposes of the law of property and the law of contract. Next, the capitalist must have the effective capacity to control the functioning of the means of production in its possession. This involves two things. First, since means of production take the form of commodities, their control must involve the capitalist in some definite form of monetary calculation with regard to decisions on pricing and purchasing, the scale of production, and so on, and also with regard to the monitoring of the different parts of the production process. Second, the capitalist requires some means to implement its decisions: it must be able to issue instructions to its employees and it must possess the means of more or less effective supervision of their conduct. Similarly, if we consider the agent of separation, the labourer, it is clear that this too must be legally recognised as an agent for the purpose of the law of property and the law of contract. It must also be able to receive and to act on instructions and it must have the capacity (or at least the potential) to work the means of production in question.

These points tell us something but they do not tell us a great deal about the conditions of existence of the agents of possession and separation implicated in capitalist production. If agents are to be the agents of capitalist production there must be a law of contract and of property which recognises them as agents. If agents are to engage in monetary calculation then, since monetary calculation is not an inborn human attribute, definite modes of calculation must be culturally available and they must be disseminated through definite forms of training. Similarly for the labourers—if they are to work the capitalist means of production then the techniques of working them must be culturally available and there must be some means of training agents in their use. In these cases certain features of the legal system or of culturally available techniques of calculations and of working appear as conditions of existence of capitalist forms of possession and separation and of the agents implicated in them. We have seen that the relations of production do not generate their own conditions of existence and they do not govern the forms in which they are provided. The concept of capitalist relations of production entails certain abstract and general conditions which forms of law or of culturally available techniques must satisfy if they are to be compatible with capitalist production. But within those conditions there may be considerable variation in the forms of law of property and of contract and in the forms of monetary calculation and of working.

There is nothing here to tell us that the agents of capitalist production must be human individuals. The capitalist must be recognised as an agent for the purposes of the law of contract and the law of property but there is no reason why the category of agents recognised for such purposes should be restricted to human individuals. The category of agents capable of operating as a capitalist is a function of the legal system of the social formation in question. For example, a series of Acts in mid-nineteenth century Britain, beginning with the Joint-Stock Companies Act of 1844, established the possibility of joint-stock, limited liability companies. Before that time agents capable of functioning as capitalists were, with some exceptions, restricted to the category of human individuals satisfying certain minimum conditions and to partnerships (with unlimited liability) formed by such individuals. The Act of 1844 and those that followed it established a new category of economic agent capable of functioning as a locus of decision and of entering into contracts with employees and other agents. The shareholder's liabilities are limited to the portion of his shares not paid for (if any) and his rights are limited to receipt of the Annual Report, the right to attend an Annual Meeting and any special meeting that may be called, the right to vote on a limited range of matters affecting company policy, and a right to share in whatever remains if the company is broken up and after outstanding obligations have been settled. The joint-stock company is a legal agent and a locus of economic decision distinct from its shareholders. It is an excellent example of an agent that is recognised by law for certain purposes and is not recognised as an agent at all for others: it may own property and enter into contract but it cannot marry. In this case the forms of British commercial law allow the possibility of agents that are specific to a strictly limited set of social relations. As for the other attributes required of an entity if it is to function as an agent of capitalist possession, it is clear that these do not require that the agent be a human individual. A capitalist must be able to calculate in commodity terms, and it must be capable of issuing instructions and of supervising the work of its employees. But there is no necessity in the concept of capitalist possession for those tasks to be performed by a single human individual. Calculation, for example, may be effected by an organisational apparatus involving both individuals and machines (e.g. computers, tabulators, and sorters, etc.) so that the products of calculation can in no way be reduced to the work of any human individual. Calculation, supervision, and the issuing of instructions may be performed by one individual or by an apparatus of employees. But if capitalist calculations and supervision *may* be performed by an apparatus there is no necessity for the capitalist to be a human individual.

Related points may be made with regard to the capitalist labourer and with regard to the agents of other forms of possession and separation. While the prevailing form of separated agent of capitalist production is certainly the human individual, the well-known examples of gang-labour in nineteenth-century Britain and of labour-only sub-contractors at the present time are sufficient to indicate the possibility of other forms. In feudal Europe it is clear that the place of feudal possessor of the land may be occupied by human individuals (feudal lords), by religious communities or by other corporate bodies (towns and cities). As with capitalism, it is the specific form of law in Europe which allows entities other than human individuals to function as a locus of economic decision, occupying the position of possession in feudal relations of production. Precisely similar points apply to conditions of slavery where what may operate as a slave-labour owner is a matter of legal definition. It is a function of the forms of law as much as of the relations of production as such.

These examples show that there is no necessity to identify economic agent and human individual. What *may* function as an agent of production, either of possession or of separation, is dependent first on the forms of possession and separation involved and then of the specific forms taken by their conditions of existence. In particular, to be an economic agent presupposes legal or customary recognition as an agent for the purposes of the pertinent relation, it presupposes the cultural availability of and dissemination of the appropriate forms of calculation and techniques, and, in the case of agents other than human individuals, it presupposes the possibility of delegation of certain tasks and performances to other agents so that performances of the agent may be directly effected by human individuals or organisational apparatus. But none of these points are peculiar to economic agents. They are pertinent to the conceptualisation of all kinds of social agent. If an agent is to function as an agent in certain relations it must be recognised as an agent for the purposes of those relations, it must be able to reach decisions and to act on them and in many cases it must be able to delegate tasks and performances to other agents. A full discussion of these requirements cannot be attempted in the context of the present chapter but it may be necessary to comment briefly on each of them.

Consider first the question of recognition. The significant points to notice here are first that the necessity of recognition as a condition of existence of agents ensures that agents must always be specific to particular social relations or categories of relations, second, that recognition is not reducible to intersubjective relations between humans and third, that social relations cannot be reduced to the agents engaged in them. To say that an agent must be recognised is to say that the conditions of existence of an agent for the purpose of a particular social relation are not reducible to the agent itself. Thus there can be no category of agent that is inherently capable of entering into all social relations. To function as a capitalist is to be recognised as an agent of the relevant type by law and by other pertinent economic agents—but that recognition cannot be effected by the would-be capitalist itself. To be an agent in a social relation is to be recognised as an agent for that relation but recognition for one relation does not entail recognition for all others. An agent recognised for the purposes of commercial relations may not be recognised for the purposes of marriage or kinship. Agents are always specific to definite social relations or categories of social relations and, conversely, there may be social relations that are specific to definite categories of agents—relations between States would be one example.

To see that recognition is not reducible to intersubjective relations it is sufficient to consider the case of capitalist economic agents. If an agent is to operate as a capitalist it must enter into commercial and contractual relations with a variety of other economic agents, it must be a legal subject of the State (for purposes of taxation, etc.) and it may have to act on behalf of the State, say, in the collection of taxes from employees and customers. This means that it must be recognised as an agent of the appropriate kind by other economic agents, by various organs of the State apparatus and by the system of commercial law. Recognition in these cases is clearly not a matter of subjective or intersubjective relations between humans: it is not a matter of one human subject acknowledging the humanity of another. For a capitalist to be recognised as an economic agent by other economic agents means to be able to buy and sell from them, to be able to exchange contracts, and to initiate or suffer legal proceedings in cases of default. Establishing these conditions is not always unproblematic: ICI may have little difficulty in obtaining recognition from actual or potential trading partners, but new or small enterprises may well need to furnish evidence of their status as *bona fide* economic agents. Legal recognition is one condition of existence of capitalist economic agents but it cannot constitute economic agents as such. If parliament were to enact legislation recognising the M6 motorway as an agent for purposes of commercial law that would in no way constitute the M6 as an economic agent. To be an agent is to be recognised as such by other pertinent agents and to be a locus of decision and action.

Legal recognition is a condition of existence of all agents engaged in relations that are subject to legal regulation. There are other relations, for example, friendship in capitalist societies and all relations in society without law and therefore without the possibility of legal recognition. But in all cases recognition of some kind is a condition of existence of an agent for purposes of a determinate social relation. The case of friendship clearly presupposes recognition by all parties involved of the others as agents of the appropriate kind. In other societies numerous categories of social relations are regulated by custom. Many kinship systems, for example, clearly prescribe the types of social relation open to different categories of agents. To be an agent in a social relation is to be recognised as an agent of the relevant type by other pertinent agents and by law or custom. Entities that are not recognised as agents play no part in any social relations. They are not social agents at all. This dependence of agents on recognition by other pertinent agents and by law or custom ensures that social relations in general cannot be reduced to the agents engaged in them.

If there are ultimate agents whose actions are constitutive of social relations then social relations are reducible to the agents engaged in them. We have argued above that to be a social agent is to be an agent in one or more social relations and that to be an agent in a social relation is to be recognised as an agent of the relevant type by other potential agents and by law or custom. The dependence of agents on recognition by other potential agents and by law or custom ensures that social relations cannot be reduced to the agents engaged in them. If the satisfaction of their conditions of existence as agents cannot be effected solely by the agents themselves then the agents cannot be constitutive of the relations. Any contrary argument must be circular in the sense that it presupposes what it has to establish. Consider the case of commercial relations in a capitalist economy. We have seen that to be an agent in these relations is to be recognised as an agent for that purpose by other pertinent agents and by law. To argue that the system of commercial relations is nevertheless reducible to the constitutive acts of agents is to argue that the agents of those relations only appear to be dependent on recognition, that the *true* agents of those relations do not have recognition as one of their conditions of existence, and, further, that recognition by law is itself reducible to the constitutive acts of agents. The difficulties of sustaining such a line of argument are clear. We have already seen that the forms of recognition of economic agents by other agents are in no way equivalent to the decision of free human subjects to recognise each other as subjects. But consider the matter of legal recognition. It may be argued that the legal apparatus of the State is dependent on the delegated actions of a variety of agents and therefore recognition by law is equivalent or reducible to recognition by agents. This argument fails, for what is pertinent here is not recognition by any agent but rather recognition by agents recognised by law as its representatives. In the last resort legal recognition depends on recognition by a court of law and by appropriate members of the legal apparatus of the State. The argument manifestly presupposes what it has to establish. But to argue that the law itself depends on recognition by agents and that legal recognition is therefore ultimately reducible to the constitutive acts of agents whose recognition constitutes the law is to fail even more drastically. First, the legal apparatus of the State is clearly not reducible to its recognition by agents. Second, the argument also presupposes what it needs to establish, namely, that the agents whose recognition is pertinent are reducible to human subjects.

Social relations, then, cannot be reduced to the agents engaged in them. In particular, they cannot be reduced to the constitutive acts of human individuals. It follows that the actions of organisations and collectivities cannot be reduced, in principle or otherwise, to the actions of individual human subjects. Thus the behaviour of a joint-stock company as a locus of decision and action cannot be analysed as if it were merely the creature of its major shareholders, directors, and senior managers. Directors and managers may be dismissed and shareholders may sell up without necessarily affecting the survival of the company or its recognition as an economic agent by other agents and by law.

Now consider the question of decisions. There are numerous cases where the locus of decision clearly cannot be identified with individual humans, the boards of companies, legislative bodies, bureaucratic apparatus and so on. What is required of an entity if it is to be a locus of decision is first, definite means of reaching decisions and second, definite means of effecting them. The second may involve both attributes of the agent and its position within definite social relations, for example where action depends on or requires the instruction of other agents. We return to this point in the discussion of delegation below. The question of decision involves the question of calculation. Decision depends on the formation of a definite conception of the situation of possible action. (It may also involve other features, for example, voting, but these need not be considered here.) Let us use the term calculation to refer to the process of formation of a definite conception of the situation of possible action. Calculation in this sense is presupposed in any decision. It is not restricted to quantitative analysis and its pertinence is not limited to the action of economic agents in a monetary economy. Political decisions are made on the basis of some conception of the conditions in which the decision is taken and in this sense they always presuppose some definite calculation. What is involved in this notion of calculation and what are its conditions of existence? It is clear, to begin with, that calculation cannot be reduced to a function of the human individual. It may be a function of definite organisation involving the action of a plurality of human individuals together, in many cases, with machines and other means of calculation (computers, card sorters, paper, etc.). For example, the central-purchasing decisions of large retail chains depend on calculations involving the processing of information through several distinct organisational levels. That calculation is performed by an organisational apparatus, not by any one human individual.

A more important point is that the conditions of calculation are never reducible to attributes of the calculating agents or to an epistemological relation of knowledge. In addition to the forms of organisation and the material means of calculation that are frequently involved, calculation always involves the processing of definite materials, reports, estimates, etc., by the use of definite conceptual and discursive means of calculation. Political decisions, for example, are made on the basis of some conception and analysis of the pertinent conditions. They therefore depend on the reports and observations employed and on the concepts, forms of argument, and other discursive means involved in the formation of that conception. There are two issues here. First, it follows from the critique of epistemology in Chapter 8 that the agent's conception of its situation of action cannot be conceptualised in terms of an epistemological relation of knowledge. As in *conception* it has, *inter alia*, definite conceptual and discursive conditions of existence, and it provides conditions of existence of definite types of decision and action, but there can be no question of it providing the agent with a more or less adequate *knowledge* of its situation. Second, to say that calculation, political, economic, or whatever, presupposes definite conceptual and discursive means of calculation is to say that it depends on social and cultural conditions that are in no way reducible to the attributes of the agent of calculation itself. It depends on the one hand on the social conditions of existence of its means of obtaining materials for analysis (e.g. the political condition in which State or party officials produce reports) and on the other on the cultural availability of the conceptual and discursive means of calculation and on the social conditions in which agents may acquire the capacity to deploy these means of calculation.

It is necessary to insist on these points since they are obscured in those discussions which seek to present numerical calculation in general, and monetary calculation in particular, as the height of rationality. Examples of such positions can be found in the economic theory of Böhm-Bawerk, the sociology of Weber and a host of related and derivative positions. One example will be enough to illustrate what is at stake. Consider Chayanov's arguments concerning the nature of peasant economy in *The Theory of Peasant Economy*. He argues that the family labour farm is the unit of production: the family, equipped with means of production, uses its labour-power to cultivate the soil and receives as the result of a year's work a certain amount of goods (*The Theory of Peasant Economy*, p. 5). Since it does not employ wage labour and its products are not produced as commodities, the peasant economy lies outside the range of forms of conceptualisation appropriate to economic calculation in the capitalist economies.

> This family labour product is the only possible category of income for a peasant or artisan family labour unit, *for there is no way of decomposing it analytically or objectively*. Since there is no social phenomenon of wages, the social phenomenon of net profit is also absent. Thus it is impossible to apply the capitalist profit calculation. (*ibid*., emphasis added)

The labour product is conceptually indivisible and Chayanov usually refers to it as a single labour income. The basic organisational feature of the peasant farm is that 'the family as a result of its year's labour receives a single labour income and weighs its efforts against the material results obtained' (*ibid*., p. 41). The family's economic activity is a function of its '*subjective* labour-consumer balance' (p. 46, emphasis added). The subjectivity of peasant calculation is necessitated, in Chayanov's account, by the absence from the farm of the categories of wages, prices, profits, etc., employed in capitalist calculation.

There are many problems with Chayanov's conception of peasant economy, but what is particularly important for the present discussion is his treatment of the difference between the use of monetary and of non-monetary categories in economic calculation as equivalent to the difference between objective and subjective forms of analysis. Whilst monetary economic calculation is or may be objective, non-monetary calculation must be subjective. The notion of the objectivity of monetary calculation depends on the conception of money as providing an objective measure of relative values. Leaving aside the question of money, which is discussed in another chapter in this book, it is clear that this conception involves a positivist epistemological conception of measurement. Here the objectivity of a measure is a matter of its correspondence with real properties of the objects measured: monetary calculation is objective because prices represent true relative values; other forms of economic calculation are not objective because they fail to represent relative values. In the absence of positivist epistemology this conception of measurement cannot be sustained. Measurement is always a function of definite conceptual and discursive means of measurement. To claim that objectivity or rationality is attributable to one set of categories only is to claim for that set of categories an unwarranted and indefensible discursive privilege.

But there is also a serious confusion in the treatment of non-monetary economic calculation as subjective. To claim that the family labour income is conceptually indivisible, that 'there is no way of decomposing it analytically or objectively', is to confuse two distinct questions, namely, the question of the conceptual and discursive means of calculation and the question of the effects of the constitution of the calculating agent on the calculation itself. Calculation depends on definite conceptual and discursive means and it depends on the practices of the calculating agent in deploying those means. In this sense the 'subjectivity' of the agent is always pertinent to the results of calculation—but that in no way precludes the pertinence of the conceptual and discursive means employed. The absence of monetary categories in no way prevents the peasant household from deploying concepts and arguments in reaching the decision to plant just so much corn, so many potatoes, and so on. To claim that, in the absence of the approved monetary categories, calculation must be subjective is to deny the pertinence of concepts and forms of argument in non-monetary calculation: it is to reduce it to an expression of the essential subjectivity of the agent.

Finally, there is the question of delegation. We have used the example of the joint-stock company to argue that there may be economic agents other than human individuals and, more generally, that there is no necessity to identify agent and human individual. Agents require definite means of reaching decisions and definite means of effecting them. In the case of agents other than human individuals satisfaction of these requirements depends on other agents acting on behalf of the agent in question—signing cheques and contracts, issuing instructions, supervising the work of others, and so on. In these cases actions are delegated to other agents so that under certain conditions the actions of delegated agents are recognised as acts of the responsible agent itself. Thus, subject to specific conditions, the signature of an officer of a company on a contract will be recognised as binding the company itself to that contract. Similarly, under appropriate conditions, instructions issued by members of senior management may be recognised as the company's instructions. The delegation of action in this sense depends on the recognition by other pertinent agents and sometimes by law or custom that certain specific agents may stand in for others. The use of delegation is not of course restricted to agents other than human individuals. It is possible, for example, for an individual to instruct a solicitor or an accountant to act on his behalf on certain matters so that certain of their actions may be legally recognised or acts of the individual concerned. However, the main interest of delegation lies in the fact that it allows for the possibility of agents all of whose actions are dependent on delegation. The joint-stock company is one obvious example but there are many others, States, churches, football teams, communities, etc. All the actions of a State, for example, are dependent on the actions of other agents. The conditions of existence of such non-human agents must therefore include the conditions of existence of delegated agents and the conditions in which they may be recognised as delegates.

Agents and human individuals

Before concluding this chapter it may be necessary to comment on the implications of these arguments for the conceptualisation of classes and class-relations. Marxism has traditionally maintained that classes do consist of human individuals and, in particular, that relations of production are essentially relations between classes, that is, between human subjects as members of distinct classes. In this conception the joint-stock company, or the religious order functioning as a feudal landowner in medieval Europe, can only appear to function as an independent locus of decision while in fact it is the creature of one or more human subjects, of its large shareholders, directors, and senior managers in one case and of bishops, abbots, and the like in the other. This conception raises questions of the position of managers, in particular, of the connections between class position on the one hand and technical function in the social organisation of production which will be discussed in the following chapter. What is significant in the present context is that human subjects must be conceived as the ultimate agents of social life in the sense that their actions alone are irreducible in principle to those of other agents and are essentially non-delegated.

We have seen that positions of this kind are fundamentally essentialist. They depend on the presumption that to be a locus of decision is to partake of a decision-making essence, which is located at the level of the human subject. The human subject itself may be conceived as the constitutive agent of social life or as the bearer of functions determined by its social position. Both positions are equally untenable and they provide no means of conceptualising the conditions of existence and the effectivity of the particular actions of particular agents. If agents are constitutive of social life then there are features of their actions (ultimate values or whatever) that have no determinate condition of existence. We have seen that the dependence of agents on recognition is sufficient to establish that they cannot be conceived as constitutive of their social relations. On the other hand to conceive as Althusser does, of agents as effects of the structure is to make it impossible to conceptualise the specificity of individual agents and their actions: it is to reduce all agents to expressions of a single inner essence, the structure. In Althusser's conception the essentialisation of the subject reinforces the essentialisation of the structure. It is precisely because all agents are subjects and therefore endowed with the subjective faculty of experience that the structure is enabled to impose on agents the forms of consciousness appropriate to their position in the structure.

In the absence of such essentialism there can be no basis for maintaining that agents must be conceptualised as human subjects. We have argued that social relations are irreducible to the constitutive actions of agents and that there may be agents other than human individuals. This does not mean, of course, that there are no significant differences between agents. Agents have definite social conditions of existence and those conditions and the forms in which they are secured govern the types of relations and practices in which agents may engage. In particular, different categories of agent may well be privileged in the forms of legal and customary recognition in so far as they assign, say, differential capacities and responsibilites to human as opposed to other types of agents—so that, for example, human individuals may be held responsible for certain actions of the non-human agents they are employed to direct. However, the forms of legal or customary privilege accorded to human individuals in such cases does not mean that agents other than human individuals are reducible to the human agents who direct them. But if there may be agents other than human individuals it follows that the membership of classes, as categories of economic agents, may include agents other than human individuals, for example, joint-stock companies. Two consequences should be noted here. First, this conclusion provides further proof of the absurdity of attempting to conceptualise classes as social forces in terms of the actual or potential class-consciousnesses of individuals: if there are agents other than human individuals then the actions of those agents cannot be conceptualised simply as a function of the consciousnesses of human subjects. For the same reason it is impossible to sustain the Althusserian notion of ideological apparatuses reproducing relations of production by endowing human subjects with subjectivities appropriate to their positions. Second, the example of joint-stock companies raises the possibility of a capitalism in which all means of production are possessed by non-human economic agents—a capitalism without 'capitalists'. In addition to raising the question of the position of managers this possibility also problematises conceptions of the distinctions between capitalism and socialism. If there may be a capitalism with no class of individual human capitalists and in which all human agents of production are employees how would that differ from socialism? We will return to this question in the concluding chapter.

Finally, it may be necessary to insist we have not argued that human individuals cannot be conceived as loci of decision: but rather that, under definite social conditions, there may be agents other than human individuals, and that social relations cannot be reduced to the constitutive actions of agents. If it is to operate as a social agent the human individual is dependent on definite conditions of existence, recognition by other pertinent agents and by law or custom, the cultural availability of appropriate discursive and conceptual means of calculation, and the conditions in which agents may acquire them, and so on, on the one hand, and the capacity of the human individual to acquire and to deploy their conceptual and discursive means on the other. The second set of conditions pose a problem which we have not attempted to discuss here, namely the problem of the condition of existence of such a capacity on the part of the human individuals, while the first ensures that those individuals cannot be the constitutive subjects of social life.

Chapter 12

Economic Class-Relations and the Organisation of Production

This chapter is concerned with the relationship between economic class-relations on the one hand and the division of technical functions in the organisation of production (technical division of labour) and the distribution of the social labour force into a variety of activities (division of social labour) on the other. It argues, in particular, that while the technical division of labour and the division of social labour are not independent of the structure of economic class-relations there need be no direct correspondence between class membership and the performance of certain technical functions in the organisation of production. We have argued that the social formation must be conceived as consisting of a definite set of economic class-relations together with the economic, political, and cultural forms and relations in which their conditions of existence are secured. Classes are categories of economic agents defined by their possession of or separation from the means and conditions of production. Economic class-relations encompass those engaged in the organisation of production either as possessors or as separated non-possessors. In this sense there is no reason to suppose that economic class-relations must encompass all members of the social formation. This point has often been disputed. For example, Poulantzas appears to argue that the division of the members of a society into classes is exhaustive and that there can be no social groupings external to classes:

> the class struggle and the polarization it involves does not and cannot give rise to groupings alongside of or marginal to classes, groupings without class membership, for the simple reason that this class membership is nothing more than the class struggle,

> and that this struggle only exists by way of the existence of the places of social classes. (*Classes in Contemporary Capitalism*, p. 201)

We have seen already that the notion of the primacy of the class struggle must be problematised but even if it were accepted Poulantzas's 'simple reason' would not entail the conclusion we are asked to draw. Classes defined on the basis of struggle need bear no relation to the taxonomic definition which Poulantzas effectively employs. Class struggle can exist only if there are classes but it does not follow that class struggle can exist only if all members of society belong to classes.

But, to return to the general argument, we have seen that it is necessary to distinguish between economic class-relations on the one hand and the forms in which their social conditions of existence are secured on the other. Capitalist relations of production, for example, depend on the satisfaction of their legal and political conditions of existence by definite apparatuses, organisations, and practices. But those organisations and practices are neither the emanations nor the products of capitalist relations of production themselves. State functionaries and other agents may be engaged in those practices and organisations without being in any way directly implicated in capitalist economic class-relations. Poulantzas claims that the heads of State apparatuses belong to the bourgeois class 'chiefly because they manage the State functions in the service of capital' (*ibid.*, p. 187). But again there is no necessary connection between the reason he gives and the conclusion he wishes to draw. The fact that State apparatuses provide certain of the conditions of existence of capitalist relations of production does not entail the conclusion that the members of those apparatuses themselves participate in capitalist production-relations.

Economic class-relations involve agents active in the sphere of production and distribution either as possessors or as separated non-possessors of certain of the means and conditions of production. A social formation may also include agents engaged in practices which provide conditions of existence for its economic class-relations but it does not follow that those agents need be members of the economic classes concerned. This chapter will therefore be concerned primarily with the differentiation of functions in the social organisation of production and distribution and its relation to the structure of economic class-relations.

Marxists have frequently made use of Marx's distinctions between labourer and non-labourer and between productive and unproductive labour and his comments on the double nature of supervision to argue for a correlation between the distribution of agents into classes on the one hand and the performance of particular functional tasks on the other. The labourer/non-labourer distinction has been examined in Chapter 10 where we argued that the notion of possession presupposes the performance of certain tasks of co-ordination and supervision by or on behalf of the possessing agent. If those tasks are not performed, then either production does not take place or effective possession passes into the hands of other economic agents. Thus the role of effective possession always involves the performance of certain tasks that are necessary to the production process. The categories of labourer and non-labourer are therefore totally inadequate to the analysis of economic class-relations and they involve a gross misrepresentation of the role of the possessing agent in the organisation of production. This chapter will therefore concentrate on Marx's discussions of productive and unproductive labour and the double nature of supervision and management and on the way they have been taken up to provide the basis for a demarcation between the functions of the bourgeoisie, proletariat, and petty bourgeoisie in the organisation of production and distribution. A final section considers the concepts of management and capital both in relation to these discussions and with reference to the possession of the means of production by agents other than human individuals.

Productive and unproductive labour

Distinctions between productive and unproductive labour have been used by many Marxists as a means of differentiating between employees who are engaged primarily in productive labour and therefore belong to the proletariat and employees who are unproductive and therefore members of the petty bourgeoisie. This section examines Marx's distinctions and the way they have been used to erect class distinctions within the ranks of the employees of capital. Marx draws two distinct but interrelated types of distinction between productive and unproductive labour which are distinct and incompatible. One depends on the argument that certain functional tasks are essentially unproductive whether they are performed by capitalists or their employees while the other is clearly hegemonised by the theory of value. It cannot therefore be retained in the form that Marx presents it. We shall see that these distinctions cannot provide a coherent foundation for the division of employees of capital into classes.

Marx's main discussions of productive and unproductive labour appear in *Theories of Surplus Value*, vol. 1, ch. 4 and addendum 12, *Capital*, vol. 2, in connection with the costs of circulation, and *Capital*, vol. 3, in connection with non-industrial forms of capital and profit. There is also a short discussion in Marx's draft ch. 6 for *Capital*, vol. 1, 'Results of the Immediate Process of Production'. In these discussions Marx is concerned with labour that is or may be considered productive from the point of view of capitalism. He therefore distinguishes between 'productive labour in general', that is, labour which results in a use value, and labour that is productive from the standpoint of capital. Marx's first type of distinction is therefore between labour that must be considered productive or unproductive *from the standpoint of capital*—however productive it may be from some other point of view.

> Productive labour, in its meaning for capitalist production, is wage-labour which, exchanged against the variable part of capital (the capital which is spent on wages), reproduces not only this part of the capital (or the value of its own labour power), but in addition produces surplus-value for the capitalist. . . . Only that labour is productive which produces capital. (*Theories of Surplus Value*, vol. 1, p. 152)

The labour of petty-commodity producers is therefore unproductive from the standpoint of capital. But what of those who perform tasks in exchange for money? Labour is productive if it produces surplus value for a capitalist and it is unproductive if it 'is not exchanged with capital, but *directly* with revenue, that is, with wages or profit' (*ibid.*, p. 157). This distinction, therefore, has nothing to do with the material characteristics of the labour or the product. Rather it derives 'from the definite social form, the social relations of production, within which the labour is realised' (*ibid.*). The performance of a service may be productive or unproductive depending on whether the service is sold by a capitalist who pays the labourer to perform it or is purchased directly by the consumer of the service from the performer with no capitalist intermediary. Marx gives the examples of cooks, actors, musicians, prostitutes, whose labour may be productive or unproductive depending on the nature of the economic relation in which it is performed. The labour of an employee may be either productive or unproductive. It is productive only if it is engaged in the production of commodities for sale by the purchaser of the labour power.

In this sense the category of productive labourer includes all employees who contribute to the production of commodities for a capital 'from the actual operative to the manager or engineer (as distinct from the capitalist)' (*ibid.*). Marx returns to this point elsewhere in *Theories of Surplus Value* and in the draft chapter 'Result of the Immediate Process of Production'. For example, he refers to the effects of the capitalist division of labour: 'the unskilled labourers in a factory [who] have nothing directly to do with the working up of the raw material . . . the workmen who function as overseers . . . the works engineer [who] in the main works only with his brain, and so on. But the totality of these labourers . . . produce the result' (*ibid.*, p. 411). But this differentiation of technical functions:

> in no way alters the relation of each one of these persons to capital being that of wage-labourer and in this pre-eminent sense being that of a *productive labourer*. All these persons are not only *directly* engaged in the production of material wealth, but they exchange their labour *directly* for money as capital, and consequently directly reproduce, in addition to their wages, a surplus-value for the capitalist. Their labour consists of paid labour plus unpaid surplus labour. (*ibid.*, p. 412)

Marx's discussion of this first distinction between productive and unproductive labour is clearly hegemonised by the theory of value but it also has a central point that is not dependent on value formulations, namely, that productive labour is labour performed at a definite position within capitalist relations of production.

But Marx also makes a second distinction which depends on the view that certain tasks are *essentially unproductive*. Surplus value derives from productive labour but it can be realised for the capitalist only on condition that commodities enter into circulation. The realisation of surplus value therefore seems to depend on the performance of other tasks that are not themselves productive of value, they belong to the *faux frais* of capitalist production and not to the process of production of value. For this distinction the material character of the labour is decidedly pertinent. In the case of the transport industry, for example, Marx argues that labour is productive precisely because it does result in a material change in the object of labour: 'Its spatial existence is altered, and along with this goes a change in its use value, since the location of this use value is changed' (*ibid.*, p. 412). But the more significant points here concern Marx's treatment of buying and selling, merchants' capital and money and banking capital as involving tasks which are intrinsically unproductive. Perhaps the clearest discussion of this position occurs in *Capital*, vol. 2, ch. 6, 'The Costs of Circulation'. Marx argues that there are costs which are necessary to capitalist production but are nevertheless not productive.

Since the capitalist enterprise depends on the purchase and sale of commodities, Marx argues that the time of buying and selling is a necessary part of the time in which the capitalist functions as a capitalist. But the sphere of circulation effects only the distribution of already produced commodities and the conversion of value in commodity-form to value in money-form or *vice versa*. Thus the time and labour involved in purchase and sale are not creative of value: 'Nor can the miracle of this transformation be accomplished by a transposition, i.e., by the industrial capitalist making this "work of combustion" the exclusive business of third persons, who are paid by them instead of performing it themselves' (*Capital*, vol. 2, p. 130). This argument turns on the notion that certain functions are essentially unproductive and that therefore the labour engaged in them cannot be productive under any circumstances:

> If by a division of labour a function, unproductive in itself although a necessary element of reproduction, is transformed from an incidental occupation of many into the exclusive ocupation of a few, into their special business, the nature of this function is not changed. (*ibid.*, p. 131)

The worker in circulation may perform a function necessary to capitalist production but '*intrinsically his labour creates neither value nor product.* He belongs to the *faux frais* of production' (*ibid.*, emphasis added). Marx employs the same argument with regard to the costs of book-keeping and again, in *Capital*, vol. 3, with regard to labour employed by merchant's capital and by money and banking capital. These are merely capital functioning in the sphere of circulation where neither value nor surplus value are created. Thus even if labourers are employed merchant's capital 'does not act as capital by setting in motion the labour of others, as industrial capital does, *but rather by doing its own work*, i.e. performing the functions of buying and selling. . . .' (*Capital*, vol. 3, p. 294, emphasis added). The basic principle at work is clear. Industrial capital is the primary form of capital and all functions which are unproductive when performed by the industrial capitalist remain unproductive when they are performed independently:

> Since merchant's capital is absolutely nothing but an individualised form of a portion of industrial capital engaged in the process of circulation, *all questions referring to it must be solved by representing the problem primarily in a form, in which the phenomena peculiar to merchant's capital do not yet appear independently*, but still in direct connection with industrial capital, as a branch of it. (*ibid.*, p. 298)

Merchant's capital must be analysed without reference to its distinctive features.

We thus have two related principles of demarcation between productive and unproductive labour. The first distinguishes labour performed in capitalist enterprises by the non-possessors of the means of production from labour performed under other conditions, while the second separates off certain functions performed within or by capitalist enterprises as being essentially unproductive. We will return to the examination of these principles in a moment, but first it is necessary to indicate how they may be used as a means of demarcation between classes of economic agents. The first principle distinguishes non-possessors engaged in capitalist production from all other economic agents, that is, it defines an economic class in the sense of this chapter, as a category of economic agents defined in terms of their position of non-possession with regard to capitalist means of production. The second imposes a further differentiation within this category between those employed in productive functions and those whose functions are intrinsically unproductive. It is this differentiation which has been employed as the basis of a proposed distinction between proletariat and petty bourgeoisie within the ranks of non-possessors employed by capitalist enterprises. It will be sufficient to consider Poulantzas's discussion in *Classes in Contemporary Capitalism* as illustrating this type of proposal.

Poulantzas argues that there are capitalist wage labourers who are not members of the working class. Instead they form part of the petty bourgeoisie. The working class is not defined solely by reference to its position with regard to the means of production but rather by productive labour. Poulantzas adopts Marx's distinction between productive and unproductive labour except for one significant correction. Consider first the correction. To avoid the ambiguities in Marx's position Poulantzas proposes to go beyond the basic definition of productive labour in terms of surplus value:

> We shall say that productive labour, in the CMP, is labour that produces surplus-value while directly reproducing the material elements that serve as the substratum of the relation of exploitation: labour that is directly involved in *material* production by producing use-values that increase material wealth. (*Classes in Contemporary Capitalism*, p. 216)

Now, while there are points at which Marx argues from the material character of the labour, we have seen that it is not the material characteristics that are decisive but rather the production of surplus value. Poulantzas acknowledges Marx's argument on this point and then claims 'what Marx is seeking to avoid at all costs is the confusion of productive labour with useful labour, the general utility of labour and its product' (*ibid.*, p. 218). Here Poulantzas adopts the time-honoured practice of reading into Marx positions that are manifestly contradicted by the text. When Marx affirms that his definitions are 'not derived from the material characteristics of labour . . . but from the definite social form, the social relations of production, within which the labour is realised' (*Theories of Surplus Value*, vol. 1, p. 157) he really means that the material characteristics are crucial, and when he refers to 'actors, musicians, prostitutes' (*ibid.*, p. 166) engaging in productive labour he means that their labour is essentially unproductive. Poulantzas therefore excludes service workers from the ranks of the working class.

But the main distinction concerns the production of surplus value. Wage labourers in the sphere of circulation and employees of financial enterprises do not produce surplus value and are therefore no part of the working class:

> These wage-earners simply contribute towards redistributing the mass of surplus-value among the various fractions of capital according to the average rate of profit. Of course, these wage-earners are themselves exploited. . . . Surplus-labour is extorted from wage-earners in commerce, but these are not

> directly exploited in the form of the dominant capitalist relation of exploitation, the creation of surplus-value . . . their remuneration is an unproductive expense and forms part of the *faux frais* of capitalist production. (*Classes in Contemporary Capitalism*, p. 212)

Other authors, e.g. Carchedi, may reserve the term 'exploitation' to refer to the extraction of surplus-value while concurring with the central point of Poulantzas's conception. The working class is defined by the production of surplus value and capitalist wage labourers who do not produce value belong to the petty bourgeoisie. In this way Marx's distinctions between productive and unproductive labour appear to allow for class differentiation within the ranks of capitalist wage labourers.

While these definitions of proletariat and petty bourgeoisie depend on Marx's distinctions between productive and unproductive labourers within the ranks of capitalist wage labourers, they are clearly not required by it. There is nothing in his discussion to ensure that Marx's solution to a problem posed within the theory of value, namely, the distinction between labour that produces value and labour that does not, should be taken as defining two essentially different classes of wage labourers employed in capitalist enterprises. There is no reason why the working class should not rather be defined as including all non-possessing economic agents engaged in capitalist production. The conception of a non-proletarian class of capitalist wage labourers is a possible but not a necessary consequence of Marx's distinctions.

We can now return to the examination of Marx's distinctions between productive and unproductive labour. We have seen that while Marx's discussion of the first distinction is hegemonised by the theory of value it nevertheless has a central point that is not dependent on value-theory, namely, that labour is productive from the standpoint of capital if it is performed in capitalist enterprises by non-possessing economic agents in return for wages. However, the second distinction that Marx draws, within the ranks of capitalist wage labourers, is impossible to sustain in any form. Not only does it have no meaning outside the context of the labour theory of value which, as we have shown, must be rejected. But, even if the theory of value is retained Marx's distinction cannot be sustained in the form that he makes it. There are certain functions that are intrinsically unproductive although they are absolutely necessary for capitalist production. Since they are intrinsically unproductive they remain so even if they are performed by labourers in return for wages. The essentialism of this argument is apparent: certain activities are essentially unproductive and certain capitals, although they may happen to employ wage labourers, do '*not act as capital by setting in motion the labour of others*, as industrial capital does, *but rather by doing its own work*' (*Capital*, vol. 3, p. 294, emphasis added). The mere fact that non-industrial capitals may set labour in motion cannot affect their essentially unproductive character because the functions they perform are essentially unproductive. Marx's position here clearly depends on an essentialisation of the functions of industrial labour: labour employed by industrial capital is essentially productive, that employed by other capitals is not.

But Marx's essentialisation of certain functions conflicts with his insistence that the definitions of productive and unproductive labour are derived not from the material character of the labour but rather from the 'definite social form, the social relations of production, within which the labour is realised' (*Theories of Surplus Value*, vol. 1, p. 157). To establish the contradiction here we must recall first Marx's treatment of the services performed by actors, prostitutes, and so on. Their labour is unproductive from the standpoint of capital if it is purchased by the consumer of the service directly from the labourer concerned. It is productive from the standpoint of capital if the consumer buys the service from a capitalist who pays a wage labourer to perform it. Consider the case of a capitalist enterprise which acts as a sales or purchasing agent for industrial capitalists by selling their products or buying raw materials and components in return for a fee or commission. Are the wage labourers employed by this enterprise productive or unproductive? They are clearly unproductive in terms of Marx's argument that the functions of buying and selling are intrinsically unproductive. But if we follow Marx's argument in the case of services we must conclude that the sales force employed by this enterprise consists of productive labourers. They perform a service for industrial capitalists and the consumer buys the service from a capitalist who pays wage labourers to perform it. The contradiction is clear. Either the material character of the labour is decisive or it is not. If it is not then it cannot be argued that certain functions are intrinsically unproductive. But if certain functions are intrinsically unproductive of value then the material character of the labour must be decisive. In the one case the mere fact that labour is employed in buying and selling or by a finance capitalist enterprise has no bearing on whether it is productive or not. In terms of Marx's arguments, for example, we would have to say that the labour of buying and selling is productive under some conditions and unproductive under others. In the other case it is the material character of the labour that determines whether it is productive of value or not. But to say that would be to define value not as Marx does in terms of abstract labour but rather in terms of an arbitrary decision that only certain concrete kinds of labour deserve to be called productive.

Thus, even in terms of his theory of value, Marx's distinction between productive and unproductive capitalist wage labourers is extremely problematic. Since the theory of value itself cannot be sustained we must conclude that there is no coherent foundation for the division of capitalist wage labourers into those that are productive and those that are not. There is therefore no foundation for the attempts by Poulantzas and others to erect a class distinction on the basis of a division of functions among capitalists' employees.

The double nature of supervision and management

A second major type of attempt to erect a class distinction within the ranks of capitalist wage labourers is based on Marx's discussion of the double nature of supervision and management. Marx's argument is presented most clearly in *Capital*, vol. 3, ch. 23, 'Interest and Profit of Enterprise'.

> The labour of supervision and management is naturally required wherever the direct process of production assumes the form of a combined social process, and not of the isolated labour of independent producers. However it has a double nature.
>
> On the one hand, all labour in which many individuals cooperate necessarily requires a commanding will to coordinate and unify the process, and functions which apply not to partial operations but to the total activity of the workshop, much as that of an orchestra conductor. This is a productive job, which must be performed in every combined mode or production.
>
> On the other hand—quite apart from any commercial department—this supervision work necessarily arises in all

> modes of production based on the antithesis between the labourer, as the direct producer, and the owner of the means of production. The greater this antagonism, the greater the role played by supervision. Hence it reaches its peak in the slave system. But it is indispensable also in the capitalist mode of production, since the production process in it is simultaneously a process by which the capitalist consumes labour-power. (*Capital*, vol. 3, pp. 383–4)

Once again, Marx's comments do not in themselves entail a class division within the ranks of non-possessors between those who labour and those who supervise their labour. But it is easy to see how they could be used in support of such a division. Commenting on the second aspect discussed by Marx, Poulantzas claims: 'In this last aspect, supervision represents part of the *faux frais* of capitalist production' (*Classes in Contemporary Capitalism*, p. 226). The work of supervision and management is productive in one aspect and unproductive in another. Poulantzas argues that the mode of separation of the labourer from their means of production implies that there is no division or co-ordination of tasks that is purely technical in character. On the contrary management and supervision under capitalism is always 'the direct reproduction, within the process of production itself, of the political relations between the capitalist class and the working class' (*ibid.*, p. 228). It is for this reason that the agents of supervision and management, the NCOs of capitalist production, must be considered petty bourgeois rather than working class:

> The reason why these agents do not belong to the working class, is that their structural class determination and the place they occupy in the social division of labour are marked by the dominance of the political relations that they maintain over the aspect of productive labour in the division of labour. Their principal function is that of extracting surplus-value from the workers—'collecting' it. They exercise powers that derive from the place of capital, capital that has seized hold of the 'control function' of the labour process; these powers are not necessarily exercised by the capitalists themselves. (*ibid.*, pp. 228–9)

Poulantzas argues that relations of production 'are expressed in the form of powers which derive from them, in other words class powers; these powers are constitutively tied to the political and ideological relations which sanction and legitimize them' (*ibid.*, p. 21). He adds that these relations 'are themselves present . . . in the constitution of the relations of production' (*ibid.*) Relations of production are constituted by political and ideological relations and these relations 'sanction and legitimize' definite class powers in the organisation of the production process. Economic class-relations are effectively reduced to relations of domination. The capitalist factory is therefore conceived as structured by the despotism of capital over labour. Capitalist relations of production therefore involve a fundamental division of economic agents into dominators and dominated and it is the role of management as agents of domination that allows Poulantzas to separate them off from the working class. Thus it is precisely the politicisation of relations of production that allows Poulantzas to differentiate between the working class and this section of the petty bourgeoisie—although both are equally separated from the means of production.

Poulantzas affirms the primacy of the political over the productive aspects of the labour of management and supervision, and he therefore argues for a political division between management and the working class. A different form of the argument that managers and supervisors belong to the new petty bourgeoisie is advanced by Carchedi in 'On the Economic Identification of the New Middle Class'. Carchedi distinguishes between the labour process which 'invests only the producer and the means of production' and the surplus value-producing process which 'invests also the non-producer, the non-labourer' (*ibid.*, p. 7). The capitalist mode of production is then defined as the unity of these two aspects under the domination of the surplus-value-producing process. The functions of the capitalist are therefore 'performed outside the labour process and yet inside the capitalist production process' (*ibid.*, p. 20). Now if, with the division of managerial labour, these functions are performed by employees of capital the fact that they are 'outside the labour process' ensures that those who perform them are not part of the working class: 'all those agents who perform one of these operations, no matter what their technical content, perform at the same time the global function of capital' (*ibid.*). The middle class may therefore be defined as including those who are neither fully labourer nor fully non-labourer: that is, they perform *both* the global functions of capital and the functions of collective worker.

These examples will serve to illustrate the way in which a class division among employees of capital may be erected on the basis of the 'double nature' of supervision and management. The argument turns on a separation between two parts or aspects of the capitalist organisation of production. On the one hand there is the labour process and on the other there is the process of extraction of surplus value. There are the forces of production on the one hand and the relations of production on the other. Where one involves a technical organisation of labourers and means of production the other involves non-labourers in coercive relations of domination and control. These arguments therefore do little more than extend the classical labourer/non-labourer distinction to cover those cases where functions assigned to the non-labourer are performed by certain of his employees.

Now, we have shown in Chapter 10 that the categories of 'labourer' and 'non-labourer' are totally inadequate to the analysis of class-relations and that they entail a gross misrepresentation of the functions of possessing and non-possessing agents in the organisation of production. The 'non-labourer' performs certain functions which are technically necessary to the organisation of the production process. In the case of capitalist production, for example, enterprises produce commodities and attempt to sell them and they purchase elements of the production process, means of production, raw materials, labour-power, in the form of commodities. If these elements are not purchased in appropriate quantities relative to one another then production cannot take place at all. Further, since the elements of the production process are the property of the capitalist and the labourers are separated from them, production can take place only as a function of co-ordination by or on behalf of the capitalist. Thus certain definite functions of monetary accounting, budgeting, purchasing and selling and of co-ordination must be performed by or on behalf of the capitalist if production is to take place.

But, if the functions of the capitalist are necessary to the existence of capitalist production then there can be no division of the capitalist production process into a sphere of the labour process on the one hand and a sphere of labourer/non-labourer relations on the other. The concepts of relations of production and forces of production do not designate two distinct things. Rather they function jointly as the means of conceptualising the structure and organisation of definite production processes. Carchedi's position is simply absurd: there are no 'functions performed outside the labour process and yet inside the capitalist production process' ('On the Economic Identification', p. 20). Poulantzas's argument is less immediately absurd but it is no less problematic. First, the productive aspect and the 'relations of production' aspect of co-ordination and supervision are interdependent and inseparable. There can be no relations of production if no production takes place and there can be no production without some definite form of possession of the means and conditions of production. To say that one is dominant over the other while each is clearly dependent on the other involves precisely the doctrines of ontological primacy considered and dismissed in Chapters 8 and 9—it is to say that the dominant relations call into being their own conditions of existence. Second, the politicisation and ideologisation of relations of production involves the conflation of *economic* relations, definite forms of possession of and separation from the means and conditions of production, with their political and ideological conditions of existence. To say that management and supervision internalises within the factory 'the political relations between the capitalist class and the working class' (*Classes in Contemporary Capitalism*, p. 228) is to confuse the political conditions necessary for capitalist production to exist with the organisation of capitalist production itself. Some form of co-ordination is always required when many individuals co-operate in production. But production can take place only if the means and conditions of production are subject to some definite form of possession—whether that form be communal, capitalist, feudal or whatever. It follows that the tasks of co-ordination, like all other productive tasks, can take place only under conditions of some definite form of possession. This dependence of the mode of co-ordination on the form of possession ensures that modes of co-ordination will vary from one form of possession to another. But it cannot follow that non-possessors engaged in co-ordination constitute a different class from those whose labour is co-ordinated.

Management and capital

Finally, consider the relations between forms of possession and forms of direction of capital by economic agents who are themselves separated from the means of production. The conventional notion of management is a very diffuse one, extending in many cases to any non-manual employee with administrative responsibility. Here 'management' will be used in a more specific sense to refer to performance of the functions of an exclusive possession by non-possessing agents. In the case of capitalist possession 'management' refers to the direction of the operations of a capital. Managers are economic agents employed to exercise the capacity of direction on behalf of a capital. We have seen that attempts to distinguish within the organisation of capitalist production between labourer and non-labourer or between productive and unproductive labour cannot be sustained. These proposed distinctions cannot therefore justify the allocation of managers to a class of non-possessing wage labourers distinct from the proletariat. Similarly the double character of supervision and management does not entail a class distinction between non-possessors who perform the functions of capital from those who do not. Sections of management may form a specialised and highly paid component of the capitalist labour force but that does not define a distinctive type of class position in the sense of the possession of or separation from the means of production. Many authors have used the high remuneration of senior managers as an index of their capitalist character on the grounds that they are essentially paid out of the profits of the enterprise (e.g. Poulantzas, *Classes in Contemporary Capitalism*, p. 229, Carchedi, 'On the Economic Identification', pp. 54–9, Braverman, *Labour and Monopoly Capital*, p. 404f). But this suggestion is entirely circular. It is precisely because these highly paid employees are thought to be really capitalists in disguise that their salaries can be separated from the labour costs of the enterprise: because they do not form part of the labour costs they must be paid out of profits.

We have argued in Chapter 11 that there may be economic agents other than human subjects. Such agents depend for their conditions of existence on the delegation of functions to other agents—for example, where the signature of a senior manager is necessary to make a contract. Joint-stock companies as economic agents depend on the delegation of the functions of direction of their capital on to members of a management structure. Managers serve as the representatives of the capital of a joint-stock company or trust. They do not exercise this function by reason of possession of the means of production which they direct, rather they are *combined* with the means of production by an economic decision (to engage certain numbers of functionaries) made on the part of the capital.

In respect of the mode of combination with the means of production they are in the same position as wage labourers (although generally with greater contractual obligations on the part of the employer). Although managers direct the actions of a capital, it and not they is the legal subject responsible for the obligations and the possessor of the receipts which follow from those actions. No amount of performance of the function of direction confers on the manager the capacity to alienate or appropriate the means of production in question, or even the right to continue to exercise the function of direction.

The manager is separated from the means of production and yet directs them. What is entailed in the manager 'representing' or 'directing' a capital? It will be necessary to define the functions entailed in the operation of any 'capital' in order to comprehend and separate the different functions combined and confused in the conventional notion of 'management'. In order to deal with this question one must first examine a concept which might appear to offer a solution, the 'capitalist'—is not the manager merely a substitute for the subject the capitalist?

The simple combination of the social and technical divisions of labour produces their fusion in a human subject, the 'capitalist', who exercises his functions by reason of possession. This fusion of possession and function has led to the practical identity of the human subject and the economic subject (locus of exercise of economic functions) in Marxism. Whereas classicism and neo-classicism found the economic subject on a definite human nature (in the one case, needs and attributes, in the other, a certain calculating psychology) Marx conceives the capitalist as a 'personification of capital'. The capitalist is the incarnation of a social force, it is an empty subject which occupies an economic place ('capitalist') and receives through its capacity of experience the appearances of the structure which confer on it the subjectivity appropriate to its place. Marx avoids a naïve anthropology or psychology through this use of the left Hegelian incarnation structure (cf. Rancière). The effect, however, is similar to that of psychologism, the functions vanish into the subject, but with the difference that the subject in turn vanishes into the structure. The capitalist is a mere 'aliquot part' of the total social capital and the experience of the appearances of the structure by capitalists is universal in form. It is the structure which generates the forms of recognition which sustain it. The differential effectivity of calculation and organisation is set at nought. The conception of the capitalist as personification of capital is in its own way as unenlightening as is 'economising' as a universal form of human calculation.

We have argued that the conditions of existence of capitalist economic agents must be analysed in terms of the conditions of recognition of entities as economic agents, the possibilities of the delegation of functions onto other agents, and the cultural conditions of economic calculation. Consider, for example, the relationship between the legal subject and the economic subject with respect to a capital, between the form of a possession and its functioning. Legal subjectivity is a recognition of the form of possession (in capitalism legal differences in the form of property are not reflections of pre-existing forms of possession; legal recognition itself generates difference, without an appropriate legal *form* joint-stock companies could not exist). In the person of the 'capitalist' legal subject and economic subject coincide. In the joint-stock company the pertinent legal subject for the capital as a whole is the company itself (shareholders' obligations extend only to their portion of the capital). The unity of the company is a unity of recognition as an entity capable of certain actions (possession, alienation, contracting, etc.)—it is a locus of possession different from human subjects. The possessing and the economic subjects are combined here too (*the economic subject must be operative at the level of effective possession*)—it is the company as combined money funds which is the capital and it is this capital which must be directed. Economic subjectivity is not human subjectivity, it is possession in operation. Hence economic subjectivity must be defined abstractly. *Economic subjects must be defined as the locus of exercise of the function of direction of a possession*—this locus corresponding to the form of possession.

But direction of what? The concept of 'means of production' is inadequate to define what is directed in capitalism. The production of commodities is merely one medium of expansion of money capital. Financial and commercial capital do not necessarily entail the direction of 'means of production': markets for financial assets, consumer credit, sale of financial commodities (insurance, etc.), the speculative purchase of commodities, all pertain to the circuit M—M^1 and entail no direct contact with industrial capital. Financial capital indicates the need for a more abstract definition of a 'capital'. *A 'capital', the form of economic subjectivity in capitalism, can only be defined as whatever money funds are operated by a single direction. This direction will be exercised within the form of an exclusive possession* (*whether or not the funds directed are so possessed*). These definitions may appear elliptical, but they are not empty. Possession and function are combined to define a unit of economic operation: direction defines economic subjectivity, it is whatever funds are directed, the form of possession indicates the limits and the objects of direction, in this case the expansion of the money capital of an exclusive possession.

Marx defines the unity and limits of a capital in a different way. The analysis of the form of capitals is hegemonised by the theory of surplus value and its distribution. Industrial, commercial, and interest-bearing capital are differentiated on the basis of the mode in which they share in the surplus value. Industrial capital is the primary form of capital, it must be because capital is conceived as a process of self-expansion of value derived from the exploitation of labour-power and realised through the sale of commodities. The primary objects of analysis are the distributive relations between the fractions of capital (redistributing surplus value) and tendencies in the production and realisation of surplus value which transcend the enterprise. Marx does not need to theorise the capitalist enterprise, its form and functions. Capitals are designated by a subject, the capitalist as possessor and agent, and by a process of generation—all capitals represent a certain pool of surplus value drawn from the labourers in a definite labour process. Capitals are unified by their *origin*: in the process of exploitation of labour which creates capital and through the redistribution to other claimants in the capitalist class. A capital is defined essentially in production; the 'capitalist' is the possessor of the surplus value produced. Once the concept of capital as the self-expansion of value is abandoned then the unity of a capital ceases to be conceivable as the process of its own generation. The rejection of the theory of value necessitates the theorisation of the enterprise; without value the limits, operations, and financing of the enterprise become problematic objects for theorisation. Hence to ask, what is a capital?, what is it that is directed?, is a consequence of abandoning value and the problem of the source of profit.

The abstract conception of a capital as whatever funds are subject to a direction serving an exclusive possession becomes inevitable once value is displaced and credit as a source of financing is supposed. To understand further *what* is directed it is necessary to introduce certain formal concepts relating to financing, since financing is the determinant of what funds are available to a capital. These terms are concerned with things which are partly a consequence of and also impose conditions on a directive agency. These concepts are the *source*, the *level* (relative to a prevailing social scale), and the *objects* of capital funds. A capital is determined in its objects by its sources and level of finance. Financial and industrial capital may be differentiated in terms of their sources of financing. Financial capital centralises money funds, which function as capital in the form of credit and interest. Industrial capital is a recipient of credit (including the sale of share issues), but it has in addition another source of finance, retained profits. Both of these forms of financing depend upon the investment of capital funds in some definite branch of commodity production and the sale of commodities at prices which permit the payment of interest, of dividends, and/or the retention of investment funds. Capitals may be differentiated in terms of the level of access to finance. This has a crucial effect on the specific objects of its operations within the general division of financial and industrial capital. In finance capital a certain scale is imposed in different types of financial operations by the prevailing conditions of competition (different levels of centralisation/financing will be necessary in branch banking or hire purchase, for example, new enterprises will tend to develop in areas not dominated by large competing centralisers of credit, again cf. hp). In industrial capital technical forms impose certain necessary levels of financing, this is one of the dominant conditions of competition. Different branches of production require different levels of capitalisation and different forms of access to finance.

A complex of (formally or otherwise) related enterprises function as a single capital if they are subject to an agency of direction with regard to their sources and level of financing. We will now attempt to define the four levels of function involved in the direction of the operations of any capital (industrial capital will be used for illustration, but analogues of functions 2, 3 and 4 are to be found in financial institutions like banks and insurance companies, concerned with the technical planning of rates of interest and periods of loan, and the co-ordination of departments).

1 *Direction of Investment*: the central function here is the calculation of financing (source and level of funds), the definition of the areas of operation of the capital—this will take the form of

an overall investment decision or plan. The temporality of decisions here relates to the *turnover of investment*; period of reproduction of the capital as a whole (fixed and circulating).

2 *Production Planning*: as a consequence of basic investment decisions this level involves decisions as to the products, type of production process, general level of production, etc.; this involves calculations of investment costs and production prices relative to the funds available and the rate of profit anticipated in the period of turnover of investment. This level entails accounting and technical calculation—it will (depending on the enterprise) serve as the technical basis for the financial decisions at level 1.

3 *Production Operation*: decisions as to the purchases of raw materials, labour-power, etc., are made on the basis of assessment of market conditions within the constraints imposed by the financial strategy. The temporality of decisions relates to the period of *turnover of production* and concerns the level of application of and turnover of circulating capital.

4 *Co-ordination and Supervision*: the integration of the phases of a process of production and the maintenance of production performance.

Functions 1 and 3 involve decisions which directly affect the nature and level of economic operation of the enterprises—they are functions which in some sense must be united in a single agency of calculation and decision. These functions define the *economic subject*—the agency of direction of a capital. Functions 2 and 4 are in general technical consequences of or factors in economic and operational decisions, and are subordinate to them. Co-ordination is a necessary function of the technical composition of the process of production. Supervision, where it is concerned with monitoring the performance of personnel in the process of production, is a necessary operation of capital, but one which may in practice be carried out without managerial specialists through payment systems or forms of work organisation.

Functions 1 and 3 are those specific to the economic subject. They require non-technical economic calculation and decisions ('non-technical' in the sense that it is concerned with defining objectives which are not given by previous decisions). Functions 2 and 4 are technical calculations or decisions subordinated to the ones above—in any complex enterprise they will be conducted by specialist personnel. 'Managers' performing functions 1 and 3 are specialists hired to act as agents of an economic subjectivity, directors of capital. Specialists performing functions 2 or 4 exclusively are technical functionaries ancillary to the economic subject. These statements define functions not the social essences of subjects. 'Managers' are not capitalists by reason of function, nor are they necessarily differentiated from the rest of the technical specialists. It is the differentiation of the tasks, their relation to calculation and economic operation which is our concern, not the 'sociological' characteristics of their occupants.

The two broad divisions of functions may be characterised as involving 'economic' calculation and 'technical' calculation. Ignoring the problem of direction has led to ignorance of its effects in Marxism and a rejection of the effects of direction because of its absurd representation in managerialist views. The problem of direction raises the questions of the existence and effectivity of forms of investment strategy and their connection with forms of calculation. Calculation, in which immediate operational decisions based on existing market information are dominant and set the forms of investment strategy, exists in both industrial and financial capital. It may be analysed in terms of the sources of finance and the objects to which it is in consequence directed (branch banking versus investment banking—periodicity of turnover of funds centralised). Calculation, in which strategic decisions tend to dominate operational ones, corresponds to a lengthening in the period of turnover of invested funds, and this may have technical (scale of investment necessary) or financial (periodicity of funds centralised, terms of credit) determinants. These questions of mode of direction require investigation but this is only possible on the terms of an analysis of forms of financing and conditions of technical competition. The sources and level of financing cannot be investigated independently of definite financial systems.

The existence of distinct functional tasks, the difference in forms of calculation, pose the question of the formation of managerial and specialist cadres. Questions of the market for managerial labour, training, functional differentiation, in general the organisation of management as a labour force, have been neglected by Marxists. The same is true of the development and dissemination of forms of calculation. The market for managers and specialists will depend in its characteristics on the degree of specialisation of enterprises, the degree of concentration/centralisation of capital, the level of development of non-capitalist administrative apparatuses, etc. The differentiation of the agents of economic subjectivity from technical functionaries, the formation of a distinct stratum of managerial personnel concerned with 'direction' is a tendency observable in several advanced capitalist economies. The systematisation of processes of calculation and business administration, the rigorous training and competition of specialists, may very well (other questions aside) directly affect the conditions of inter-enterprise competition and the general performance of enterprises. Specialist management can be argued to have had a direct and radical effect on the scale, organisational and productive efficiency of industrial capital, as much as its being a consequence of change in technical complexity, periods of turnover and size of operations. The effectivity of specialist and skilled agents on the economic subjects whose operations they support cannot be discounted as Marxists have tended to do and must be investigated.

Managers direct capital funds but do not possess them. This separation of possession and the performance of function corresponds to the development of centralised or socialised capital. These forms of capital are connected with the development of finance capital and the transformations in the scale of investment and periods of turnover in certain branches of industrial capital. As the capital funds necessary to the operation of enterprises have been transformed in scale and enforced by competition so the figure formed by the unity of possession and function in the person of the capitalist has receded. Managerial ideologues like Berle and Means conceive the development of joint-stock capital and management as a separation of *ownership* and *control*. This position is absurd, it identifies individual titles to wealth with effective possession and human with economic subjectivity. Possession and function are *combined* in the enterprise, the possessing subject and the economic subject correspond. The function of direction is supported through recourse to a specialist labour market, which, like all others, depends on non-possession. The units which *possess* as capital (and which separate the working population from) the means of reproduction of labour-power are non-human, legal-economic subject, enterprises. These forms of possession require that the function of direction which they separate from all other functions be performed by specialists who act as agents of the economic subject. These forms systematically reproduce these specialist as non-possessors, as servants of socialised capital. Capital controls its managers.

The social division of labour of socialised capital creates a unique category of technical specialists, directors of the means of production. The combination of possession and function is preserved in that direction as an activity differentiated from all others and placed at the service of an exclusive possession. The social and technical divisions of labour are combined and separated: direction is a function monopolised by possession, and direction serves possession; direction is, however, a specific function in a technical division of labour and its occupation depends on performance. 'Managers' cannot appropriate what they direct; what they direct can exist as the capital which it is only in a socialised form. Performing the function of direction of capital (or the means of production equivalent in other modes) does not result in possession. Capitalism in its socialised forms retains the consequence of possession in separation, it is 'capitals' which exist not 'capitalists'. The performance of the technical task makes possible the existence of a social form, that is 'capitals' as economic subjects, and also the continuance of the relations of production and the social division of labour of capitalism. Class-relations continue to exist but the possessors in separation are not necessarily human subjects; the operation of the relations of production is sustained by paid functionaries separated from the means of production.

Chapter 13

Conclusion

These chapters have proposed a fundamental reconstruction of the classical Marxist conceptions of the structure of the social formation, classes and economic class-relations. Their arguments are neither complete nor definitive but they do open up significant areas of further work in Marxist theory. This conclusion outlines some of these areas first, in relation to the structure of the social formation, classes, and economic class-relations. Their arguments classes and economic class-relations.

The structure of the social formation

In the classical conception the social formation is an articulated structure of economic, political, and ideological levels dominated by a specific mode of production. The economic level is held to play the role of 'determination in the last instance' in that it determines the character of and relations between each of the levels. Nevertheless the political and ideological levels are 'relatively autonomous': they exercise a reciprocal effect on the economy and in certain cases they may occupy the place of dominance in the social formation. We have argued that this conception involves a particular rationalistic epistemology in which relations between concepts are transposed on to relations between the social relations and practices specified in those concepts. A relation between the concept of an economy and the concepts of its conditions of existence is transposed on to a relation of determination between the economy and the political and ideological levels. The economy determines these levels 'in the last instance' by calling in to being its own political and ideological conditions of existence.

In opposing this conception we have argued that connections between social relations, institutions, and practices must be conceived not in terms of any relations of determination, 'in the last instance' or otherwise, but rather in terms of conditions of existence. This means that while specific social relations and practices always presuppose definite social conditions of existence they neither secure those conditions through their own action nor do they determine the form in which they will be secured. Thus, while a set of relations of production can be shown to have definite legal, political and cultural conditions of existence those conditions are in no way determined or secured by the action of the economy. The arguments of Chapters 8 and 9 have shown that analysis in terms of conditions of existence and the forms in which they are secured entails the rejection of the doctrines of 'determination in the last instance' and its Althusserian variant, 'structural causality', of the closely related doctrine of the necessary correspondence of relations and forces of production, and finally of the conception of the social formation as organised into a number of distinct and unitary structural levels. We have therefore argued for a displacement of mode of production as a primary object of Marxist conceptualisation in favour of social formation conceived as a definite set of relations of production together with the economic, political, legal, and cultural forms in which their conditions of existence are secured.

Four implications in particular should be noted here. First, it follows that political practices, institutions, and ideologies can no longer be conceived as reducible more or less directly to the effects, expressions, or representations of economic relations. Political institutions and practices may provide certain of the conditions of existence of economic class-relations but they do not express those relations or represent the interests of the classes engaged in them. It is necessary to abandon the traditional Marxist practice of reading into political and ideological forms and relations the classes, class fractions, or interests they are alleged to represent. But to abandon that practice is to problematise the greater part of the classical Marxist analyses of politics, the State, and ideology which are characterised precisely by the reading of political and cultural phenomena for the classes and interests represented. The necessary reworking of the Marxist theories of politics and ideology has not been attempted here but it is clearly an urgent theoretical task.

To insist on the analysis of social relations and practices in terms of their conditions of existence is not to say that there are no connections between political practices, institutions, and ideologies on the one hand and economic class-relations on the other. It is to say that those connections cannot be conceived in the way that Marxism has tended to conceive them. Political institutions and practices do not represent the structure of economic class-relations, but they may provide some of their conditions of existence. What is at stake here is the specificity of political issues and struggles and the State apparatuses, parties, or other political forces active in relation to them. To say that political issues and forces are not reducible to effects of economic relations is to insist on their specificity. It is to say that the interests represented in political organisations and practices are not determined elsewhere: they are constituted in the field of politics itself. Similar points may be made with regard to cultural and ideological forms and practices: to say that they are not reducible to something else is to say that they must be taken seriously with regard to their specific content and its effects. We have seen in particular that the effectivity of culture and ideology cannot be reduced to the formation of agents' consciousnesses appropriate to their positions in the structure of the social formation.

Second, to insist on analysis in terms of conditions of existence and the forms in which they are secured is to insist that no ontological primacy and no necessary discursive priority can be accorded to any specific relations or set of relations. The connections between economic relations and other social relations cannot be analysed in terms of the type of ontological primacy assigned to the economy by the doctrines of determination in the last instance or structural causality; the connection between relations and forces of production cannot be analysed in terms of the necessary correspondence of the one with the other, and so on. The order of discourse in the analysis of social relations and the connections between them is not given in the order of social relations themselves: it is a consequence of definite political ideologies and specific political objectives. The discursive primacy accorded to economic relations in Marxism and more generally in socialist discourse cannot be conceived as an effect of the ontological structure of reality. On the contrary it is the effect of a definite political ideology and a definite political objective, namely, the objective of a socialist transformation of capitalist relations of production. The concepts of relations of production, classes, and other concepts of Marxist theory acquire political pertinence in the formation of concepts of definite social formations. At this level Marxist analysis can never be reduced to a disinterested academic exercise since it always depends on political problems as a necessary point of departure, albeit a problematic one. Political problems cannot be taken simply as they arise and are specified in political debate. They require critical theoretical evaluation and they may require reconstruction, but they are nevertheless of fundamental importance for the conceptualisation of definite social formations as arenas of political practice. The mode in which political problems are posed and theorised depends on the level of development both of politics and of Marxist theory and on the extent to which they are inscribed one in the other. *Mode of Production and Social Formation* has suggested that one reason for the signal failure of Marxist analyses of modern British capitalism lies in the weakness of the 'left' in this country, its doctrinaire gesture politics, its failure to engage major political issues and forces and its consequent failure to generate political problems for theorisation.

Third, the proposal to conceptualise the social formation as consisting of a definite set of relations of production together with the economic, legal, political, and cultural forms in which their conditions of existence are satisfied requires a reconsideration of the nature of socialist politics and of the forms of socialist political practice that are possible. The classical conception of the structure of the social formation presents it as dominated by a definite mode of production except for relatively short periods of transition between the domination of one mode and the domination of another. The capitalist mode of production is either dominant or it is not. If not, then the social formation is in transition or it is dominated by some other mode of production. It is easy to see how this conception can generate a distinction between reform and revolution. Reformist modes of political practice aim at social amelioration and real social changes, but they leave the essential structure of the dominant mode of production intact. Revolutionary political practice aims at displacing that mode of production by overthrowing the State apparatuses which secure its dominance. Reform is concerned with the surface phenomena of the social formation while revolution tackles the essential structure in its den. In terms of these conceptions socialist politics in capitalist society are necessarily revolutionary. They may be insurrectionist or they may hope to achieve their ends through peaceful means but they always aim at the more or less rapid overthrow of the essential economic structure of capitalist society.

But if the classical conception of the structure of the social formation is displaced then that dichotomy between reform and revolution must collapse. If the social formation is not conceived as governed by the essential structure of a mode of production and *its* corresponding forms of State, politics, and ideology then the options facing socialist politics can no longer be reduced to a matter of confronting this essential structure or else refusing to do so. Socialist politics can no longer be conceived as necessarily oriented towards the one big push that finally knocks capitalism out of the way and clears the ground for something else. This means that socialists should be concerned with expanding the areas of socialisation and democratisation in the social formation and that existing struggles to these ends cannot be judged diversionary merely because they fail to confront the overall structures of State power and the economy. What kinds of struggle are concretely possible will of course depend on the structures and powers of the State apparatuses, on current forms of politics and political ideologies—and there are well-known cases where serious socialist politics could not be other than revolutionary. But that is always a function of definite political conditions and not of capitalist relations of production as such. For example, we have seen that economic class-relations can be conceived only in relation to specific processes of production and distribution. This means that economic class-relations always have a definite field of application: they cover some areas of production and distribution and they do not cover others. Most advanced capitalist societies have removed significant areas of education from the sphere of commodity forms of distribution and several have done the same for the distribution of medical care. The fact that the supply of education and in some cases of medical care are not completely subsumed under commodity forms of distribution is not due to any essential feature of capitalism or to the intrinsic properties of education and medicine. It is the product of definite political conditions and struggles. But if non-commodity forms of distribution can be achieved within capitalist society then the democratisation and expansion of non-commodity forms into other areas of the economy, their removal from the field of application of capitalist economic relations, represent possible objectives of socialist politics. Socialists need to argue in particular cases and in general for the importance of non-commodity forms of distribution and production. Similar points may be made with regard to the development and expansion of forms of popular democratic control. Where political conditions make limited struggles for the democratisation and socialisation of particular areas of social life possible it would be folly for socialists to treat them as diversionary and reformist.

Finally, these arguments call into question the pertinence frequently accorded to class analysis for socialist political calculation. We have argued that there are no necessary political or ideological effects of classes. Political practices, institutions, and ideologies are not generated as effects of the structure of economic class-relations but they may provide some of their conditions of existence. The pertinence of economic class-relations for socialist political calculation does not derive from any supposed ontological primacy or effectivity of the economy for the determination of political and ideological forms. On the contrary, it is the political objective of the socialist transformation of the forms of possession of and separation from the means and conditions of production which ensures the central importance of these forms for socialist political analysis. The analysis of economic class-relations provides the starting point of socialist political calculation but it is necessary to go beyond that analysis to the investigation of the forms in which their political, legal, and ideological conditions of existence are secured, and to the conditions of their transformation. But those forms and conditions are not given by the identification of economic class-relations as such.

Classes and economic agents

We have argued in Chapter 10 that classes must be conceived as categories of economic agents occupying definite positions with regard to particular forms of possession or of separation from the means and conditions of production. Economic class-relations are constituted by the possession-in-separation of certain of the conditions necessary to the process of production. In some cases the form of possession requires that the tasks of direction and control of the production process are performed by or on behalf of the possessing agent while in other cases the possessing agent merely exercises control over the allocation of certain of the conditions of production to particular units of production. The capitalist farmer is an example of the first type and the owner of the estate from which he rents his land is an example of the second. Where capitalist farming is conducted on landed estates there are economic class-relations between the landowner and the farmer and between the farmer and his labourers. The arguments of Chapters 11 and 12 have established that the category of economic agents may include agents other than human individuals and that there is no direct and necessary correspondence between the performance of the technical functions entailed in control of the conditions of production and economic class-position. A capitalist may perform the tasks of direction and supervision himself and he may employ others to do so on his behalf. If managers and directors are employees of a capital then they are separated from the means and conditions of production. The mere fact that they perform functions of the capitalist cannot suffice to place them in a class different from that of other wage labourers.

These arguments have serious implications for the conceptualisation of economic class-relations and they require in particular that the concepts of communal possession and of classless societies be problematised. If classes are conceived as categories of economic agents then the possibility of agents other than human individuals must completely transform the traditional conceptions of classes as consisting precisely of human individuals. We have defined effective possession of the means of production as involving the capacity to control the conditions in which these means enter the production process and the capacity to exclude others from their use. Since production always presupposes some effective control of the means and conditions of production it can take place only under some definite form of possession. Possession may be communal or private and it may be distributed between several different economic agents but if the means of production are not possessed at all then production cannot take place. This means that once classes are defined as categories of economic agents rather than as large bodies of people then the notion of societies without classes can no longer be sustained. Communal possession involves a class of communal agencies of possession. Communal possession of the means and conditions of production certainly precludes the presence of a possessing class of human individuals but it nevertheless involves the presence of agents with effective possession of the means of production and the capacity to exclude others from their use. It follows that the traditional Marxist distinction between communal and class-based forms of production cannot be sustained. Communal possession means the absence of class-relations in the traditional sense. It does not mean the absence of a class of agents of possession but it does mean the absence of a class of possessing human individuals.

Consider for example the Meillassoux, Terray, Rey debate on the question of whether the elders in lineage society constitute a possessing class as against the cadets and others. *Pre-Capitalist Modes of Production* argued that functional differences do not entail class-relations and that, far from constituting a class the elders act as executors or functionaries of a communal, lineage property. However, to say that the elders do not constitute a class is not to say that there is no distinct category of economic agents with effective possession of the means of production. Elders do not form a class any more than the managers discussed in the last chapter, but that does not mean that there are no classes in lineage societies. If the lineage and sections of the lineage have exclusive possession of certain crucial means of production then both elders and cadets are separated from possession of those means. Membership of the lineage is a condition of participation in the production process and the lineage may, through its representatives, exclude certain individuals from the production process, or penalise them in other ways.

We have seen that there may be a capitalism in which possession devolves on to agents other than human individuals. The distinction between capitalist and socialist production cannot then be made in terms of the presence or absence of a possessing class of human individuals. Socialists will have to reconsider what is meant by communal possession of the means of production. This means, in particular, that it is necessary to develop concepts of communal agents of possession and of the possible modes of communal possession-in-separation of the means and conditions of production. The following discussion has two objectives. First, it shows that there can be no system of production in which the labourers are in no way separated from their conditions of production. It follows that production always involves economic class-relations and the possession-in-separation of at least some of the means and conditions of production. Second, it presents a tentative and provisional outline of some of the consequences of these arguments for the conceptualisation of economic class-relations in contemporary socialist societies.

First, consider what conditions would be required for the non-separation of labourers from the totality of their means and conditions of production. There seem to be three possibilities:

1 There is no social organisation of production capable of sustained reproduction. Production is a matter of individual human agents and of such temporary and intermittent collectivities as chance encounters may allow. The means of production are primitive and rudimentary at best and there can be no instruments of production whose production or use requires the employment of a plurality of labourers. In this case of primitive non-separation there are no reproducible agencies of production other than human individuals and in the absence of organised social life there is no apparent basis for the long-term reproduction of even those agents. Primitive non-separation effectively postulates a speculative pre-social phase of human existence.

2 A society of autonomous producers who exchange commodities amongst themselves under conditions such that no economic agent can monopolise the conditions of production of any other agent. In this case commodities must be produced and exchanged in proportions sufficient to ensure both the reproduction of the conditions of production for all economic agents and the existence of an adequate supply of all socially necessary products. In effect, commodities are exchanged at their values, that is, there is no systematic deviation of the relative prices of commodities from the relative labour-times required to produce them.

The idea of such a society is absurd. If the individual commodity producers are indeed autonomous and subject to no supra-individual mode of possession-in-separation then there can be no social mechanism to ensure that the various commodities are indeed produced in appropriate proportions at the appropriate times. Products are produced as commodities by autonomous producers. They are not produced according to a social plan. Thus there is no social means of ensuring that economic agents can acquire the conditions of their economic reproduction through commodity exchange. This means that there will be economic agents who cannot persist as autonomous petty-commodity producers. On the other hand if there were a social mechanism to ensure that all economic agents could acquire the conditions of their economic reproduction through commodity exchange, for example, if production were regulated by a social plan, then the individual producers would not be completely autonomous and crucial conditions of production would be in the effective possession of the communal agencies and not of the individual producers. A society of petty-commodity producers not separated in any way from their means and conditions of production is impossible.

3 The community possesses the means and conditions of production. But what is this community? If it and its communal agents of possession have definite organisational forms with definite social conditions of existence then individual human agents will be separated from the means of production possessed by communal agents. To conceive of communal possession as representing a state of non-separation on the part of human individuals is to suppose that those individuals are not separated from the communal agents of which they are a part: human subjects are submerged in an intersubjective communion in which the will of each is the will of all. The absurd romanticism of this position is evident—and it is well represented in many of the classical descriptions of the utopian communist society. The free and full development of each human individual takes place in a realm of social harmony—see for example the passage from Morgan's *Ancient Society* which Engels quotes approvingly to conclude *The Origins of the Family, Private Property and the State*. Social harmony is an effect of the absence of scarcity and the consequent realisation in society of essential human qualities:

> Then for the first time man, in a certain sense, is finally marked off from the rest of the animal kingdom, and emerges from mere animal conditions into really human ones. . . . Only from that time will man himself, with full consciousness, make his own history. . . . It is the ascent of man from the kingdom of necessity to the kingdom of freedom. (*Anti-Duhring*, p. 336)

Similar sentiments are expressed from time to time in the pages of *Capital*.

But, setting aside the doubtful appeals of utopian romanticism, it is necessary to recognise that communal possession always involves definite communal agents of possession and the consequent separation of the labourers from at least some of their conditions of production. The social organisation of production always involves economic class-relations and the possession-in-separation of certain of the means and conditions of production by a definite category of economic agents. These agents may be private or communal but there can be no social organisation of production that is not subject to some definite modes of possession and the correlative separation of labourers from some of their means and conditions of production. Marx's claim 'that the *existence of classes* is only bound up with *particular historical phases in the development of production*' (Marx to Weydemeyer, 5 March 1852) depends on the identification of human individual and economic agent which is ubiquitous in Marxism. The notion of a classless society and the conception of joint-stock companies and credit institutions as forms transitional to socialism are results of the same fundamental error.

Now, consider the question of socialism and, in particular, the problem of conceptualising relations of production in contemporary socialist societies. Most work on socialist production and distribution has been concerned with its possibility or with its technical operation as an 'economy'. The literature is dominated by the problems of planning as an economic technique, price formation, the role of incentives, 'efficiency' relative to capitalism, and so on. The pioneering work of Charles Bettelheim represents only the beginnings of an attempt to theorise the conditions of possession of the means and conditions of production under socialism. Discussion of relations of production in contemporary socialist societies has been limited either to the bland assertion that the means of production have indeed been socialised since they are now the legal property of a State which represents the interests of society as a whole or to the debate over whether senior members of the State and party bureaucracies and directors of State enterprises represent a possessing class, a 'State bourgeoisie'. On the first point, once we distinguish the question of the economic relation of possession from the question of its political and legal conditions of existence it is clear that the legal form of State property cannot simply be identified with the effective socialisation of production. As for the debate over the 'State bourgeoisie', it is noteworthy that the problem of a possessing class has been posed in terms of whether a certain category of human individuals constitute a class. The most rigorous form of the argument that Russia and the socialist economies of Europe (but not China) are dominated by a

State capitalism has been advanced by Bettelheim in *Economic Calculation and Forms of Property* and again in his Introduction to *Class Struggles in the USSR: 1917–1923*. We will return to his arguments in a moment. But first notice that the arguments of Chapters 11 and 12 concerning the possibility of economic agents other than human individuals and the class position of managerial employees have cut the ground from under much of the State capitalism debate. That debate is organised around the question: are the relations between one category of employees (the 'State bourgeoisie') and another (workers in State enterprises) class-relations or not? A negative answer to that question leaves open the further question of the relation between State enterprises in the Soviet Union and their employees. We have argued that a wage labourer performing functions of direction on behalf of a capital is, however highly paid, nevertheless separated from possession of the means of production. Similar arguments apply to members of the State and party apparatuses and directors of State enterprises in the Soviet Union. The mere fact that they may perform functions of direction in the system of State enterprises or in particular enterprises does not mean that they are any the less separated from possession of the means and conditions of production.

We can now return to Bettelheim's analysis of the system of state enterprises in the USSR. Bettelheim poses the question of the significance of commodity-relations within the system of State enterprises and between enterprises and workers and he argues that the system of State enterprises is characterised by a double separation. First, the units of production are separated one from another and their exchanges take a commodity form. Second, the workers are separated from their means of production with the sole exception of their labour-power which they sell to enterprises in exchange for wages. The system of State enterprises may be considered socialist precisely to the extent that enterprises and the relations between them are subject to a superordinate control by a State planning apparatus which is itself dominated by the working class. But the State apparatus is far from being dominated by the workers. On the contrary it is: 'the place where the means of repression directed against the workers are constructed, the place where the power to utilize the means of production and to dispose of its products is concentrated' (*Economic Calculation and Forms of Property*, p. 98). Bettelheim therefore argues that capitalist economic-relations are dominant and that the legal form of State ownership, far from representing the socialisation of the economy, merely enshrines the collective private property of the State bourgeoisie. In the Introduction to the English edition of *Economic Calculation* Barry Hindess has argued that Bettelheim's conclusions concerning the capitalist character of the USSR fail on two counts. First, he fails to distinguish the question of the political relations obtaining within the State apparatus and that of the economic relations in which that apparatus is implicated in the system of State enterprises. The *political* character of the State apparatus, the fact that it is very far from being subject to popular democratic control by the workers is not sufficient to show that capitalist *economic* relations are dominant in the system of State enterprises. Second, if a single private property in the system of State enterprises is to represent a form of effective possession then it must subordinate commodity-relations between enterprises through its control over the material and financial conditions of economic reproduction of State enterprises. To argue that the legal form of State property represents a capital is to argue that the State planning apparatus has no effective control over the provision of conditions of production at the level of the enterprise. It is to argue for the effective decomposition of the system of State enterprises. But that is far from being the case in the USSR and the socialist economies of Europe.

How do these arguments stand in the light of the analysis of classes and economic agents developed in this text? First, we have seen that the question of economic class-relations in the system of State enterprises can no longer be posed as a question of the relation between one category of employees and another. It concerns relations between possessing and non-possessing economic agents. In the system of State enterprises we have a double system of possession-in-separation involving relations between enterprises and their employees on the one hand and enterprises and the State planning apparatus on the other. Enterprises are the agents of possession at the level of the immediate production process. They purchase means of production and labour-power in the form of commodities and they engage specialist wage-labourers to perform the functions of management and direction. At this level we have capitalist possession-in-separation and capitalist economic class-relations between enterprises and their employees, from director to manual labourer. But the enterprises themselves are subject to a superordinate form of possession on the part of the economic planning apparatus of the State. The State planning apparatus has effective possession of certain conditions of production through its capacity to set prices, its regulation of access to the purchase of machinery and other means of production, and so on. At this level then we have a form of communal possession and a corresponding separation of enterprises from certain of their conditions of production. The system of State enterprises therefore represents a double set of economic class-relations involving both capitalist and non-capitalist economic forms. Where the system includes people's communes in addition to State enterprises the set of economic class-relations is more complex, since the people's commune form represents a move away from capitalist possession-in-separation.

Consider the connections between the system of State enterprises and its social conditions of existence. We have seen that any set of economic class-relations must have definite economic, legal, political, and cultural conditions of existence. The system of State enterprises involves definite means and processes of production and it presupposes the legal form of State property, the legal recognition of the enterprise as an economic agent and some legal form of wage-labour contract. It presupposes political conditions in which these legal forms are effective and it clearly presupposes that definite forms of economic calculation are operative at the levels both of the enterprise and of the planning apparatus. These legal, political, and cultural conditions cannot be interpreted as the more or less adequate expression of the interests of the proletariat, the 'State bourgeoisie', or any other class that may be invoked. They provide the conditions of existence of economic class-relations but they do not represent classes. Economic class-relations cannot determine the form in which their political conditions of existence are secured—the suppression of harmless cranks, religious minorities and political dissidents in the USSR is not an effect of its economic class-relations—but the precise form in which those conditions are secured may well have definite economic effects. For example, political conditions may well have significant effects on the conditions of wage-bargaining, the range of wage and salary differentials, the forms of regulation over enterprises by the State planning apparatus and its capacity to control black-market distribution and unauthorised commercial relations between enterprises. To say that economic class-relations cannot determine the precise form in which their conditions of existence are satisfied is to say, among other things, that those forms and their effects may be subject to political conflict and debate. But there is nothing in economic class-relations as such to ensure that there will be political forces aiming at their transformation. Capitalist economic class-relations do not guarantee the emergence of socialist political forces, and the system of State enterprises does not guarantee the emergence of significant political forces aiming at further socialisation of the economy. The system of State enterprises is not an intrinsically transitional economic form.

But what is entailed in the further socialisation of such an economy? Socialism is concerned with communal possession of the means and conditions of production under popular democratic control. Further socialisation of the system of State enterprises must therefore involve complex transformations in at least three respects. Two of these concern the suppression of commodity-relations and the third concerns the nature of the communal agent of possession. Commodity-relations in the system of State enterprises involve a double separation: enterprises are separated one from another and workers are separated from their means of production. To say that enterprises are separated one from another is to say also that the agent of communal possession, in this case the State planning apparatus, is in no position to direct the production process itself: it may regulate the conditions in which production takes place but its control over production is limited by the intermediary of distinct agencies of possession at the level of the enterprise. Further socialisation therefore requires increasing control by the communal agency over production and distribution and the consequent suppression of commodity forms of distribution. Now consider the separation of the workers from their means of production. We have argued above that the social organisation of production always involves some form of possession-in-separation. What is important at this level is not whether the workers are separated but the nature of their relation to the directing agent of possession. The suppression of commodity-relations between workers and enterprises and the democratisation of relations between the agent of possession and its employees is a second aspect of the further socialisation of the system of State enterprises. Finally, the agents of communal possession in the USSR and other socialist economies are manifestly not subject to popular democratic control—although there are significant differences with regard to the extent and possible effects of popular initiatives. What is significant here is not merely the fact of possession by a communal agency but also the character of the communal agent of possession, the extent of its subjection to popular democratic control by the mass of the working population.

These points do no more than indicate some of the problems confronting the analysis of economic class-relations in contemporary socialist societies and they suggest what is involved in the further socialisation of their economies. Political institutions, practices and ideologies cannot be read as reflecting the interests of a class or of the whole people. The interests represented in politics cannot be defined independently of the political means of their representation. They are not constituted elsewhere and then represented within the sphere of political struggle. On the contrary they are constituted by definite political ideologies and by the practices of political organisations. This means that political institutions and debates must be analysed in terms of the specificity of their forms and conditions of conflict, the issues at stake and the forces engaged in them and in terms of the possibilities of transformation of political and economic relations in the social formation in question. The political conditions for further socialist transformations may well be more propitious in some cases than in others—and in some they are extremely unpropitious at present. But it is essential that Marxists should not be misled as to the significance of the legal form of State property or of the absence of a class of individual human agents of possession. At their best these features represent no more than the beginnings of the socialisation of production and they clearly provide no guarantee of further movement in a socialist direction.

Bibliography

Althusser, L., *For Marx* (London, Allen Lane, 1969).

Althusser, L., *Lenin and Philosophy* (London, New Left Books, 1971).

Althusser, L., *Essays in Self-Criticism* (London, New Left Books, 1976).

Althusser, L. and Balibar, E., *Reading Capital* (London, New Left Books, 1970).

Anderson, P., *Lineages of the Absolutist State* (London, New Left Books, 1974).

Bettelheim, C., *Economic Calculation and Forms of Property* (London, Routledge & Kegan Paul, 1976).

Bettelheim, C., *Class Struggles in the USSR: 1917–1923* (Brighton, Harvester Press, 1977).

Böhm-Bawerk, E. von, *Karl Marx and the Close of his System,* published with Hilferding, R., *Böhm-Bawerk's Criticism of Marx* (ed. P. M. Sweezy) (London, Merlin Press, 1974).

Braverman, H., *Labour and Monopoly Capital* (London and New York, Monthly Review Press, 1974).

Carchedi, G., 'On the Economic Identification of the New Middle Class', *Economy and Society*, 4, 1, 1975.

Chayanov, A. V., *The Theory of Peasant Economy* (Homewood, Illinois, Irwin, 1966).

Engels, F., *The Origin of the Family, Private Property, and the State,* and 'The Part played by Labour in the Transition from Ape to Man', both in Marx and Engels, *Selected Works* (see below).

Engels, F., *Anti-Dühring* (Moscow, Progress Publishers, 1969).

Hegel, G. W. F., *The Science of Logic* (London, Allen & Unwin, 1969).

Hilferding, R., *Le Capital financier* (Paris, Minoir, 1970), translation of *Daz Finanz Kapital* (Vienna, 1910).

Hilferding, R., see Böhm-Bawerk.

Hindess, B., *The Use of Official Statistics in Sociology* (London, Macmillan, 1973).

Hindess, B., *Philosophy and Methodology in the Social Sciences* (Brighton, Harvester Press, 1977a).

Hindess, B., 'Humanism and Teleology in Sociological Theory', in Hindess, B. (ed.), *Sociological Theories of the Economy* (London, Macmillan, 1977b).

Hindess, B. and Hirst, P. Q., *Pre-Capitalist Modes of Production* (London, Routledge & Kegan Paul, 1975).

Hindess, B. and Hirst, P. Q., *Mode of Production and Social Formation* (London, Macmillan, 1977).

Hirst, P. Q., 'Althusser and the Theory of Ideology', *Economy and Society*, 5, 4, 1976.

Hirst, P. Q., 'Economic Classes and Politics', paper presented at *Marxism Today*, and Communist Party Sociology Group conference on 'Class and Class Structure', November 1976.

Lecourt, D., 'Lenin, Hegel, Marx', *Theoretical Practice*, 7/8, 1973.

Lenin, V. I., *The Development of Capitalism in Russia, Collected Works*, vol. 3 (1957). All volumes of *Collected Works* are published by Lawrence & Wishart, London.

Lenin, V. I., *What is to be Done?, Collected Works*, vol. 5 (1963).

Lenin, V. I., *The Agrarian Programme of Social-Democracy in the First Russian Revolution*, *Collected Works*, vol. 13 (1962).

Lenin, V. I., 'The Discussion of Self-Determination Summed-Up', *Collected Works*, vol. 22 (1964).

Lenin, V. I., 'A Great Beginning', *Collected Works*, vol. 29 (1965).

Lukács, G., *History and Class Consciousness* (London, Merlin Press, 1971).

Marx, K., *Capital*, 3 vols, Chicago, Kerr, 1909–1915.

Marx, K., *Capital*, vol. 1 (Harmondsworth, Penguin, 1976).

Marx, K., *Capital*, vol. 1 (London, Lawrence & Wishart, 1967, for parts 1 & 2; 1974 for part 3); *Capital*, vol. 2 (Moscow, FLPH, 1961); *Capital*, vol. 3 (Moscow, FLPH, 1962, for parts 1 & 2) (Progress Publishers, 1966, for part 3).*

Marx, K., *Theories of Surplus Value*, 3 vols (London, Lawrence & Wishart, 1969, 1972).

Marx, K., *Economic and Philosophical Manuscripts of 1844*, in Marx and Engels, *Selected Works*, vol. 3 (London, Lawrence & Wishart, 1975).

Marx, K., *A Contribution to the Critique of Political Economy* (London, Lawrence & Wishart, 1971).

Marx, K., *Grundrisse* (Harmondsworth, Penguin, 1973).

Marx, K., *The Eighteenth Brumaire of Louis Bonaparte*, in Marx and Engels, *Selected Works*.

Marx, K., *Critique of the Gotha Programme* in Marx and Engels, *Selected Works*.

Marx, K., *The Communist Manifesto*, in Marx and Engels, *Selected Works*.

---

* The Soviet edition of *Capital* has been used except where indicated in the text. Since different printings of this edition vary as to pagination the printings used have been listed to make it possible to check references.

Marx, K. and Engels, F., *Selected Works* (1 vol. edn) (London, Lawrence & Wishart, 1968).

Marx, K. and Engels, F., *Selected Correspondence* (Moscow, FLPH, n.d.).

Medvedev, R., *Let History Judge* (London, Macmillan, 1972).

Meillassoux, C., *Anthropologie économique des Gouro de Côte d'Ivoire* (Paris/The Hague, Mouton, 1964).

Morgan, L. H., *Ancient Society* (1877) (New York, Meridian Books, 1967).

Poulantzas, N., *Political Power and Social Classes* (London, New Left Books, 1973).

Poulantzas, N., *Classes in Contemporary Capitalism* (London, New Left Books, 1976).

Rancière, J., 'The Concept of "Critique" and the "Critique of Political Economy"', *Theoretical Practice*, 1, 2, 6, 1971/'72, and *Economy and Society*, 5, 3, 1976 (first published in Althusser, L. *et al.*, *Lire le Capital*, vol. 1 (Paris, Maspero, 1965)).

Revai, J., 'A review of *History and Class Consciousness*', *Theoretical Practice*, 1, 1971 (first published in *Archiv fur die Geschichte des Sozialismus und der Arbeiterbewegung*, xi, 1925).

Rey, P.-P., *Colonialisme, neo-colonialisme et transition au capitalisme* (Paris, Maspero, 1971).

Rey, P.-P. 'The Lineage Mode of Production', *Critique of Anthropology*, 3, 1975.

Ricardo, D., *Principles of Political Economy and Taxation, Works* (ed. Sraffa), vol. 1 (Cambridge University Press, 1951).

Rubin, I. I., *Essays on Marx's Theory of Value* (Detroit, Black & Red, 1972).

Smith, A., *The Wealth of Nations, Works*, vol. 2 (reprint of 1811–12 edn) (Aalen: Otto Zeller, 1963).

Sraffa, P., *Production of Commodities by Means of Commodities* (Cambridge University Press, 1961).

Stalin, J. V., *Dialectical and Historical Materialism* (New York, International Publishers, 1972).

Stalin, J. V., *Economic Problems of the USSR*, in *Selected Works* (ed. Davis) (California, Cardinal Publishers, 1971).

Stalin, J. V., *Economic Problems of Socialism in the USSR*, in *Selected Works* (ed. Davis) (California, Cardinal Publishers, 1971).

Terray, E., *Marxism and 'Primitive' Societies* (London & New York, Monthly Review Press, 1972).

Weber, M., *The Protestant Ethic and the Spirit of Capitalism* (London, Allen & Unwin, 1965).

Weber, M., *The Theory of Social and Economic Organisation* (New York, The Free Press, 1964).

